SHOPS

SHOPS

A Manual of Planning and Design

David Mun

THE ARCHITECTURAL PRESS : LONDON

ACKNOWLEDGEMENTS

I would like to express my gratitude to the British Multiple
Retailers' Association and the National Association of Shopfitters
for their advice and help with my enquiries.

My appreciation to the librarians and staff of the Royal Institute of
British Architects Library, the Library of the Department of the
Built Environment at the Polytechnic of the South Bank (in
particular to its Manufacturers and Materials Division) and to the
photographic library at the Architectural Press.

I owe a particular debt to all the manufacturers and trade literature
writers who, uncredited, produce so much invaluable information.

My appreciation to all the retailers, architects and shopfitters who
in any way assisted me and to my friends who encouraged me and
especially to my wife for her tolerance and support.

Finally my thanks to Maritz Vandenberg, Patrick Gillies and Alan
Brunstrom, who helped produce this book.

Frontispiece: Plaza boutique, London, designed by Anthony Price

First published in 1981 by The Architectural Press Ltd: London

© David Mun 1981

ISBN: 0 85139 610 0

British Library Cataloguing in Publication Data
Mun, David
  Shops: a manual of planning and design.
  1. Store fixtures
  1. Title
  690'.5'21   HF 5521
ISBN 0-85139-610-0

Library of Congress Cataloging in Publication Data
Mun, David.
  Shops, a manual of planning and design.
  Bibliography: p.
  1. Stores, Retail. 2. Stores, Retail — Decoration. 3. Store fixtures.
I. Title.
NA6220.M86 725'.21 81-11115
ISBN 0-89397-112-X AACR2

Photoset by Alacrity Phototypesetters, Banwell Castle,
Weston-super-Mare
Printed in Great Britain by Mackays of Chatham Ltd

Contents

Picture acknowledgements

(Unless otherwise stated photographs are by the architects)

Bert J Anderson, p62 (bottom); Brecht-Einzig, p30-31; Gianni Celada, p37; Martin Chaffer, p42 (bottom); Robert Hill, p22 (top and bottom); Hubermann, p58, 59, 64 (bottom right), 90 (middle and bottom left); Horst Kalo, p91; A Kawasumi, p56 (top), 57; Edgar Kyman, p66; E Locatelli, p61 (bottom left); John Maltby, p42 (top); Norman McGrath, p65, 67; Mario Mullas, p60; David Mun, p90 (bottom right); Pacozinski, p90 (top right); Ezra Stoller, p38; Tim Street-Porter, p23, 28 (bottom right), 62 (top), 63 (bottom), 90 (top left); Studio 3, p18 (bottom), 19 (bottom); Colin Thomas, p24.

1
SETTING UP A SHOP

1.1 INTRODUCTION

Changing patterns

Retailing methods and shopping patterns have changed to keep abreast with rapidly changing social conditions. Recent causes for changes have been:

1 Increases in population and in the level of personal earnings.
2 Increase in private and decrease in public transport facilities.
3 The development and wider personal ownership of labour saving devices and food storage equipment such as microwave ovens and freezers.
4 The development of credit cards and credit purchasing schemes.
5 Larger scale and more sophisticated forms of advertisement.
6 The increased range of goods available because of technological developments and international trading.

These factors have influenced changes in shop planning and retailing methods. Personal service has given way to self service or assisted service; display techniques have developed for mass display with customer inspection and self selection; purchase scales have risen from small to bulk.

The same period has seen a continuous reduction in the number of retail outlets with the share of the market moving away from the independent retailer towards the larger multiples. Figure **1.1** illustrates this shift, the main reasons for which are:

1 Replacement of old shops by new ones is leading to closures by businesses unable to pay the higher rents.
2 Multiples and co-operatives are rationalising their policies by closing down smaller units and opening fewer larger ones.
3 The competition from multiples has made it difficult for many independents to stay in business.
4 Restrictions of credit have taken a larger toll on small businesses.
5 Large shops such as supermarkets have led to large quantities of goods being handled by fewer outlets.

The only fields in which independents have fared particularly well are those too specialised for competition from multiples, such as antiques, health foods, gift shops and so on.

Architects and parties concerned with shop buildings and installations should keep up with new developments so that they may anticipate the resultant effects on their personal field.

1.2 FEASIBILITY

Market research

As a preliminary process in setting up a shop it may be necessary to establish the level of market demand for the proposed business so as to ascertain whether the venture will be economically viable. Market research and feasibility studies reduce the element of risk in such enterprises. They will indicate the number of potential customers, their needs and preferences and determine whether the proposed project can be accommodated.

Research of this order is usually undertaken by the client or by independent consultants. Local trade association surveys, retail and telephone directories and publications by government sources require to be examined and enquiries need to be made through estate agents or local planning authorities.

Site grading

Grading		Observations
Grade 1	Exclusive	Established high class neighbourhood; shops tend to offer personalised service to a small clientele and to supply luxury goods; high standards of finishes and the maximum degree of customer comfort are desirable
Grade 2	Shopping centre	Mostly in city centres or commercially developed centres; types of shops are those mainly offering comparison goods where customers carefully select for quality, variety and price; some specialised service shops are also to be found here; high standards of finishes are desirable
Grade 3	High street	Busy shopping area to serve local district; shops offer a combination of comparison and convenience goods and a combination of self service and assisted service; a wide range of shops offering different services is also to be found; standards of finishes vary widely depending on the neighbourhood
Grade 4	Local	Few small units to serve a predominantly residential area; shops deal mainly with convenience goods; there has been a considerable reduction in the number of this type of retail outlet in favour of Grade 3 sites where units are larger and in greater numbers so as to provide customers with a wider choice and lower costs; standards of finishes are medium to low

continued

	1957	1966	1971	1975	1981
Department Stores	5	5	5	5	5
Multiple Shops	24	32	35	39	42
Co-operatives	12	9	7	7	6
Mail Orders	2	4	5	6	7
Independents	57	55	48	43	40

1.1 *Table showing the share of trade for different types of retail outlets (figures up to 1971 derived from* Report on the census of distribution and other services, *HMSO, 1971, subsequent figures estimated)*

Site grading

Grading	Observations
Grade 5 Resort and terminal	These sites are usually found in hotels, transport terminals or holiday resorts; shops depend on magnetism of site to attract customers, who are usually in the process of moving from one place to another; types of goods and finishes are dependent on the standards set by the main magnet

Site selection

Considerations affecting the selection of site for any particular shop are:

Considerations	Details
1 Location	*Whether exclusive, popular or low grade*: this gives an indication of the relative affluence and social preferences of the local population (see observations on site grading above) *Whether prominently visible or sheltered*: the more visible a shop is (eg on a main street rather than off it) the better its trading potential
2 Site parameters	*Gross and nett floor area, frontage and depth*: check that nett area and proposed plans suit the trading activities intended and that the frontage suffices for the client's needs for window display *Other usable areas* (upper floors or basement): customers generally prefer shopping on the ground floor only; if only two floors are used it is sufficient to have stairs, which should be located near the main entrance; if there are to be more than two floors a lift or escalators may be required *Future expansion of the site*: if this looks possible plan so that it may be carried out with minimal cost and disturbance
3 Neighbourhood	*Character of neighbourhood and adjacent properties*: assess if there is need for protection against litter or vandalism *Size and level of illumination of near-by signs*: if the neighbourhood is brightly lit the proposed shop will have to compete for attention *Neighbourhood moving up or down market*: assess likely changes in the area and what it will look like in 5 to 10 years' time
4 Competition	*Quality or quantity of local competition*: is the area saturated for a particular trade? how distant and important are major competitive shopping areas, eg shopping centres in town and big hypermarkets just out of town? (note that some trades benefit if the site has an established trade, eg books, antiques, collectors' items, hardware and so on)
5 Economic activity	*Magnetism of additional customer sources* (eg tourism, theatres, hotels, banks, transport terminals and large space users such as department stores: this may indicate type of goods likely to sell well, such as souvenirs and gifts, types of convenience goods such as chemists and newsagents, or comparison goods
6 Economic data	*Local rents, rates and premiums, labour availability and salaries*: assess overheads and availability of staff
7 Transport	*Availability and frequency of public transport, customer and staff parking, off street loading and unloading facilities*: good transport facilities are essential; where goods are heavy or bulky, delivery services will be necessary; premises next to bus stops tend to get congested pavements
8 Environmental conditions	*Whether exposed or sheltered from the sun, prevailing winds, traffic noise and pollution*: recessed entrances with deep lobbies give some protection against the elements
9 Restrictions	*Restrictive covenants on tenancy leases*: check for restrictive covenants on type of merchandise permitted, design, materials, services and operation restrictions (see separate subsection on restrictive covenants below)
10 Services	*Availability and condition of engineering services on site* (electricity, water, gas, drainage, lighting, heating and communications): assess the problems and costs involved in upgrading or supplying these services

Types of tenure

Properties may be under any of the following types of tenure:
Freehold: owner occupation with or without residential or commercial premises above the shop.
Leasehold: tenant paying rent to landlords. Period of lease may determine quality of finishes as there is no point in using expensive finishes on short lease properties. Clients may intend only a short tenure to test the market. Restrictive covenants should be understood.
Joint occupancy: situations where a number of shops are associated in a joint venture. For the architect this may mean dealing with a number of clients or a number of architects representing the other clients. A typical situation is when a retailer takes an area in a department store. The architect for the retailer has to deal with the architect from the department store in determining the design policies of their respective clients.

Restrictive covenants

Most leasehold agreements contain some form of restrictive covenant or covenants which must be understood and followed by the tenant. Architects are advised to check on these restrictions to determine how they affect the design and specification of the shopfitting. Usually all drawings have to be submitted to the landlord's architects for the landlord's formal approval.
The main restrictions in shop installations are:

Restrictions	Details
1 Design	Usually kept to the elements in the shopfront; may only affect small details or may involve essential design considerations
2 Materials	Impositions on constructional or more frequently on finishing materials: usually concerned with shopfront elements
3 Reinstatement	The lessee is responsible for the upkeep of the building and for reinstating it to its initial condition at the end of the lease: may influence design or detailing of fixtures
4 Services	Restrictions may be imposed on the type of services permitted: some may be compulsory, eg sprinklers; others may be shared, eg goods handling, refuse
5 Period of lease	The period of the lease may determine cost limits; short periods do not warrant expensive materials
6 Merchandise	There may be restrictions on the type of goods to be sold so as to limit competition between tenants selling the same goods; the range of goods to be sold may also be restricted, eg butchers or fishmongers may not be permitted to rent shops in the development
7 Operation	There may be restrictions on how premises operate, eg opening hours, lighting levels, noise restrictions and so on

Cost limits

The client must assess his trading capability at the outset in order to determine if the project is feasible. The trading capability is often expressed in terms of cash turnover per year. From this figure the client can assess the size of shop, number of staff, quantity of goods held in stock, running and maintenance costs and the capital for building and fixtures. He should determine whether he prefers a higher running and maintenance cost in order to keep capital costs to a minimum or whether he is prepared to permit a higher capital allowance so as to take advantage of tax relief where applicable. The client's policy on this should be established at the outset because it will affect the design of services such as lighting, heating and ventilation, and influence the choice of materials for finishes.

1.3 THE CLIENT

Types of client
Clients likely to be concerned with shop installations may be divided into two groups: those concerned with the shopfitting of the individual retail unit or those concerned with the development of the building structure.

Shopfitting clients

Independent retailer
He may own more than one shop (usually under ten) or just the one shop with residential accommodation above. He will normally specialise in one type of merchandise. Although independent retailers represent about 78 per cent of retail outlets they have only about 40 per cent of the total trade.

Multiple group
This is a chain organisation on a local, regional or national basis which normally owns more than ten shops. Each group normally specialises in a particular trade, eg shoes, men's wear, chemist, etc. They represent 18 per cent of the retail outlets and control about 42 per cent of the total trade.

Co-operative group
This is a locally based multiple store group owned by its customers and connected with a manufacturing or wholesale organisation. It may be specialist or comprehensive in the range of merchandise it sells.

Variety chain store
This provides a wide selection of goods at relatively low prices which are supported by manufacturing or wholesale organisations.

Department store
This retails a wide range of goods and services at various prices under one roof. Areas in department stores are sometimes sub-leased to other clients such as a manufacturer or an independent trader providing specialist service or goods.

Manufacturer
He will often provide showrooms to display and sometimes also to sell his products.

Wholesaler
He can range in size from an individual trader providing cash and carry services to a discount store operating through a chain of warehouses.

Nationalised industry
(Gas, Electricity, Post Office or Telecom showrooms.)

Service
He will be an independent or multiple group client who provides a specialised service, eg an optician or hairdresser.

Developer clients
The type of clients who are concerned with shop building structures are:

Speculative developer
This is usually a property company which builds units for leasing as shops with or without foreknowledge of a particular tenant's specific requirements and provides only the essential requirements of the building structure and service terminating points.

Local Authority
Similar considerations apply as to the specialist developer. Planning is usually determined by committees rather than by individuals.

Liaison with client
In the case of large organisations the client should be asked to appoint an individual with whom the architect can deal as the organisation's representative. If more than one person has to be involved in representing such an organisation the areas of responsibility may be allocated as follows:

Policy planning and administration: to relate to the organisation's established corporate image and to maintain constraints over design and materials.

Stock and staff requirements: to deal with needs of the particular branch under discussion (eg type, size and range of goods, number of staff and nature of accommodation to be provided).

Service requirements: to deal with specialised display equipment or services developed for or by the client organisation, eg standardised transport vehicles for goods handling.

1.4 SHOP BUILDINGS

Basic types
Shop buildings may be one of the following types:
(a) Individual unit
(b) Shopping centre
(c) Market

Individual unit
This is the most common type of shop building and consists of units of whatever size fronting on to a street in a city centre, suburb or small town. The main types of sites on which units of this nature are located are as follows (see Fig **1.2**):

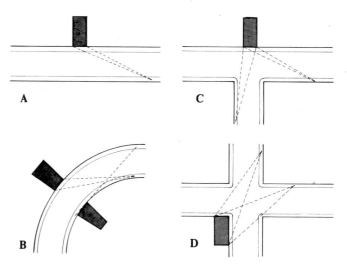

1.2 *Types of street site*
A normal high street: *visibility factor is dependent on the width of the street* B curved street: *the outer curve holds the more prominent sites but gives frontages narrower than rear widths. The reverse is true for the inner curve* C 'T'-junction: *the most prominent sites are at the head of the 'T'* D Corner: *shops so situated have longer facades but this limits the amount of wall space and causes increase in heat loss plus solar heat gain*

Street site
For obvious reasons the most common type of site adjoins the street. It has a low visibility factor which is dependent on the width of the street. Where service yards are not available shops are subjected to obstructions by vehicles loading or unloading off its single frontage.

Curved street

The outer curve holds the better sites because frontages may be seen for considerable distances from both directions. On the outer curve the frontage tends to be smaller than the back of the unit. On the inner curve the reverse is true.

T-junction

The best position is at the head of the T which is visible from a great distance by both pedestrians and traffic.

Corner sites

Such sites are more valuable than those with only one frontage for the following reasons: the greater frontage permits more display windows, there is a choice on which street to place the main entrance, daylight distribution is better, there are greater facilities for natural ventilation, and obstruction on the main frontage by vehicles loading or unloading is avoided. The disadvantages are that pedestrians may congest at road junctions, wall storage space is lost and there is greater exposure to solar gain and heat loss.

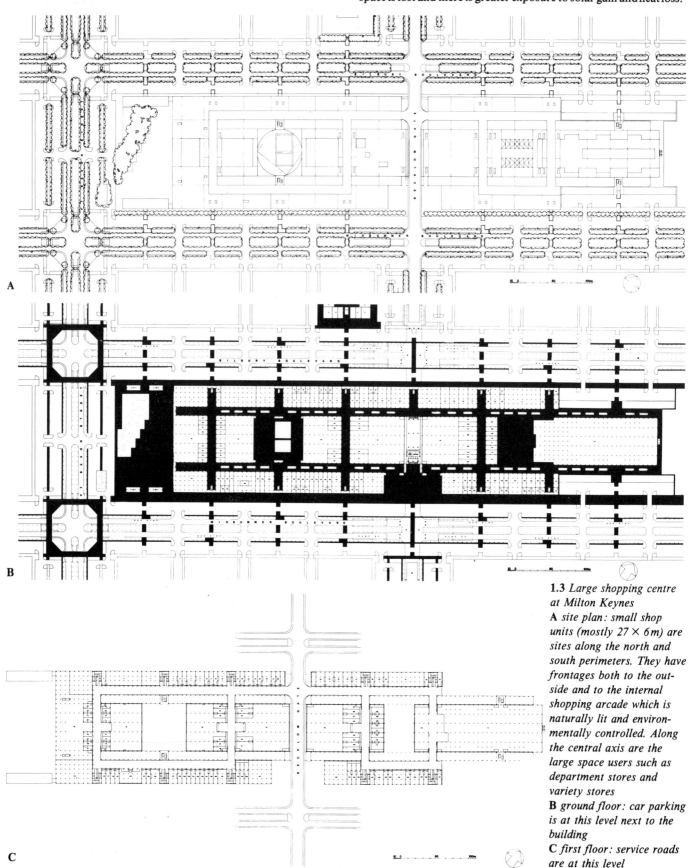

1.3 *Large shopping centre at Milton Keynes*
A *site plan: small shop units (mostly 27 × 6m) are sites along the north and south perimeters. They have frontages both to the outside and to the internal shopping arcade which is naturally lit and environmentally controlled. Along the central axis are the large space users such as department stores and variety stores*
B *ground floor: car parking is at this level next to the building*
C *first floor: service roads are at this level*

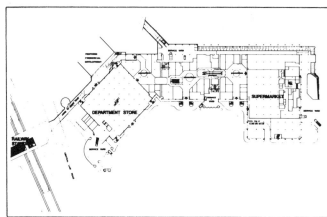

1.4

Sloping sites
These sites are not generally liked by customers especially if goods have to be carried up-gradient. Window design may cause problems since internal treatment may be required to the steps on the window base.

Sunny or shaded sites
In high latitude countries the sunny side of the street is preferred because people like to walk under the sun. If there is a choice it is better to have the side of the street which gets morning sun, as this is warming and the air clear. Sunny sites do have some disadvantages which are:
(a) greater heat gains,
(b) rapid deterioration of perishable foods on window displays,
(c) damage to goods caused by colour fading, and
(d) expenses of solar control mechanisms such as blinds, special solar control glass or mechanical plant.

Shopping centre
Shopping centres or precincts are the product of speculative building by Local Authorities or property developers. They may form a row of shops as an infill to existing streets or consist of a group whose frontages are served by a traffic-free pedestrian precinct or 'mall'. This may be open-air, with or without canopy protection or enclosed with partial or fully controlled environmental conditions.

Examples in the last category include Brent Cross in London, Eldon Square in Newcastle and the new Milton Keynes shopping centre (Fig **1.3**). Most shopping centres produce their own briefing

1.5

1.4 *Noarlunga Centre, shopping centre, South Australia, designed by Cameron, Chisholm and Nicol. The top lit shopping mall is on two levels with escalators helping shoppers to the upper level*
1.5 *Same. Ground floor plan*

guides on design, services and planning which should be studied and complied with. Usually building units are finished as a 'shell' with service points terminating in appropriate positions. Tenants are required to fit out to the standards set by the landlords. Public and common spaces are finished and controlled by the landlord's agents. Some other shopping centres are shown in Figs. **1.4** to **1.11**.

1.6 *Belconnen Mall Shopping Centre, Canberra, Australia, design by Cameron, Chisholm and Nicol. The round concrete columns are painted white and the tubular steelwork is painted red. The shops slot in between the columns and sometimes break forwards*

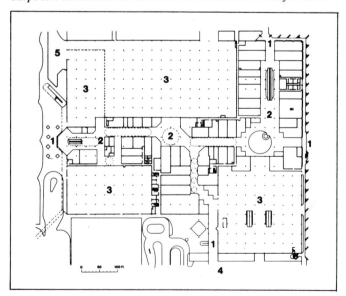

1.7 *Same. Upper shopping level key plan*
1 *entry* **2** *mall* **3** *supermarket* **4** *car park* **5** *service area*

1.8 *Same. The steel roof truss is clad with solar control glass which lets some daylight into the shopping mall*

1.9 *Park Circle shopping development, South Melbourne, Australia, designed by McIntyre and Partners. Steel truss canopy over the shops provides protection against inclement weather*

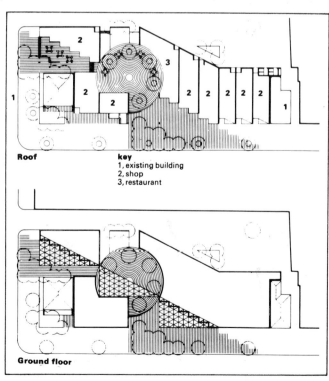

1.10 *Same. Central area: view to restaurant showing outdoor seating area. The restaurant is considered an asset because it attracts the public outside shopping hours*

1.11 *Same. Plans of roof and ground floor. The shop development is planned on a road junction: this encourages passers-by to take a short cut through the development and shop on the way*

Market

The traditional market is mainly associated with agricultural towns where shows of livestock and agricultural produce draw the rural population into the town. An essential requirement for this type of market is a central paved space on which the stalls may be erected on market days. This space is usually surrounded by structures, invariably in the form of shop buildings, as a protection against winds (Fig 1.12). The perimeter shop buildings will include at least one public house together with shops trading in convenience goods or in goods which require a high degree of hygienic control (such as chemists, butchers and fishmongers). The main types of goods sold in the stalls or kiosks are fruit and vegetables, poultry and dairy products, clothing, gifts, toys, household goods, second hand articles, antiques and crafts. A modern variation of the traditional open market is the market hall, formed within large buildings where the sheltered environment provides for all-weather shopping. This form of building resembles a scaled-down version of the shopping centre, except that units are not enclosed by structural walls or fitted with shopfronts. For security reasons units may be contained by side and back partitions and fitted with front security grilles. Some of the reasons for the recent growth in the number of market halls are that big properties in the town have become vacant because they are uneconomical for single tenants; that halls provide the small spaces and relatively low rents required for a large number of small enterprises; that capital expenditure for fitting and running such spaces is low and that the leases for them are generally short term.

1.5 RANGE OF GOODS AND SERVICES

Types of goods

The complete range of goods for sale in shops is too extensive to set out in detail but it may be said to fall within one or other of two broad categories:

1 Convenience goods: those bought for daily needs in chemists, supermarkets, newsagents and so on

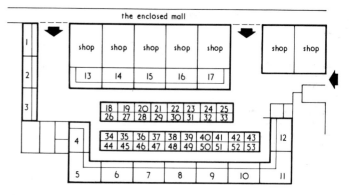

1.12 *Typical layout of market stalls adjoining small shop units (reproduced from* Enclosed Shopping Centres *edited by Clive Darlow, Architectural Press, 1972)*

2 Durable or comparison goods: those which customers compare for quality, variety and price eg shoes, clothing, furniture etc.

Within each shop, goods may be further sub-categorised as follows:
(a) Demand goods: essential goods which customers visit shops for eg in men's wear this would include suits, coats, trousers and jackets;
(b) Semi-demand goods: a category between demand and impulse eg in men's wear this could include shirts, woollens and sportswear; and
(c) Impulse goods: small and low cost goods bought on the spur of the moment eg in men's wear this would be ties, underwear, umbrellas and jewellery (cuff links, tie pins).

Types of specialist shops

The main types of independent specialist shops or the uses to which such buildings may be put are:

Category	Shop type	Goods classification		
		Demand	Semi-demand	Impulse
A Food				
Food products are 'convenience' goods. Individual retailers are widely disappearing giving ground to multiples who run chains of stores	1 Baker: foods may be baked on the premises or be delivered from main bakeries; some shops have sidelines eg catering for the office luncheon market by offering sandwiches, heated snacks, hot soups and beverages	Bread, rolls	Pies, snacks, fresh yeast cakes	Pastries, biscuits
Most foods are also now being sold from supermarkets rather than small shops	2 Butcher: compete very well against supermarkets as customers like to get cuts to order instead of pre-cut pre-packed foods found in supermarkets	Fresh and frozen meat and poultry	Meat products and game	Canned foods, preserves, eggs
Department stores however tend to stock exotic imported foods in their food halls as these give higher profit margins than mass-produced local brands of food	3 Confectioners: usually integrated with other goods such as those found in newsagents and tobacconists; goods can only be classified as a 'demand' commodity if the shop caters exclusively in confectionery such as hand made chocolates and sweets	Hand made confectionery, newspapers, tobacco products	Ices, crisps, stationery	All types of confectionery
	4 Delicatessen: mainly found in areas of high immigrant communities	Fresh cured meats, dairy products and imported foods	Grocery and staple foods	Confectionery
	5 Fishmonger: numbers are decreasing, giving ground to frozen foods	Fresh fish and shellfish	Cured and frozen fish	Canned foods, game, eggs
	6 Frozen foods: rapidly growing industry due to widespread developments in home freezers; combines the convenience of long storage life and cheaper food by bulk purchasing	All types of frozen foods	Freezer machines, micro-wave ovens, and freezer food containers	Cookery books and magazines
	7 Greengrocer: some shops have adjoining sidelines in selling flowers or plants	Seasonal fruits and vegetables	Off-season and imported fruits, eg mangoes, passion fruit	
	8 Health foods: a relative newcomer due to fashion for 'natural' foods	Staple foods, grains, cereals, dried fruits, dairy products	'Home made cooking', cakes, biscuits	Magazines, nuts
	9 Off-licence: if alcohol is sold together with other types of foods such as in a supermarket, the department must be segregated as sale of alcohol to minors is prohibited	Liquor, wine, beers		Crisps, nuts, tobacco products, confectionery
	10 Patisseries: often adjoining a tea house; cakes may be baked on the premises or delivered from main suppliers	Pastry, fresh cakes	Bread, rolls, home made confectioneries, fresh ground coffee	

Category	Shop type	Goods classification		
		Demand	**Semi-demand**	**Impulse**
B Clothing and footwear				
These are generally considered to be 'comparison' goods	1 Bridal and evening wear: found mainly in the more exclusive areas	Bridal and evening gowns	Nightwear, underwear	Gloves, hats, handbags
Small shops have fared well against competition from department and variety stores as they are more susceptible to quick changes of fashion	2 Fabric and haberdashery: now mainly found in department stores	Fabrics, haberdashery	Pattern books and stencils	
	4 Maternity, baby and child: clothing for this category is usually sold in conjunction with other associated goods such as prams, cots, nappies, etc	Utility clothing, associated furniture and equipment		Toys
	5 Men's wear: can be advantageously sited with similar types of shops as customers like to have a wide choice of styles and prices	Coats, suits, trousers, shirts, jackets	Raincoats, woollens	Shirts, underwear, gloves, umbrellas, accessories, eg belts, jewellery etc
	6 Women's wear: comment on siting same as for men's wear	Dresses, coats, blouses, shirts, skirts, jeans		Underwear, hats, gloves, leather goods and small jewellery
	7 Footwear: most cater for men and women with segregated areas for each; children's footwear is found with women's as mothers tend to do most of the shopping; can be advantageously sited in area with similar shops as customers like to have a wide choice of styles and prices	Casual, utility, fashion and sports footwear	Sandals, slippers, wellingtons	Polishes, creams, brushes and other leather goods eg handbags, belts
	8 Sportswear: this is often associated with shops selling sports equipment eg tennis rackets, golf clubs etc	Popular sports clothing, footwear eg tennis shoes	Less popular sports eg aikido, scuba-diving	Cheap goods, eg darts boards, table games
	9 Woollen goods: only in cold weather climates, and sales are dependent on season	Sweaters, pullovers, cardigans		Hats, scarves, gloves
C Household goods				
These are both 'convenience' and 'comparison' goods	1 General store: goods are distinctly separated and categorised: *a* Living room furniture *b* Dining room furniture *c* Kitchen furniture, appliances and accessories *d* Bedroom furniture *e* Bathroom accessories *f* Linen and towels *g* China and glass *h* Lighting *i* Outdoor furniture *j* Wall and floor coverings	Generally all large pieces of furniture		Generally all small and cheap items
Most of the goods are for sale in composite shops such as variety stores, hypermarkets, department stores, and discount warehouses	2 Toys: toys for children and games for adults			
Specialist stores may deal in just one of the categories a-j	3 China and glassware: mostly expensive and hand made goods suitable for gifts			
	4 Second hand furniture: vary from antique furniture in elegant shops to 'junk' in dilapidated warehouses			
	5 Do-it-yourself: this is a rapidly growing industry and the number and size of shops are increasing accordingly	Paint, brushes, accessories, wall and floor covering materials and appliances	Hardware, tools, ironmongery, timbers, gardening equipment	Books and manuals
D Other goods				
As these cover a wide range it includes both 'convenience' and 'comparison' goods	Antiques*			
	Art dealer and picture framer*			
*Denotes shops which appreciably benefit next to other shops selling similar type of goods especially in areas of established reputation	Bookseller	Best sellers, general fiction, popular non-fiction	Literature, specialist subjects	General fiction, paperbacks, cards and stationery
	Car, bicycle and motor cycle salesroom and accessories	Vehicles, accessories and tools		Accessories
	Chemist: large stores are branching out and widening their range of goods	Prescriptions, general medicines	Toiletries, photographic goods, stationery, household goods	Cosmetics
	Florists	House plants, flowers		Accessories, guide books
	Gifts and souvenirs			Mostly impulse goods
	Hobbies, stamps, fishing, hunting, etc*: require very small areas and are ideally suited in 'market hall' building types	Mostly demand goods		
	Jewellery: goods are both impulse and demand	Watches, rings, bracelets, personal jewellery	Silverware, clocks, coins	Lighters, tie pins
	Leather goods: goods are both impulse and demand			
	Pets and animal foods	Pets, animal foods	Accessories, guide books	
	Newsagents: large stores have a wide range of goods	Newsprint, tobacco goods	Stationery, ices, cards	Confectionery, beverages, crisps

Category	Shop type	Goods classification		
		Demand	**Semi-demand**	**Impulse**
	Photographic goods	Cameras and accessories	TV, radio and electric goods	Films, cleaning kits
	Records and music	Latest releases, popular albums and singles	Other records, cassettes, sheet music, cartridges	Accessories, cleaning kits, music books, blank tapes, posters
	Showrooms: manufacturers independently or in joint association with other manufacturers display and sell their products; goods may be sold or just be on exhibition with customers being referred to dealers	Types of goods are varied: eg lighting, cars, cameras, furniture, kitchen and bathroom equipment		
	Specialist equipment: comments as for showrooms above	Types of goods are varied: eg religious, medical, business etc		
	Sports goods	Sports equipment and clothing	Camping equipment and less popular sports eg scuba-diving	Games, toys
	Toys: for all ages; specialist shops cater for adult games, eg chess centres			

Other categories of use for shop premises are as follows:

Category	Shop type	Comments
E Service In these shops goods are not sold, but a service is afforded for a fee	1 Dry cleaner and launderette	There is considerable demand for these services particularly in middle to low income areas with a transient population; customers choose nearest facility, otherwise there is no competition
	2 Hairdresser	High demand in all areas; competition for clientele is great; customers choose premises for service and comfort of interior
	3 Hire service	Goods on general hire include: television sets, cars, clothing, mechanical and plant equipment
	4 Optician	Here is a combination of direct goods sales eg sunglasses, glass frames and lenses, and a service from the optician
	5 Shoe repairs and key cutting	Only a small area is required; primarily should be sited where there is a large flow of pedestrians eg at transport terminals or incorporated in a composite shop
	6 Travel and other agencies	There are various types of agency: airline, boat, coach or railway company, tour operator, travel agent, theatre booking agent and *bureau de change*
F Offices Shop premises may be used by professional bodies to serve the community	1 Doctor's surgery 2 Dentist's surgery 3 Accountant's office 4 Architect's office 5 Interior designer's office 6 Surveyor's office	Optimum sites are in semi-residential areas where the balance of rents and catchment market is correct
G Miscellaneous uses Shop sites used for general amenity services	1 Bank, *bureau de change* 2 Betting shop 3 Employment agency 4 Estate agent 5 Funeral director 6 Gas and electricity showroom 7 Post Office 8 Printer 9 Public house 10 Restaurant, café, snack bar	

Table I Distribution and particulars of retail shops in Great Britain

Type of shop	No. of shops	% distribution	Average no. of persons engaged per unit	Average unit floor area (m²)
Grocers	105 283	19·7	5	57
Other foods: bakers, butchers, fishmongers, greengrocers, off licences	92 524	17·3	5	30
Newsagents, tobacconists, confectioners	52 064	9·7	5	31
Clothing and footwear: men's, women's and children's	81 279	15·2	5–6	73
Household goods: domestic furniture, floor coverings, antiques, second-hand furniture, art dealers and picture framers, radio and electrical shops (hire and repair), ironmongers and hardware, china and glassware, wallpaper and paint	70 342	13·2	4	87

Type of shop	No. of shops	% distribution	Average no. of persons engaged per unit	Average unit floor area (m²)
Other non-food retailers: booksellers, stationers, chemists, photographic and optical goods, cycles and motor accessories, jewellery, leather goods, sports goods, florists, toys, pets and pet foods	66 724	12·6	4.5	51
Service trades: launderettes and dry-cleaners, hairdressing and manicure, shoe repairs	61 090	11·4	4-5	31
Department stores and variety and general household stores	4 775	0·9	66	1066

Source: *Report on the census of distribution and other services*, HMSO, London, 1971

Composite shops using large spaces

Goods which used predominantly to be sold by specialist shops are now increasingly being sold by the larger composite shops which cover a wider range and type of merchandise. The main types of composite shops are:

(a) Department store: provides a comprehensive range of goods (foods, clothing and footwear, household goods, other goods and services) at a wide range of prices. It is virtually a series of shops contained under one name and roof. Sales are by a combination of self service, assisted service and personal service. Provisions for credit and goods delivery usually included. There may be space concessions for specialist manufacturers: eg toiletry stands.

(b) Variety and general household store: provides for certain types of goods (foods, clothing and footwear, household goods and other goods) at relatively low prices. Mostly self and assisted service on cash and carry basis. Credit facilities may be available.

(c) Supermarket: retails mainly in foods with some additional sidelines in clothing and household goods.

(d) Hypermarket: provides a comprehensive range of goods (foods, clothing and footwear, household goods and other goods) at relatively low prices. Sales are predominantly self service with some assisted service. Mainly cash and carry. Substantial parking facilities are required and consequently only found in suburban areas.

2
TYPES OF SHOP

2.1 FOOD

Categories

The wide range of shops dealing with food products may be categorised as follows:

Shop type	Customary products	Additional products
1 Supermarket	Most types of foods, generally sub-divided into the following departments: grocery, bread and cakes, greengrocery, meat and poultry, fish, dairy, florist, tobacco and cigarettes, confectionery, off-licence and delicatessen	Popular household goods, clothing, foot-wear and other cheap goods
2 Grocer	Canned foods, dairy products, sauces, preserves, beverages, biscuits, spices, dry goods, confectionery	Popular household goods, paper pro-ducts, toilet requisites, detergents, pet foods
3 Butcher	Fresh and frozen meats, meat products, poultry	Canned foods, eggs, preserves
4 Fishmonger	Fresh and frozen fish, shellfish, cured fish	Poultry, canned foods, eggs, preserves
5 Baker	Bread, cakes, biscuits, pies	Luncheon snacks: hot soup, hot pies, sausages, sandwiches
6 Greengrocer	Fresh vegetables and fruit	Flowers and plants
7 Confectioner	Chocolates, sweets, beverages, cigarettes, tobacco	Stationery products, cards, wrapping paper, newsprint
8 Specialist foodshop	Health foods, frozen foods, delicat-essen, off-licence	

Recent development has seen the tendency towards coalescence leading to the formation of larger shops, in particular super-markets which sell most types of foods and many household goods.

Type of service

Personal service

In traditional shops goods are sold from behind the counter and are displayed on the counter or on shelves behind it and also to a limited extent on the customers' side.

In fishmongers the customer selects from a large display slab and the assistant takes up the order, prepares, weighs and wraps at the counter. In greengrocers the vegetables and fruit are kept on racks or crates along perimeter walls and the customer moves round to select while an assistant collects, weighs and puts in a paper bag or the customer's shopping basket. In supermarkets personal service is limited to the delicatessen counter where goods must be cut, weighed and packed to order. Supermarkets offering cigarettes for sale also provide personal service for security reasons.

Self service

This provides for maximum stock display per square metre of floor area using the minimum number of trained staff. Ideally entrances and exits should be sited separately. The customer should be encouraged to traverse a route filled with as many types of goods as possible. These are collected in shopping baskets or trolleys and taken, for paying and collection, to checkout units near the exit.

Grocer

The traditional grocer's shop offering personal service has virtually disappeared to make way for the self service establishment. Figure 2.1 shows how a transition from the first type to the second may take place. The planning and layout of large self service food shops is covered later in this section under the heading 'Supermarket'.

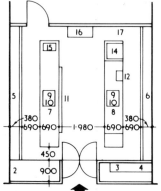

2.1 *Grocer's shop*
Overall width: nearest controlling dimension (BS 4330) is 5·4m or 5·7m.

1 *double entrance door* **2** *shop window with display bed 760mm above pavement and half height screen at the back* **3** *bacon window with marble display bed, one step shelf and half height screen at back* **4** *hanging rail for bacon, etc above* **5** *display shelving* **6** *marble shelves at 450mm centres* **7** *counter with shelf below* **8** *marble counter with shelf below* **9** *scales* **10** *cash register* **11** *semi-recess to receive biscuit tins (240mm high × 220mm × 230mm)* **12** *cheese cutter* **13** *bacon slicer (requires 920 × 960mm)* **14** *marble butter slab and screen* **15** *coffee grinder* **16** *egg display* **17** *bacon or ham hanging rail*
If this traditional layout is to be self service the perimeter shelves **(6)** *are usually replaced by dry goods display fittings, the counters are removed and a central gondola installed. A frozen food display cabinet is essential and may replace one window display* **(2)**

Butcher

A typical butcher's layout is given in Fig 2.2.

Coldstores

Most butchers have two cold stores to keep frozen and chilled provisions. The freezer allows the butcher to buy in bulk and keep stock for several weeks. The storage temperature ranges from -24°C to -30°C. The chiller allows cut frozen meat to thaw slowly without condensation forming on the surface of the meat. It also serves to store meat for immediate sale without deterioration for several days. The chiller temperatures range from -2°C to 4°C.

Construction
The following points should be checked prior to the installation of coldstores:
1 All ceiling, floor and wall surfaces must be free from damp penetration.
2 All surfaces must be firm and free from materials which might get detached.
3 Floors must be, or must be made to be, loadbearing.

Commercial coldstores are usually built by specialist firms from sectional components. The sections are bolted together on site and can be dismantled easily for use elsewhere if required. The construction consists of timber framework clad with panels of sheet metal on ply and compressed asbestos insulation board. Floors are cast with granolithic concrete reinforced with weld mesh to a thickness of 35 to 75mm. Chiller rooms have rebated doors with resilient gaskets. The acceptable clear opening size is 1850mm high × 700mm wide. The sill usually takes up the form of a step up into the cold room with a rebate on the bottom edge of the door. Freezer room doors, also known as 'super-freeze' doors, have the appearance of a rectangular slab closing over the door opening, overlapping it all round by approximately 80 to 100mm. The door seals are made from felt strips approximately 70mm wide screwed to the door so that when the door is shut the opening is completely sealed off. Heater cables are arranged round the door opening in the area covered by the gasket. The cables are channelled to the fascia of the door and covered with an aluminium or copper strip. For safety, low voltage heating cables are used. These are rated at about 10 volts per metre, with the transformer fitted in a convenient position near the door.

Fittings
Because of the high humidity in coldstores all fittings must be adequately protected against corrosion. The usual finishes are stainless steel or chromium plating. Wire shelves have polythene coatings. The main fittings are hanging rails and shelves. Meat hanging rails may be cantilevered off the walls or hung from the ceiling. Wall fittings or side rails are usually made from 40 × 7mm flat rolled steel supported by brackets projecting about 65mm from the wall. Ceiling hangers are of approximately the same size and hung at about 750mm centres. Shelves are usually 300mm, 375mm or 450mm deep and constructed from sheet steel or wire mesh. Interior lighting should be sealed against moisture penetration and the lamp may be protected by wire mesh as a protection against accidental breakage. All wiring should be sheathed in copper, rubber or plastic. Metal conduits should be avoided because of the risk of condensation.

Preparation room equipment
(a) Butcher's block: a very solid timber table with a 175mm top in beech; it is generally available in two sizes: 1200 × 600mm and 1800 × 750mm and is used for chopping or sawing carcasses to smaller size.
(b) Boning-out and cutting table: may be constructed from a stainless steel frame which is easy to clean and a beech cutting board which can be removed for cleaning or replacement: generally available in two sizes 1200 × 600mm and 1800 × 750mm; used to reduce carcasses by cutting them down to smaller pieces such as chops, steaks, joints, etc.
(c) Setting-out table: similar to the boning-out table with additional racks for plastic containers of various sizes under the worktop; usual size 1200 × 600mm.
(d) Wrapping table: incorporates rolls of plastic film in widths up to 450mm in which meat is wrapped and the seal hot welded; a hot air unit is attached which causes the film to shrink tightly over the

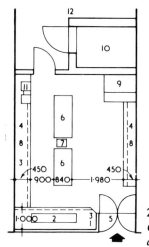

2.2 Butcher's shop
Overall width: nearest controlling dimension (BS 4330) is 4·5m or 4·8m.
1 *marble finished concrete slab 920mm above floor level laid to fall to a small curb at the window end* 2 *12·7mm plate glass shelf suspended at eye level or, alternatively, hanging rails to display joints* 3 *hanging rails* 4 *extra hanging rails, although these are not always included* 5 *entrance doors large enough to admit carcass meat if deliveries are made to the front of the shop* 6 *chopping tables or butcher's blocks* 7 *scales* 8 *fixed shelf at counter height* 9 *pay desk* 10 *cold store* 11 *sausage machine* 12 *general storage, etc*

meat. Such tables are usually 1100 × 750mm and are only required in the butcher's departments of supermarkets or department stores which require pre-packaging facilities.
(e) Meat hanging rails: made from 40 × 7mm (approximately) flat rolled steel; if placed above cutting tables they must be at a minimum height of 2750mm to allow for hanging carcasses.
(f) Tray trolley: used to convey meat from one section to the next; size 600 × 400mm, height 1150mm.

Display
Meat is largely displayed in refrigerated cabinets as described in section 4.11 below. Unwrapped fresh meat should be stored at temperatures of 0·5°C to 3·0°C and prepacked meat at -2·0°C to 0·0°C. The shelf life for prepacked meat is 3 days for beef and lamb, 2 days for veal and pork and 4 hours for mince meat (which loses colour very quickly). Meat which is to be on window display should be shaded so as to prevent early damage. Colour is an important selling factor and meat in supermarkets is often divided into red meats and white meats. Tungsten is the best form of lighting since it produces less colour distortion than fluorescent lighting. If the latter has to be used, however, tubes should produce good colour rendering. ('De Luxe natural' and 'Colour 32' are recommended as they give meats a fresh and attractive look.)

Fishmonger
A traditional fishmonger's shop is shown in Fig 2.3. Fresh fish is still to be found predominantly in shops of this type because supermarkets prefer to compete only in the field of prepacked frozen fish. The reasons for this are that:
1 The business of purchasing, cutting and preparing fish requires trained staff.
2 Fish cutting and preparation operations are messy and look unhygienic in supermarket environments.
3 Fresh fish produces strong smells which would penetrate other supermarket goods.

Coldstores
The construction and fittings for suitable coldstores have already been discussed under 'Butcher' above. Usually only one coldstore is required to keep provisions chilled. Frozen fish is limited in bulk and may be stored in freezer cabinets.

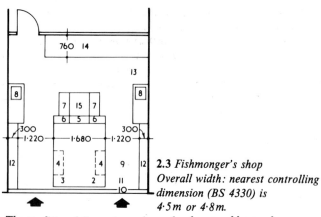

2.3 *Fishmonger's shop*
Overall width: nearest controlling dimension (BS 4330) is 4·5m or 4·8m.

The traditional form shown here closely resembles modern specialist shops. An almost invariable addition now is a frozen food refrigerated display cabinet which might replace one of the sinks shown (8). Cold storage and uncrating space is not shown but would have to be planned round a yard at the back.
1 marble finished concrete slab or refrigerated display bed. Slabs are arranged to fall 150mm from back to front. Front height 610mm above floor level 2 gutter with central trapped gulley 3 marble curb to traditional slab 4 shelves under for wrapping paper, etc 5 live fish tank if included 6 scales 7 wrapping shelves 8 sink, draining and cutting board 9 floor laid to fall to street 10 gutter cover 11 hanging rail for dried or smoked fish or poultry 12 display shelves for sundries 13 dumping space for crates or customer space for access to frozen food display 14 packing bench 15 pay desk or cash register

Display
(a) Traditional slab: made of concrete finished with marble. Slabs are arranged at an angle of about 15° so as to give better display and provide the falls for drainage. The front nosing should have an upstand to collect excessive water and prevent dripping on the customers' side. Front height should measure about 750mm from the floor. Space under the slab should be fitted with shelves to store wrapping papers, etc.
(b) Cutting table: may be constructed from stainless steel (which is easy to clean) and topped with a beech block (which can be removed for cleaning and replacing). Space under or adjacent to the table should accommodate plastic bins to collect waste. Space immediately adjacent to the table should accommodate a sink.
(c) Wrapping table: similar to a cutting table, but normally kept clean and dry. Shelving space underneath is used to store wrapping paper, bags, etc.
(d) Hanging rails for game and poultry: made from flat rolled steel measuring about 25 × 7mm. These can be hung from the ceiling or walls.
(e) Refrigerated cabinets for chilled and frozen provisions: these are discussed in section 4.11 below.

Environment
Surfaces must look clean and hygienic at all times. Impervious surfaces are easily washed and hosed down and are not affected by condensation. Noise reverberation does occur, however, and is best dealt with by using acoustic ceiling tiles. Floors should be laid to falls with iron gratings over inverted trap gulleys. There is always a conflict in fishmongers' and butchers' shops between balancing the requirements of temperature for staff comfort (16°C) and the display of provisions (-2°C to 0°C). This may be solved by using the following methods:

1 Using directional fan heaters which blow warm air towards staff and away from food.
2 Using radiant heaters placed high on walls above the food so that it is not affected.

3 Providing comfortable conditions in another room to which staff can withdraw whenever so inclined.
Adequate ventilation is required for the removal of smells. Exhaust points should be checked to make sure that they do not disturb neighbours.

Baker
A traditional baker's layout is given in Fig 2.4. Most small bakers obtain their bread from multiple bakeries where intensive methods allow for more economies. Architects who have to deal with premises where baking is done should consult at an early stage both with their clients and with the oven manufacturers to work out details. The loading will be an important factor as commercial ovens are very heavy (weighing up to 2 tons). A large amount of heat is produced which requires mechanical ventilating. The conveying of products from the bakery to the shop may also require some thought as to whether it is to be done manually, using trolleys, or mechanically using goods lifts. Cream cakes and pastries are often displayed in refrigerated cabinets. Bakeries which cater for lunch-time markets require hot display cabinets for pies, sausages, etc.

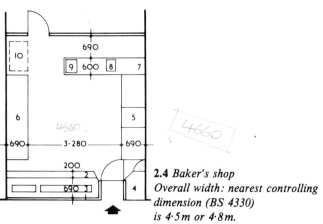

2.4 *Baker's shop*
Overall width: nearest controlling dimension (BS 4330) is 4·5m or 4·8m.

The traditional layout shown here is still widely used although frequently combined with a tea-room or restaurant in the back quarters or at first floor. Refrigerated display cases are commonly used instead of the older kind of showcases for cakes and confectionery.
1 shop window with marble or cooled display bed about 760mm above floor level 2 180mm wide shelf set 150mm above display bed and used for boxing cakes, etc selected from window display 3 pierced or slotted standards supporting adjustable brackets for forward-tilted glass shelves for cakes and 'fancies' 4 enclosed window for special display (wedding cakes, etc) 5 serving counter with bread bins or trays below 6 service counter with biscuit tins below and display cases over 7 counter with paper and cardboard box store below 8 scales 9 cash register 10 tubular rack for stock trays from bakehouse or van delivery

Greengrocer
A typical greengrocer's layout is given in Fig 2.5. Architects should establish client's requirements for delivery and unpacking of goods, washing, preparing, weighing, wrapping, waste collection and disposal.

Supermarket
Figure 2.6 shows a commodity layout scheme for a typical supermarket.

Space allocation
Architects should consult their clients about the respective amounts of space required for different purposes, for example how the available area should be subdivided to provide for a sales floor,

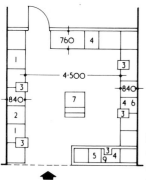

2.5 *Greengrocer's shop Overall width: nearest controlling dimension (BS 4330) is 6 m or 6·3 m.*

1 *open bins for root vegetables* 2 *slab or mesh shelves for greens (cabbage, etc) over vegetable bins, about 910mm above floor level* 3 *scales* 4 *open bins, racks or display equipment for fruit and flowers* 5 *suspended shelf for choice fruits (a high level rail for bananas is often provided here or over 4)* 6 *shelf for flowers* 7 *pay desk, sometimes replaced by a short counter, off centre, to facilitate wrapping and storage of wrapping material* 8 *the entrance may be closed by a roller shutter and left open by day or by a conventional door which can be fixed open in good weather* 9 *the shop window is often arranged so 4 and 5 make a display visible both inside and outside the shop*

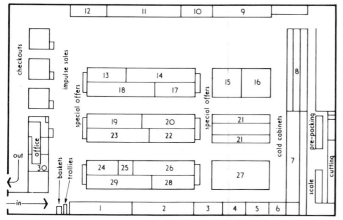

2.6 *Commodity location scheme for a typical supermarket (source: Co-operative Union Supermarkets Guide 1964). The main commodieies are marked with an asterisk.*

1 *canned vegetables** 2 *canned soups* 3 *canned meats* 4 *canned fish* 5 *sauces and pickles* 6 *delicatessen and convenience foods* 7 *meat** 8 *delicatessen* 9 *cooking sundries* 10 *paper products* 11 *dry goods* 12 *sweets and chocolates* 13 *soaps* 14 *detergents** 15 *frozen foods* 16 *greengrocery (salads)* 17 *baby foods* 18 *chemist's sundries* 19 *breakfast cereals** 20 *preserves and spreads* 21 *greengrocery** 22 *bakery* 23 *biscuits* 24 *pet foods* 25 *cold beverages* 26 *hot beverages** 27 *provisions** 28 *canned milk, cream and puddings* 29 *canned fruit** 30 *cigarettes and tobacco*

floor area subdivided by island displays known as gondolas which should form a series of corridors running lengthwise from the front to the rear. Fittings running breadthwise are not well liked: it has been found that as few as 20 per cent of customers visit areas fitted in this way compared with 80 per cent who prefer those equipped with wall fittings. Lengthwise planning also permits views of the rear from the shopfront as well as supervision by staff from the checkout points. Fittings should run in lengths between 3·5 and 7·9 m. The width between aisles should not be less than 1·35 mm or not less than 2·0 m if shopping trolleys are used. Lobbies to counters where personal service is given, such as delicatessen counters, should be a minimum of 2·0 m wide to avoid congestion. Entrance lobbies should be of adequate width to accommodate trolleys, shopping baskets, and their manoeuvering. Security-conscious premises may require the installation of turnstiles which serve to control direction of customer flow. Lobbies behind check-out counters should be about 2·0 m deep to give customers enough room to deposit their personal shopping baskets or carts before entering the store and to pack the goods they have bought into these containers after checking-in and payment.

Commodities

The location of commodities in relation to the floor plan is particularly important where refrigerated display equipment is required because this has to be put in relatively permanent positions and appropriate services have to be installed. Commodities fall under seven general categories: grocery foods, meat and poultry, greengrocery, dairy and provisions, bakery, frozen foods and non-foods. Further analysis is given in table I below. Basic rules which may be applied as to where different commodities should be put are:

1 All indisputably similar goods should be located together.
2 goods with related appeal should be located together, eg canned fruit and cream.
3 Incompatible foods should be kept apart, eg pet foods and canned meat.
2 Goods with related appeal should be located together, eg canned toiletries and cakes.
5 Small valuable items which are easy to pilfer should be located near checkout counters where they are under constant supervision, eg toiletries.
6 Commodities may be grouped by meal association, eg breakfast, lunch, tea.
7 Commodities should be broken down by value to determine whether they are demand, semi-demand or impulse goods. These should be grouped and sited accordingly, eg demand goods in rear areas, impulse goods near checkouts, and semi-demand goods in between.
8 Heavy items should be located near checkout points.

Table I Breakdown of commodities in relation to percentage of shelf area occupied

Category	Commodity	Percentage of total shelf area
Grocery foods 61·8%	Baby foods	1·2
	Canned and dried foods	5·6
	Canned and dried vegetables	5·1
	Canned and packaged soups	4·1
	Cereals	4·1
	Canned meats, fish and prepared foods	5·3
	Biscuits	8·0
	Special foods, canned or packaged	0·8
	Hot beverages (eg tea)	3·6
	Cold beverages	2·5
	Preserves	3·2
	Sauces	4·3
	Cookery needs and desserts	5·4
	Canned milk and cream	1·4
	Sugar	1·4
	Sweets and chocolates	3·5
	Pet foods	2·3

continued

for offices and staff accommodation and for storage and the handling of goods. The average figures for British supermarkets are 50 per cent for the sales floor, 20 per cent for offices and staff and 30 per cent for storage and handling. These figures can only however be taken as a rough guide because in any particular case they will be affected by such variable factors as the total floor available in relation to the turnover expected, client operation methods and the place in which the supermarket is sited.

Planning and layout

General principles for planning the sales floor are given in section 3.2 below. For all foodshops, and in particular supermarkets, the main principle to adhere to is simplicity. The ideal plan would have the perimeter walls covered with display fittings, and the remaining

Category	Commodity	Percentage of total shelf area
Other foods 18·2%	Meat and poultry	2·4
	Greengroceries	3·3
	Dairy and provisions	6·7
	Bakery	4·4
	Frozen foods	1·4
Non-foods 20%	Soap	5·7
	Chemist's sundries	5·3
	Cigarettes and tobacco	0·3
	Paper products	2·4
	Housewares	3·9
	Miscellaneous	2·4
		100·0 Total

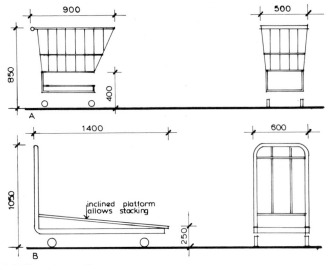

2.7 *Shopping trolleys*
A *collection trolley* **B** *cart trolley*

This table is derived from information provided by the Supermarket Association. It should be noted that shelf area in the case of commodities requiring refrigerated display does not bear a direct relationship to floor area.

Equipment
Collection baskets: commonly made from welded or woven wire mesh in aluminium or steel, chromium plated, plastic coated, or anodised and fitted with folding handles covered in plastic. Normal size (height, length and width) is $430 \times 280 \times 200$ mm and baskets are tapered for stacking. About 30 baskets should be allowed per 45 m² of selling floor area. Supermarkets with a high turnover use special carts to transport from checkout counters to entrance collection points.

Collection trolleys: commonly made from chromium plated wire mesh. Some have a basket top and a low level tray. Most types are designed to 'nest' when not in use and some incorporate a folding shelf which is used as a baby seat. Normal size (height, length and width) is $610 \times 400 \times 890$ mm.

Cart trolleys: used by staff operators in the movement of heavy or bulky goods in supermarkets and cash and carry stores. The main frame is constructed from a hollow steel box frame welded to a tubular steel back frame and handle. The loading platform measures approximately 1200×600 mm and may be plywood or steel mesh. Castors are heavy duty swivelling models with cushioned tyred wheels. Maximum loading is 500 kg, and stacking is possible on some models. Overall dimensions for height, length and width are $1050 \times 1400 \times 600$ mm. Figure **2.7** shows a collection trolley and a cart trolley.

Checkout counters: one checkout counter should be allowed per 45 m² to 60 m² of the sales floor area. Simpler types with the customer unloading and packing would call for the lower figure. More elaborate types and possibly mechanically assisted units would require the higher value. Some clients prefer the higher value for economic reasons. The counters are usually L-shaped with the register stand in front of the cashier who sits facing the interior. To the left is the checking counter. This has an inclined recess at the front for shopping baskets and is between 300 and 450 mm wide and from 1000 to 2400 mm long: anything over 1800 mm long calls for a mechanical conveyor or sloping chute. The height of the worktop is about 800 mm. Other features include: wide backs so that one customer can pack and another check at the same time; shelves under the counter for paper bags; a shelf at the back on which customers can place personal shopping baskets; a side screen to protect the cashier from draughts; moving conveyor belts and an automatic change cash dispenser. Checkout counters are illustrated in Fig **2.8**.

Cash registers: may be provided with the checkout unit or bought separately. If bought separately, they should be checked to make sure they will fit their stands. Most registers fit on a stand of 450×450 mm. The traditional mechanical registers are being replaced by electronic registers which cover the whole spectrum of retailing from registering single sales to multiplying prices per item, providing print-outs to enable customers to identify particular items

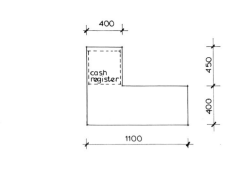

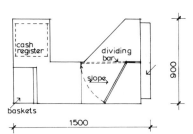

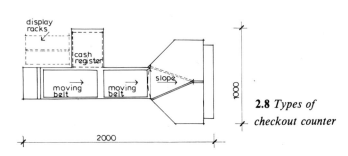

2.8 *Types of checkout counter*

purchased, separating cash sales for VAT purposes, carrying out stock control operations, recording discounts or items relating to bonus schemes and other functions. Some supermarket units are linked to an automatic change cash dispenser.

Dry goods display: 'dry goods' is taken to mean all types of goods that do not require special storage conditions and can be displayed on open shelving, or binning systems. Goods in this category are extremely diverse in size, shape, and weight. Some may be displayed on simple shelves while others require restraining by front rails, side panels or grilles. The basic form of unit is fairly standard with a fixed wide bottom shelf. This may be tilted backwards to give better visibility and should be well clear of the floor. All shelves should have price rails for insertion of prices or other information. Wall units may incorporate a canopy with concealed lighting to illuminate display, and if space is limited, this may be used to carry more goods. Island units are made up to 1·75 m high but lower units up to 1·4 m are preferable because they allow for better supervision by staff and present the customer with an open view of the store.

Factors to consider when selecting shelving and binning systems for supermarkets are:

1 Hygiene: shelf wear is very heavy and finishes must therefore be very hard to withstand abrasion without damage. They must also be easy to keep clean.

2 Strength: the system must be adequate to withstand heavy and unequal loading without becoming unstable.

3 Flexibility: units must be easily adjustable without skilled labour and it should be possible to adjust shelf heights independently.

4 Design: some units can be adjustable to compensate for uneven floors. Shelves should have built-in ticket rails for inserting price clips and other information. The unit should be free of crevices where dust might collect.

Shelving and binning systems are discussed in more detail in section 4.4 below.

Refrigerated display: selection between the various makes of refrigerated cabinets in which goods are to be displayed should take into consideration their respective appearance, finish, type of refrigeration equipment, cost, net storage volume and shelf area in relation to floor space occupied. Deep frozen food must be stored in cabinets capable of maintaining a minimum temperature of -18°C or less since expected shelf life is mainly, but not solely, dependent on this (see table II below and the note which follows it). Quick frozen or chilled food on the other hand requires cabinets suitable for maintaining temperatures broadly ranging from -6·5°C to +6·5°C (see table III below). Display cabinets may be open, closed, single-deck or multi-deck. They operate on either of the following systems:

(a) those where products are laid on a cooled surface which acts as a conductor.

(b) those where products are blanketed in a moving layer of cold air by convection or fan assisted circulation.

Architects should consult their clients on the number of cabinets required. Premises which only require a few cabinets may employ self-contained units where the refrigerant plant is incorporated in the cabinet. Premises needing a large number may however prefer them all to be remotely controlled from a separate plant. The latter may be cheaper to run; it is also easier to maintain without disturbing the customers and it takes the considerable heat and noise produced by condensers away from the sales floor. Its disadvantages are that units must be placed in relatively perman-

ent positions because of refrigerant supply pipes and that all cabinets are affected if the central plant fails. Refrigerated cabinets are considered in more detail in section 4.11 below.

Table II Recommended storage temperatures and expected shelf life of frozen food*

Commodity	Temperature (°C)	Expected storage life (months)
Meat and its by-products		
Beef	-12	5 to 8
Veal	-18	18
Veal	-18	6 to 8
Lamb	-12	3 to 6
	-23	8 to 10
Rabbit	-23	6
Poultry	-12	3
	-23	9 to 10
Seafood		
Fatty fish: herrings, mackerel, sardines, salmon	-18	2 to 3
	-29	6
Lean fish: cod, haddock	-18	3 to 5
	-29	2 to 3
Flat fish: plaice, sole	-18	4 to 6
	-25	7 to 10
Lobster, crab	-18	2
Shrimps	-18	6
Oysters, scallops, clams	-18	2 to 4
Vegetables		
Asparagus, beans, Brussels sprouts, corn on the cob, peas, spinach	-18	8 to 12
Potatoes (French fried)	-18	6
Potatoes (scalloped)	-18	1
Fruit		
Apricots, cherries, peaches, raspberries, strawberries	-18	12
	-24	18
Fruit juices	-20	9 to 12
Pre-cooked food		
Bread, rolls	-18	2 to 4
Cakes	-18	4 to 6
Pies	-18	1 to 6
Cooked meals	-18	2 to 3
	-29	5 to 7
Ice cream	-23	2
	-29	4 to 6

*Note: The above figures are only a rough guide because expected shelf life is also affected by the quality of food before it is frozen and by packaging.

2.9 *Left. Midnight Barbecue, delicatessen and foods, London, designed by Doug Patterson and Jerry Hewitt. The stylised shopfront stands out from its neighbours*

2.10 *Above. Same. Internal view with curvy counter and mirrored customers' eating worktop in white laminate*

2.11

2.13

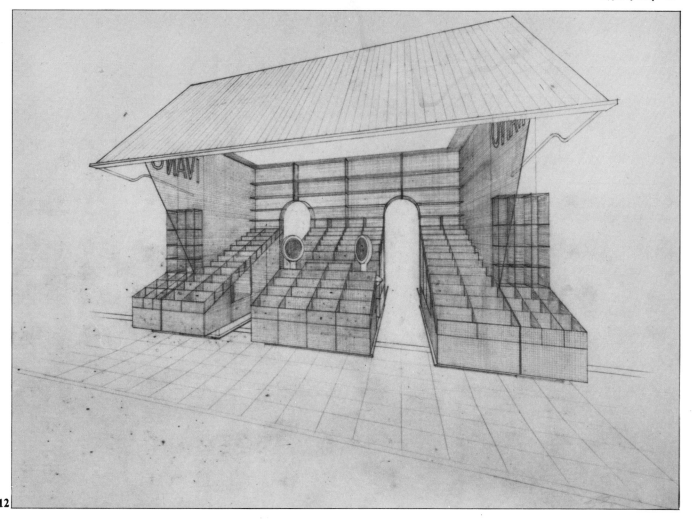

2.12

2.14

2.11 *Ivano (project) greengrocer, London, designed by Campbell, Zogolovitch, Wilkinson and Gough. When closed the curved tracked sliding doors spell the shop's name*

2.12 *Same. When open the fruit and vegetables in wire basket trolleys would slide forward on to the pavement. Side mesh grilles under the blind spell out the shop's name*

2.13 *Chalk Farm Nutrition Centre, health foods, London, designed by Rolfe Judd Group Practice. Wholesome foods are displayed on purpose-made pine shelving. The shop front has a stained glass upper section*

2.14 *Same. Looking to other sections of the shop. Dairy products are in refrigerated cabinets. Floors and all exposed timbers are sealed pine. The structural lintels and false joist are stained dark brown. Walls are fairfaced bricks as is the staircase*

Table III Recommended storage temperatures and cabinet operation for chilled foods*

Commodity	Temperature (°C)	Cabinet operation
Meat: wrapped and unwrapped, fresh	0	Fresh unwrapped meat should be displayed in cabinets equipped with gravity cooling coils
Meat: quick frozen or chilled	-4·5	Other commodities can be displayed in fan assisted automatic defrost cabinets
Offal	-6·5	
Poultry: fresh	0	When wrapped poultry may be displayed in fan assisted display cabinets
Poultry: frozen	-15	
Delicatessen: pre-packed	6·5	Unwrapped foods should be displayed in gravity cooling systems. Wrapped foods may be displayed in fan assisted units
Delicatessen: unwrapped	6·5	
Dairy products	5·5	Fan assisted display cabinets for all pre-packed foods
Provisions, bacon and cooked meats	5·5	
Fish, fresh on slab	1	Fish should be adequately iced down and the bed refrigerated to prevent too rapid loss of ice
Pastry, patisseries	7·2	Gravity cooling
Flowers	10	Gravity cooling

*Note: No shelf life is given because storage periods are relatively short.

2.2 CLOTHING

Categories
Shops dealing with clothing may be categorised into the following groups:

Shop type	Type of goods
Women's wear	Dresses, blouses, shirts, suits, coats, jackets, underwear, nightwear, hats, swimwear, knitwear, raincoats, dressing gowns, leather goods and accessories
Men's wear	Suits, jackets, trousers, coats, shirts, underwear, knitwear, ties, swimwear, belts and accessories
Unisex	Shirts, casual jackets, jeans, knitwear, leather goods and accessories
Specialist	Any of the following: bridal and evening wear, furs, knitwear, maternity baby and child wear, sportswear, outsize wear

Shops may be further classified as follows:
1 Specialists in a particular type of goods
2 Specialists for a particular age group
3 Those aiming at volume sales
4 Those concerned with limited exclusive sales
5 Branches of a multiple group
6 Independent retailers.

Service

The kind of service given may be:

Self service: this is suitable for impulse goods and pre-packed goods such as underwear, leather goods and accessories, and for units dealing with volume sales; units are generally open plan with cash desk/wrapping positions controlling the centre or at exits.

Assisted service: this is suitable for most ready to wear goods where customers have to try on for size or liking; customers select items on open display for themselves and are assisted by staff; cash desks/wrapping positions are either scattered or centralised depending on the unit size.

Personalised service: this is given mainly in exclusive shops where the clientele is limited or in premises where tailoring services are provided; usually units are small with a single cash desk/wrapping point.

Men's wear

Men's wear shops fall distinctly into one of the following types:

Traditional conservative: this is based on the view that a customer enters with a specific purchase in mind; windows display the maximum amount of goods, but the interior is subdued; the shop is usually exclusive, concerned with tailoring services on suits, coats and evening wear; a limited amount of ready to wear and mercery goods are generally available.

Fashion: this is characterised by a bold open approach and is usually concerned with fashion and marketing with the younger man in mind, mainly providing ready-to-wear clothes with some provision for alterations to suits and trousers.

Variety store: this concentrates on selling casual wear and mercery with the simplest forms of display and at the lowest prices; no alterations or services are entertained and sales is mostly self service; the vast majority of customers are women and a department of this kind is usually planned on the main traffic route of the store.

Department store: this is often a combination of all three types above; ready-to-wear goods are considered as impulse goods and accordingly placed on pedestrial routes; tailoring is regarded as exclusive and may be located in secluded locations, sometimes adjoining other male activities such as men's hairdressing; boys' wear is sold in a different department because the shopping is mostly done by women; the exception is the tailoring department specialising in school outfits which has a peak demand mainly in August and at Christmas.

A feature of tailoring shops is that they contain large samples of bolts of cloth. These are heavy and are displayed on heavy duty shelving. Standards should be spaced at 500 mm intervals or in multiples of 250 mm. The minimum total shelving run should be 20 m with shelving arranged 750 mm apart. The top shelf should not be more than 1·5 m high. The selling area can be quite small. there should be hanging space for about 20 to 30 suits, a minimum counter of 1800 × 600 mm, one or two fitting rooms about 1500 × 1200 mm and customer circulation space of about 10·0 m². Where ready-to-wear clothing or other merchandise is to be sold corresponding increases must be made in the size of the selling area.

Table IV Types of men's wear and their methods of display

Classification	Type of clothing	Display model	Stand	Clothes rail	Cabinet	Shelving	Binning
Impulse	Nightwear	*	*		*	*	
	Underwear				*	*	*
	Gloves	*	*		*	*	*
	Hats	*	*		*	*	
	Knitwear	*	*	*	*	*	
	Ties	*	*		*		
	Umbrellas	*	*		*		
	Accessories (belts, cuff links, tie pins)		*		*	*	*
Demand tailoring	Coats	*	*	*	*		
	Jackets	*	*	*	*		
	Evening and morning suits	*	*		*		
	Lounge suits	*	*	*	*		
	Trousers	*		*	*		
Ready-to-wear as above plus	Sportswear	*	*	*	*	*	*
	Dressing gowns	*	*	*	*		
	Raincoats	*	*	*	*		
	Shirts	*	*	*	*		
Boys' wear as above plus	School wear	*	*	*	*	*	
	Sports equipment		*		*	*	*

Data for display fixtures and space allocations are discussed in detail in chapter 4.

Women's wear

Women's wear shops roughly fall into the same categories as those dealing in men's wear except that the 'traditional conservative' group is replaced by 'specialists' dealing solely in bridal clothes, evening wear, furs or outsize wear. The view taken here, as with 'traditional conservative' men's shops is that the customer enters with a particular purchase in mind. Window displays exhibit the range of goods available and a high degree of customer comfort is provided in the interior. Fitting rooms should be of adequate size to permit assistants to help the customer.

Table V Types of women's wear and their methods of display

Classification	Type of clothing	Live models	Display models	Stand	Clothes rail	Cabinet	Shelving	Binning
Impulse	Nightwear		*	*	*	*		
	Underwear		*		*	*		*
	Gloves	*	*	*		*		*
	Hats	*	*	*		*	*	
	Handbags	*	*	*		*		*
	Corsetry		*	*		*	*	
	Umbrellas	*	*			*		
Demand tailoring	Coats	*	*		*	*		
	Suits	*	*		*	*		
	Ensembles (coats plus dresses)	*	*	*	*	*		
	Dresses	*	*	*	*	*		

Classification	Type of clothing	Display equipment						
		Live models	Display models	Stand	Clothes rail	Cabinet	Shelving	Binning
Demand tailoring *cont*	Evening and bridal dresses	*	*			*		
Ready-to-wear as above plus	Furs	*	*			*		
	Knitwear	*	*	*	*	*		
	Shirts, blouses	*	*		*	*		
	Skirts	*	*		*	*		
	Sportswear and slacks	*	*	*	*	*		
	Raincoats	*	*	*	*	*		
	Dressing gowns	*	*		*	*		

Live models are expensive and are only used in large shops or department stores. Where they are employed on a regular basis provisions should include a minimum space of $4 \cdot 0 \, m^2$ per model, a dressing table per pair, and a personal drawer each. There should also be hanging rails for 10 garments per model and shelving space to accommodate accessories such as hats, handbags and personal bags. Provisions on the sales floor should include a small stage approximately 6 m wide, 3 m deep and $0 \cdot 8$ m high. This proscenium stage should have side curtains and steps down to floor level. Where an apron stage is required it should measure about $1 \cdot 2$ m wide and project some 6 to 12 m into the sales floor. Its height may vary from $0 \cdot 2$ m to $0 \cdot 8$ m above the floor.

Layout and planning

The principles for the planning and layout of men's and women's wear shops follow the general line discussed in chapter 3 below but architects should also clarify the following points with their clients:
1 The percentage of the total space which should be allocated for each type of goods.
2 The average number of garments of each type that is to be accommodated.
3 The percentage of stock which is to be displayed on the sales floor and that which can remain in stockrooms.
4 The effects of seasonal variations eg whether out of season goods will be stored or disposed of in sales and whether display equipment can accommodate successive types of seasonal goods.
5 The relationship of one type of goods with another (for example coats and hats are compatible and may be displayed next to each other, but raincoats and sportswear are incompatible and have to be displayed separately).

Fitting rooms

Number

The number of fitting rooms should be determined by the client on the basis of his assessment of turnover expected and quantity of stock available.

Location

Fitting rooms should be located in the least valuable parts of the sales floor but must also be easily accessible and supervisable; in department stores this is usually solved by arranging the cubicles in an enclosure with only one common access controlled by a cash desk/wrapping counter.

Size

Sizes for individual cubicles vary depending on their function and the amount of space available. Recommended sizes are:
Limited space (eg for knitwear) $1 \cdot 0 \times 1 \cdot 0$ m or $1 \cdot 2 \times 0 \cdot 9$ m
General space (eg for ready-to-wear goods) $1 \cdot 2 \times 1 \cdot 2$ m
Assisted service (eg for tailoring services) $1 \cdot 2 \times 1 \cdot 8$ m
Curtaining is usually up to $2 \cdot 0$ m high. Where cubicles are fitted with doors these may be wired to signal lights.

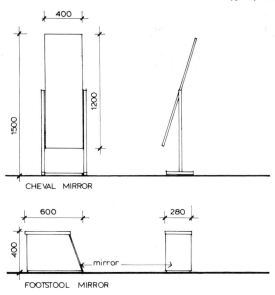

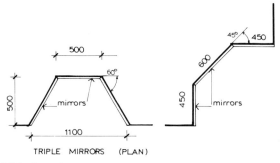

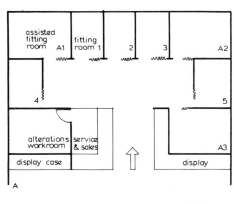

2.15 *Display mirrors*

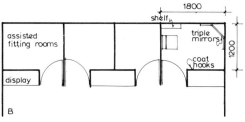

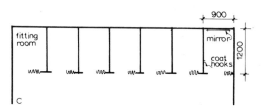

2.16 *Fitting rooms*
A *customers' entry to fitting rooms is controlled by staff at sales counter* **B** *fitting rooms with assisted service behind display cabinets* **C** *row of cubicles*

Equipment

Suitable items are:

Mirrors: where any small cubicles are not fitted with mirrors full length mirrors should be provided on the sales floor not too far from the cubicle entrances; the most useful size of mirror for cubicles is 1·5 m high × 0·75 m wide; mirrors may be folding, angled, or fitted opposite each other to give front and back views. Types of mirrors are shown in Fig **2.15**.

Coat hooks: a minimum of two coat hooks should be provided for customer's and store's clothing; alternatively there should be **hanging rails and hangers. Chair and ashtray.**

Shelf: for tailoring materials such as pin trays, chalk, pattern books and so on.

Dais: for bridal and evening wear.

Fitting rooms and cubicles are illustrated in Fig **2.16**.

Stockroom

The sizes of stockrooms vary according to the quantity of stock to be held and the scope of the client's operations. They may have to provide storage both for newly arrived stock and for out of season stock and they may also be used for unpacking, checking and marking up new stock with prices prior to its delivery to the sales floor (although the latter function is sometimes carried out in the warehouse). Packing facilities should include a table/worktop for folding and packing together with provision for storing cartons, paper, string, etc.

Workroom

This gives space for tailoring, alterations and pressing. In small shops it may be incorporated with the stockroom. Where space allows, workrooms should measure approximately 3·5 × 4·5 m and should be located adjoining the fitting room and sales floor. Equipment to be provided includes a pressing table 900 mm high which may also be used for packing, hanging rails for 20 to 30 garments, a wall bench with drawers underneath and sewing machines.

2.17

2.18

2.17 *Just Looking, boutique, London, designed by Garnett Cloughley Blakemore*

2.18 *Same. View looking up from the basement. The staircase has one side lined with mirrors which give the illusion of greater space*

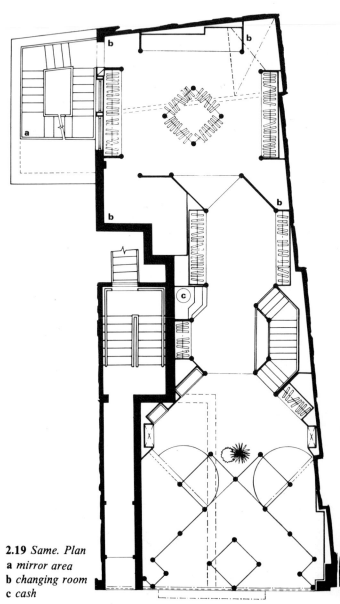

2.19 *Same. Plan*
a *mirror area*
b *changing room*
c *cash*

2.20 *Christian Dior, boutique, London, designed by Max Glendinning. This shop retains the original classical facade. During opening hours the hardwood panelled doors fold back to reveal a recessed lobby with glazed screen and doors*

2.21 *Same. Interior view looking outwards. Walls and ceilings are painted grey matching the carpet on the floor, display cases and counters. Mouldings are picked out in gloss to give more sparkle*

2.22 *Above. Same. A cluster of display cabinets with sides lined with grey carpet matching the floor. Edging trims are chrome and other finishes are interior velvet, mirror or chrome*

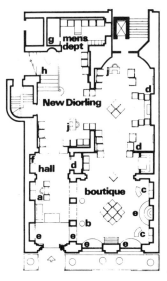

2.23 *Same. Ground floor plan.*
a *reception* **b** *belts* **c** *counter*
d *dressing room* **e** *display*
f *knitwear* **g** *changing*
h *stairs up to main salon*
j *desk*

.25

.26

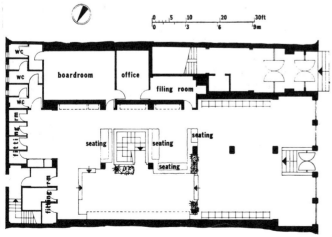

28

2.24 *John Michael, menswear, London, designed by John Michael Consultants Ltd. Shopfront in chrome and glass both clear and tinted*

2.25 *Same. View of end wall with entrance to the fitting rooms. Walls and doors are clad with tinted mirrors*

2.26 *Same. View towards the front entrance. The columns are clad with mirrors and curved chrome corner angles. On the left are display fittings. The shelvings have tubular uprights*

2.27 *Above. Same. View of stairwell to the lower ground floor. The handrail continues all round the stairwell*

2.28 *Same. Ground floor plan*

2.29

2.30

2.31

2.29 *Plaza, boutique, London, designed by Anthony Price. Night view of the facade. Goods are not displayed in the traditional manner but slide-projected on to a screen between the two entrance doors. The shopfront is glazed with a deep blue tinted glass which renders the interior invisible. Only the boldest customers dare enter*

2.30 *Same. The stylised counter houses the slide projector which lights up the window screen*

2.31 *Same. Mirrored changing rooms create multiple images*

2.32 *Same. View of the stark interior towards the changing rooms. House styles are displayed pinned to boards with colour and fabric samples*

2.32

2.33

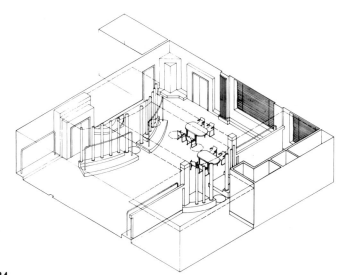

34

36

2.33 *Ellis, bridal and evening wear, London, designed by Doug Patterson and Jerry Hewitt. Interior perspective*

2.34 *Same. Axonometric*

2.35 *Above. Same. Counter detail. The base is postformed (green marbled effect) laminate with vertical fluorescent at the ends*

2.36 *Same. The curved colonnades are commercially available fibrous plaster columns painted white*

2.38

2.37

2.37 *Knitwit, knitwear, London, designed by Wilkinson, Calvert and Gough. Axonometric of interior. The stepped pyramids conceal the changing rooms and have built-in integral display cases and cash counter*

2.38 *Same. View of the shopfront with the first step of the first pyramid on the building line*

2.39 *Same. The palm trees house the light fittings*

2.39

2.40

2.40 *Altre Cose, boutique, Milan, designed by Aldo Jacobei, Ugo la Pietra and Paolo Rizzatto. A transparent lift cage takes the customers down to the basement which is used as a discotheque*

2.41 *Same. Shopfront made from tubular steel and textured perspex panels*

2.42 *Same. Clothing is displayed in perspex cylinders hung from the ceiling. On selection customers can lower these from a central panel shown in the foreground*

2.41

2.42

2.43

2.44

2.45

.46

2.43 Jeeves, shirt laundry service, London, designed by Derrick Holmes and Sydney Jacob. Sculptured forecourt view with laundry operations on the left and service shop on the right. The shirt symbol painted in outline gives an indication of the service provided. Changing the fabric behind the glass gives an impression of changing the shirt

2.44 Same. Close-up view of the service shop with the lettering on the interior bulkhead

2.45 Same. Shelving racks are painted black with chrome rails emphasizing the horizontal lines

2.46 Same. Interior view showing curved walls, ceiling and counter

2.3 FOOTWEAR

Categories
Shoe shops are of the following kinds:

Shop type	Comments
General	Usually subdivided into sections, one dealing with men's shoes, and the other with women's and children's shoes, the latter being grouped together because it is usually women who do the buying
Women's shoes	Shops which specialise are usually exclusive types and present a limited range of styles; maximum customer comfort is essential
Men's shoes	As above
Children's shoes	Usually incorporated with shops specialising in children's wear for ages up to ten years

Types of goods
The architect should consult his client on the range of goods to be sold and on the provisions which should be made for seasonal changes in demand.

Group	General range	Seasonal range	Ancillary goods
Women	Casual, sports, utility, fashion, day wear and evening wear	Sandals, boots, wellingtons	Polishes, creams, handbags, hosiery, costume jewellery and leather goods
Men and children	Casual, sports, utility and fashion	Sandals, slippers, boots and wellingtons	Polishes, creams, brushes, shoe trees

Type of service
Self service: this is suitable for cheap items such as slippers and sandals; pairs are displayed; the customer chooses style and size and pays at the counter; mostly located in variety stores where the majority of customers are women.

Assisted service: this is the most common type of service for shoe selling; stock is displayed on shelves for customer selection; the assistant collects shoes of the size required from the stockroom and helps the customer try them on; when a sale is agreed the assistant collects the money and takes it to the counter for payment, wrapping and change; for security reasons, usually only one shoe is displayed from each pair.

Personal service: this is provided mainly in exclusive shops where the clientele is limited.

Planning and layout
Plans of a shoe shop are shown in Fig **2.47**. Principles for planning and layout follow those discussed in chapter 3 below but architects should also clarify the following points with their clients:
1 The percentage of the total space to be allocated for each class of goods ie men's shoes, women's shoes and children's shoes
2 The average number of styles of each class to be accommodated and the quantities of ancillary goods to be stocked for each class
3 The effects of seasonal variations ie whether out of season stock is to be stored or disposed of in sales.

The following principles are thought to be common to all shoe shops and should be considered in the planning stages:

Location
Footwear is considered to be comparison goods because customers require a wide choice of styles, makes, prices, fittings and quality. Hence it is generally better for any shop to be grouped with other shoe shops in a locality. Potential customers may object to the limited range offered by one particular shop on its own and so be prepared to travel further afield so that they can have a wider choice from a number of shops grouped together.

Sectioning
Children's shoes are grouped together with women's shoes because women do most of the buying. Where a shop is on two floors or more it is usual to find this department on the ground floor, so that

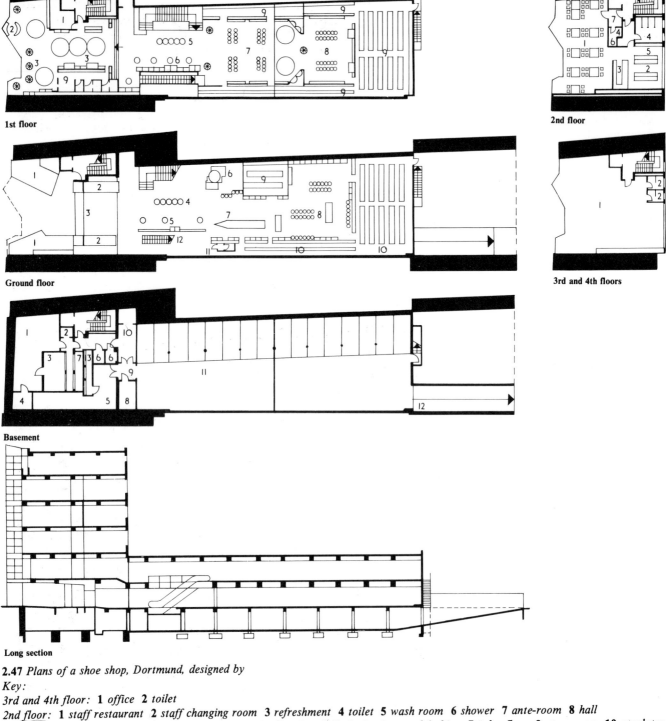

1st floor

2nd floor

Ground floor

3rd and 4th floors

Basement

Long section

2.47 *Plans of a shoe shop, Dortmund, designed by*
Key:
3rd and 4th floor: **1** *office* **2** *toilet*
2nd floor: **1** *staff restaurant* **2** *staff changing room* **3** *refreshment* **4** *toilet* **5** *wash room* **6** *shower* **7** *ante-room* **8** *hall*
1st floor: **1** *manager* **2** *expresso bar* **3** *trend-shop* **4** *toilet* **5** *cash desk* **6** *sports and fashion* **7** *sales floor* **9** *store room* **10** *escalator*
Ground floor: **1** *display windows* **2** *show cases* **3** *sinking door* **4** *cash desk* **5** *sports and fashion* **6** *creche* **7** *children's department*
8 *sales floor* **9** *stock shelves* **10** *store room* **11** *toilet* **12** *escalator*
Basement: **1** *central heating* **2** *meter room (electricity)* **3** *air conditioning* **4** *meter room* **5** *store room* **6** *cellar* **7** *air shaft* **8** *boiler*
room **9** *lobby* **10** *stowing room* **11** *garage* **12** *ramp*

women and children have the easier access. In such cases the men's department will be situated on the next floor.

Windows

The maximum amount of window display should be provided so as to make it possible to display the complete range of shoes in stock. Men's and women's shoes have to be separated for display purposes: as most shops cater for both kinds the recessed type of shopfront is favoured because it makes clear division possible on this basis. It also permits customers to inspect goods at leisure under the shelter of a protecting lobby.

Interior

Exclusive shops which only cater for a small number of customers provide for maximum customer comfort. Chairs are of comfortable types and as only a few are needed may be spaced apart. The limited stock available can be displayed on tables or special stands. General shops which cater for the mass market require the maximum amount of seating (which is usually laid out in rows) and display their stock on inclined shelves set against walls or in gondolas.

Finishes

The floor finish is an important factor affecting sales. To make customers feel as comfortable as possible in the new shoes which they are trying on, soft carpeting is therefore preferred to other types of flooring. A large number of mirrors is also desirable: these need only show the customer's feet but it is better to have full length mirrors.

Fixtures and fittings

Display shelving

Shoes on the sales floor are usually displayed on shelving fitted against walls or in gondola fittings. Shelves are inclined on a downward angle of 15° for better visibility. The maximum height should not exceed 1·5 m and shelf depth should be 300 m for men's shoes and 250 mm for women's and children's shoes. Usually only the right foot shoe is displayed for security reasons. An allowance of three shoes per 300 mm of shelving is made for men's shoes and five shoes per 300 mm of shelving for women's shoes. The space between shelving should be allocated for full length mirrors.

Binning

Binning is used for 'throw away' lines. Here shoes are displayed in pairs rather than singly because security is not so relevant. Selection is usually by self-service.

Stands

Accessories such as cleaning and polishing kits are usually displayed on stands provided by the manufacturers. Tall stands are usually located freestanding next to the cash counter or entrance. Small stands are placed on tables or counters. (A typical manufacturer's stand is shown in Fig **4.12** below.)

Chairs

The number, size and type of chairs should be established with the client. As already stated above exclusive shops will have just a few large, very comfortable chairs while general shops tend to have rows of small chairs facing the display shelves. In general bulkier chairs with armrests are preferred to those without.

Fitting stools

The fitting stool consists of a flat surface for the assistant to sit on and an inclined board for the customer to fit the shoe on. This surface is usually black ribbed rubber which is non-slip and does not show dirt easily.

Mirrors

At least one full length mirror should be provided. The higher the grade of shop the more important it is to provide an adequate number. Foot mirrors are portable. They should be inclined at an angle of 25° to the vertical and be robust but light in weight. (Fig **2.15**.)

2.48 *Sid's, shoe shop, London, designed by Lionel Stirgess. The two large display cases are freestanding inside the shop and serve both for passers-by and for customers inside*

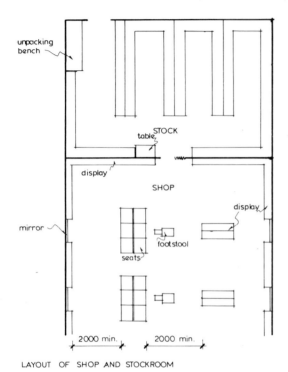

2.49 *Shoe shop layout showing section through stockroom and the relationship between shop and stockroom*

2.50 *Sacha, shoe shop project, Birmingham, designed by Wilkinson, Calvert and Gough. External perspective*

Stockroom

Stockroom shelving

Shoes in the stockroom are kept in boxes and stacked up to six boxes high per shelf. The sizes of the boxes may vary but ordinary shoe boxes average 115 mm high × 225 mm wide for men and 90 mm high × 175 mm wide for women. Shelf depths should measure 300 mm. The maximum height for shelving should be limited to 3 m and movable stool ladders are required to allow staff to reach the upper shelves. The gangway between shelves should be 750 mm wide at the minimum but where bays are over 2·5 m long it should be increased to at least 850 mm and preferably 900 mm.

Location

An important factor in planning shoe shops is the relationship between the stockroom and the sales floor (see Fig **2.49**). Stockrooms may be completely hidden or semi-hidden. Sales staff who have to travel from one room to the other are sometimes out of view for long periods and this causes some concern to customers. One solution (mainly applicable to premises where floor area is limited) is to house the stockroom on a different floor. Goods are brought directly to the sales floor through a small goods lift. While the shoes are being collected and delivered the sales person can assist another customer.

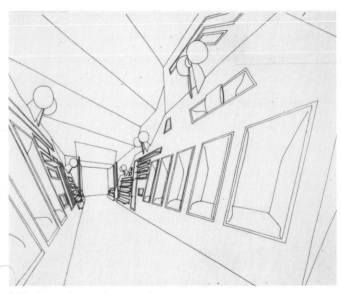

2.51 *Same. Internal perspective*

Step ladders

Step ladders should be related to the shelving height. It is preferable for them to be on rollers so that they may be moved easily and to be fitted with a safety pole so as to help staff to maintain balance. One step ladder per gangway is desirable.

Workroom

Shoe repair is a specialist service and not normally found in shops trading with new shoes. Where repair services are to be provided the following points should be determined:

1 Receipt counter: it should be decided whether this is to be incorporated with the main cash desk/wrapping counter or whether it is to be a special counter.

2 Storage: a method of storage and identification should be established for shoes brought in for repair and for those already repaired and ready for collection.

3 Machinery: this is usually noisy and foul smelling so that the workroom should be well lighted and ventilated and sited out of view from the sales floor.

While-you-wait heel bars are very popular. These are often situated in variety stores and transport terminals but are equally often independent shop units. Machinery is sited in full view in the shop. Stools should be provided for the customers.

2.4 HOUSEHOLD GOODS

Categories

The various types of shops dealing with household goods may be classified as follows:

Shop type	Type of goods
Household furniture	Living room, bedroom, kitchen, dining room and bathroom furniture and accessories
Household goods	China and glass, linen and towels, bathroom accessories, kitchen equipment, lighting equipment, cushions, upholstery fabrics, outdoor furniture and accessories
Hardware and do-it-yourself	Materials, tools, paints, wallpapers, gardening equipment, electrical and mechanical appliances, sanitary ware, and general accessories
Floor coverings	Carpets, rugs, mats, lino and tiles

Type of service

Self service: this is suitable for small items such as household goods, hardware and do-it-yourself goods; the plan is similar to that of a supermarket with goods on display on open shelves and checkout counters at the ends to control sales.

Assisted service: this is suitable for larger items such as furniture and floor coverings; merchandise or display samples are arranged on open display and customers are encouraged to walk round to inspect for style, quality, design, and size; ordering and some sales talk is done by staff.

Planning and layout

General principles relating to planning and layout are discussed in chapter 3 below (see however section 2.9 below if the shop takes the form of a showroom). Points which should be mentioned here are:

Windows

These should be simple and visually open. Shopfronts are preferred as the merchandise is generally large and viewed from medium to distant viewpoints. Shops with small types of merchandise, eg household goods, require low window sills not higher than 300 mm. Other shops with larger merchandise require no sills.

Interior

Wide traffic aisles should be provided to allow for the circulation of mothers with perambulators and the movement of large furniture. Goods should be classified into different groupings and arranged accordingly, eg living room furniture, bedroom furniture and so on. The warehouse type of sales system relies on narrowing down the selection of elaborately finished goods so as to concentrate more on low prices, bulk display, self service and high turnover.

Sales method

This depends on the type of goods and service provided. If it is self service requirements should be established for cash counters or checkout counters. If it is assisted service as in a showroom a reception desk and salesmen's desks will probably be needed.

Floor loading

Most floor coverings are heavy and awkward to handle. In new buildings floors should be designed for loadings of 700 to 1000 kg/m². In existing buildings it may be necessary to have additional structural strengthening.

Finishes

Simple finishes are preferable because retail units rely more on high turnover than competitive appearance. Floors and walls should be hard wearing, easily maintained and in neutral colours.

Display

Small goods are usually displayed on open shelving, tables, dump baskets, cabinets and stands as for 'dry goods' in a supermarket. Large goods require display techniques as in showrooms. It is necessary to determine if an open plan is required which exhibits all the merchandise or whether there should be low partitions which separate displays into different sections. Floor covering materials use a distinct range of display units. These are available 'off the peg' from specialist manufacturers, or can be designed individually.

Table VI Standard sizes of floor coverings and recommended methods of display

Item	Sizes (mm)	Display
Carpet squares	Ranging from 2285 × 1830 to 4570 × 3660 with size increases of approximately 500 in each direction	On carpet platforms ('beds') or hung on frames vertically
Body and stair carpet	Roll widths 457, 572, 686, 914, 1372	In rolls or as 1·8 m samples on platforms or hung on frames vertically
Broadloom carpet	Roll widths 1830, 2285, 2745, 3200, 3660, 4115 and 4570, and occasionally wider	In rolls or special racks
Indian and oriental rugs	914 × 610, 1525 × 1067, 1372 × 686, 1525 × 915	Usually on platforms, but may be hung vertically
Rugs	1220 × 610, 1372 × 686, 1525 × 915	Usually on platforms
Sisal matting / Haircord	Range of sizes as for body carpet and broadloom	Sisal matting and haircord: usually shown in sample books or as samples on small platforms
Underfelt		Underfelt: in sample books
Rush mats	Irregular sizes; may be circular or oval but usually not larger than 2500 diameter	On floor or platforms
Sheet linoleum, vinyl, rubber etc	In rolls 2 m wide; a space 3·7 × 2·4 m is required for cutting	Usually arranged in rolls vertically so must be retained by frames
Tiles: linoleum, vinyl, rubber, cork etc	230 × 230 and 305 × 305	On special cabinet combining platform and shelving

Workroom

It is necessary to establish if a workroom is required for repairs or work specially done on clients' commissions.

Storage

Requirements should be established concerning a storeroom for receiving goods, checking, unpacking and distribution. Adequate space should be allocated for empty crates and surplus packaging material. Good unloading and loading facilities are essential and a goods elevator will be necessary if the shop is on more than one level.

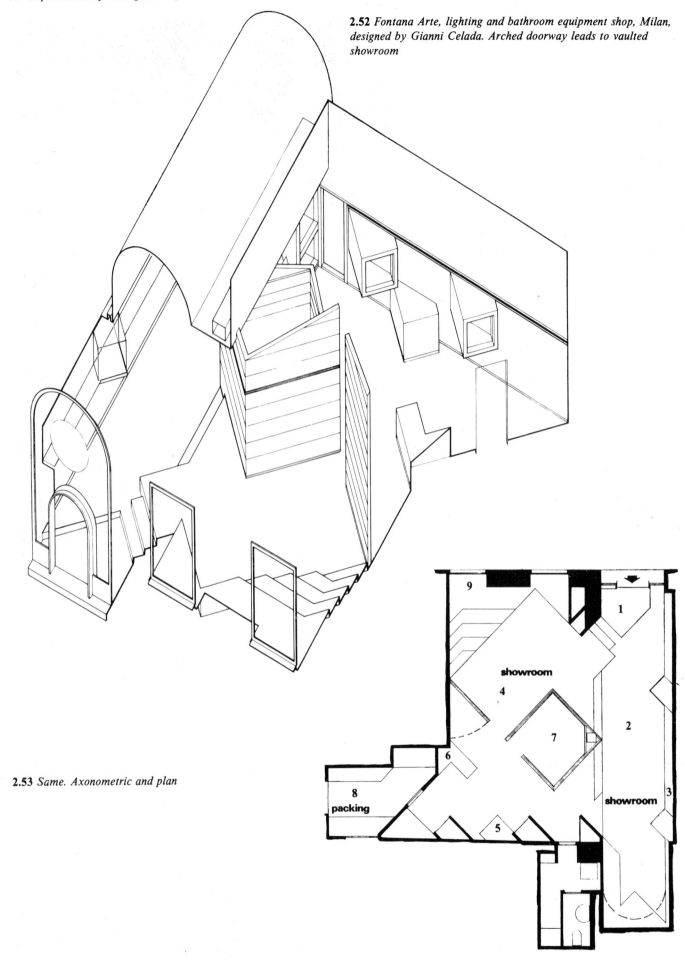

2.52 *Fontana Arte, lighting and bathroom equipment shop, Milan, designed by Gianni Celada. Arched doorway leads to vaulted showroom*

2.53 *Same. Axonometric and plan*

1 *entrance* **2** *vaulted gallery* **3** *built-in flush display* **4** *raised gallery* **5** *projecting display* **6** *counter* **7** *bathroom display* **8** *packing* **9** *window*

2.52

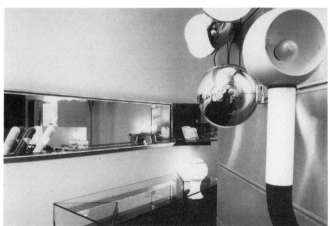

.54

2.54 *Same. Looking towards the flush display case with mirror backing. The wall in the foreground is the partition to the square island room housing the bathroom wares. It has flush lighting tracks*

2.55 *Same. Long view of vaulted gallery. The display case on the right is flush with the wall except for the two projecting showcases*

2.56 *Same. Looking over the entrance to the raised gallery on the right*

2.55

2.56

2.57

2.58

2.57 *Design Research Shop, household goods, Cambridge, Massachusetts, USA, designed by Benjamin Thompson and Associates. View from the entrance*

2.58 *Same. The open-treaded staircase does not enclose the view*

2.59 *Same. Split levels and galleries create a very fluid space*

2.59

2.60 *Best Products, household goods, South San Fransisco, designed by SITE. A project for a large American catalogue showroom merchandiser with a now well established and distinct house style. The walls are concrete blocks with an outer skin of* four foot glass modules, allowing a small gap between glass and masonry. This space is to be filled with earth and rock reflecting the regional terrain. Over it, the planted vegetation would take root and grow.

2.61 *Camera Barn, cinematic and photographic goods, New York, designed by SITE. Rather than propose major structural changes for the renovation of this facade, the project suggests enclosing the street facade with plate glass. Sandwiched between the glass* and a plexi-glass backing are a series of life-size photographs of people engaged in street activities. The retailer's window becomes the showcase within the showcase.

2.5 PETS

Commodities

Traditional: pet animals eg mice, hamsters, guinea pigs, rabbits, cats, dogs, birds, fish.
Additional: animal foods and accessories, guide books.

Planning

Pet shops require carefully controlled environmental conditions to sustain healthy living and growth of animals. Adequate ventilation is a prime concern and air change rates are determined by the following factors:
1 Number of animals in the shop and their respective rates of metabolism.
2 External and internal heat gains.
3 Temperature and humidity control.
4 Temperature difference between room and supply air.
5 Animal odour control.

Table VII   Animal room environmental data

Animal	Surface area (m^2)	Average metabolic rate at 21°C (W)	No. of animals per m^2 of floor area	Typical animal room gain (W/m^2)	Recommended temperature range (°C)
Mice	0·01	0·5	200	100	21-23
Guinea pigs	0·07	3·0	40	120	17-20
Rabbits	0·20	11·0	3·2	35	16-19
Cats	0·20	8·0	1·6	13	18-21
Dogs					
male	0·65	26·0	0·5	13	12-18
female	0·58	22·0	0·5	11	12-18

Source: Institution of Heating and Ventilating Engineers

It appears that low relative humidity (30 per cent) can cause disease especially with small rodents. Most animals require a relative humidity of approximately 50 per cent. For this reason humidification is essential in winter. In summer, temperature and humidity is adequate in Great Britain, assuming a good air change rate of 8 to 12 air changes per hour. Air distribution should be even with a low air velocity. This is best achieved with a perforated ceiling with extractors placed above the false ceiling. Food containers, bedding and storage areas should be well ventilated (6 to 10 air changes per hour), cool (10° to 15°C) and with low relative humidity to prevent mildew and mould from forming. In addition to the sales and display area pet shops require a separate room for cage washing and food preparation.

2.6 JEWELLERY

Categories

Jewellery shops are either:
1 Exclusive: dealing with luxury goods of a limited range for a small select clientele; or
2 Popular: dealing with goods for volume sales.

Types of goods

Customer	Commodities
Male	Watches, bracelets, rings, tie pins, cigarette lighters
Female	Watches, bracelets, brooches, hair pins, tiaras, necklaces, cigarette lighters
General	Silverware, clocks, coins, medals, ornamental works in gold, silver and precious stones

Service

Service is always personal, usually from across the counter. Exclusive shops may have a reception sitting area where customers sit and goods are brought over and displayed on a table. Alternatively this service may be offered in a private room.

Planning and layout

Architects should clarify the following points with their clients:

1 The percentage of total display space to be allocated for each type of goods, ie male, female, and general
2 The average number and styles of each type that is to be accommodated on display and in storage
3 The degree of security to be provided.
The following principles are thought to be common for jewellery shops and should be considered in the planning stages:

Location
Shops catering for the mass market should be sited on busy streets to draw in a large volume of trade. Jewellery is considered to be comparison goods where customers prefer a wide choice of styles, makes, prices and quality. Hence it is generally better for any shop to be grouped with other jewellery shops in a locality.

Sectioning
Personal goods for male or female customers are usually displayed on glass topped counters. General goods are displayed in glass fronted cabinets behind the counters.

Windows
Popular shops require large amounts of window to display their comprehensive range of goods. The nature and size of the goods require that they be inspected from very close distances. Invariably this causes windows to have high sills and narrow depths. Consideration should be given to providing access for staff to take out goods for direct sales and also to security arrangements to prevent pilfering. Anti-bandit laminated glass should be used on windows and showcases as this eliminates the need for unsightly security grilles.

Interior
The internal design must bear in mind the following points:

1 Customers are predominantly female.
2 The degree of luxury and sophistication must be related to the quality of the goods.
3 Background walls are traditionally plain so as not to clash with the merchandise.
4 Traditional layouts call for counters to be placed all around the selling floor. This forms a barrier with customers on one side and staff on the other.
5 Exclusive shops may have layouts with island showcases where customers are encouraged to walk round and reception areas where they sit and inspect the goods that are brought over to them.

Finishes
Display background in contact with goods is usually velvet. Traditionally dark blue or green is used for silver, platinum or diamonds, and deep crimson for gold and copper. Where the background is of only one colour it is dove grey.

Lighting
Correct lighting plays an important part because it affects sales. It may be provided by a combination of fluorescents and low voltage incandescents. Incandescent lighting is good for precious stones because it produces a sharp beam which causes bright sparkles. However on pewter and silver it gives a yellow glow which is detrimental to sales. It must therefore be counterbalanced by natural daylight or fluorescents. Special consideration should be given to the illumination of counters, showcases and display windows. Internal lighting should have concealed sources and be adequately supplied with power points so as to avoid trailing flexes.

Fixtures and fittings

Counters
The top and front are both usually made of glass with access at the

rear. There may be either a single deck on a metal stand or a full height counter with a top display deck and intermediate display levels. There should be drawers and removable trays that come out in sections and can be removed for display on request. Glass counters may require velvet mats for the display of selected goods.

Wall cabinets

Wall cabinets are used to display the larger merchandise such as clocks, pewter and silverware. Most popular types have two sections: the top part has glass sliding doors with security locks while the lower part is solid with drawers or sliding doors and is used to store extra merchandise, jewellery cases, wrapping boxes, etc.

Showcases

These should be specially designed to suit the client, having regard to whether there is to be internal illumination and to the sizes, type of glass, locking system and finishes preferred.

Chairs

The number, size and type of chairs should be established with the client. Seating should be arranged in relation to display cases and any additional pieces of furniture such as tables, coat stands, ashtrays, etc.

Security

Jewellery shops are considered high risk premises. The client should be consulted on personal requirements. These include:

Personal attack

Personal attack buttons may be fitted to manager's, receptionist's or any other desk or counter so that if there is an attack any person may push the button to trigger the alarm; they may either be 'tripped' (programmed to set off the alarm after a few seconds) or direct (to give immediate warning). Signalling devices may be bells, sirens or a telephone warning (see section 7.3 below). A security system may also be linked to operate and record on closed circuit television or on cameras.

Intruder detection

A wide choice of systems is available for intruder detection. It includes protective switches, wired panels or tubing, vibration detectors, ultrasonic sound detectors, pressure mats and 'space' detectors which register movement inside any protected area. These are discussed in chapter 7 below.

Security doors

These may be fitted to protect a high risk area containing valuable merchandise such as the workroom, safe or strongroom. The protection they offer is mainly against forcible entry or shotgun attack by raiders attempting to get in. Such doors are constructed with an internal steel lining and hung on heavy duty hinges attached to a hardwood frame fitted with metal rebates. To be termed a 'security door' the door must swing outwards so that attacks have to be transferred to the frame. Doors may be supplied with vision panels, electric locks and automatic closers. Finishing decoration may be styled to suit the general decor.

Safes

Safes vary a great deal depending on manufacturer, model and size. Before a safe is installed it should be established whether the existing floor will take the load it will impose and whether it can be brought to the required position.

Strongrooms

Strongrooms are usually built by specialist firms using either spiral reinforcements or pre-cast concrete blocks:

Spiral reinforcements: these are used mainly for in-situ work; they offer greater protection but are relatively expensive. The reinforcement consists of 12·7 mm bars wound in 127 mm diameter coils of spiral form. These are placed vertically to interlock and the common spaces are threaded with spacing rods. The process is repeated until the whole of the perimeter walls have been inter-

woven in reinforcement so as to form a solid mattress; by suitably arranging the number of rows of coils in the thickness of the 'mattress' any required degree of protection can be obtained.

Pre-cast concrete blocks: these have circular hollow cores. They are bonded in staggered courses, and reinforcing rods are threaded through (see Fig 2.62). Standard block dimensions are: thickness— 230 mm, 305 mm, 380 mm, 535 mm, or 610 mm; length — 610 mm, or 915 mm; height — 330 mm; special course heights — 203 mm, 228 mm, 280 mm; corner blocks (L-shaped) — 305 × 610 mm or 610 × 915 mm.

Roof: may be constructed by using similar pre-cast concrete blocks reinforced with steel tensioning bars or with rows of pre-cast beams reinforced with spiral reinforcement.

Floors: blocks may be built into existing concrete floors or laid on new foundations to manufacturers' details. When laying these on an existing floor it is necessary to make sure that it will take the load. A groove about 75 × 50 mm can be cut on the concrete to house the ends of reinforcing bars. If this is required the floor may be laid with a course of pre-cast blocks as for the roof construction.

Sizes: strongroom sizes should be dimensioned to suit standard block sizes. This eliminates the need for odd courses which create weak points in the strongroom. Internal dimensions for strong-rooms should not be smaller than 2·6 × 3·0 × 2·3 m (height). Sizes smaller than this become impractical to use and uneconomical to build.

Internal finishes: wall and roof surfaces should be rendered with anti-condensation plaster. The floor is usually screeded to a thickness to line with the internal threshold of the door.

Strongroom door: this should be placed so that it is able to swing

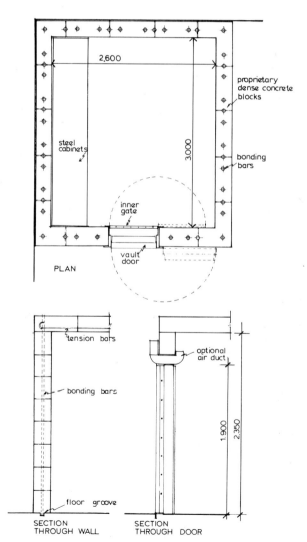

2.62 *Layout of a strongroom using reinforced proprietary concrete blocks*

2.63

through 180° to open fully. It usually consists of an outer door and an internal gate. The outer door is constructed with an outer steel plate, an internal lining material and an inner steel plate welded to the outer plate. The lining material is designed to resist attacks by oxygen cutting apparatus and drilling equipment. The door is fitted with heavy sliding bolts which lock into the sides when extended. The number of bolts varies but it is not uncommon to find seven bolts on the sides and two bolts at the top and the bottom. the internal gate consists of a steel grille which may be locked when the main door is open.

Locks: these are dealt with in section 4.10 below.

Lighting: electrical wiring should not pass through the walls. This can be achieved by having a special conduit leading to and from a concealed switch in the top hinge of the main strongroom door. this method also ensures that all wiring in the vault is dead when the door is closed and eliminates any possibility of fires started by short-circuit. The choice of lighting is purely a matter of taste.

Ventilation: this can be introduced by means of a plenum chamber built into the top of the main door.

Fittings: internal requirements should be established with the client. They may include steel cupboards, open shelving, filing cabinets, security lockers and safes.

Workroom

Space may be required for watch and jewellery repairs, engraving, designing and building commissioned works or other purposes. The security element in jewellery shops dictates that customers shall not have access to the workroom. Goods for repairs are received at the main counter or reception desk and taken by staff to the workroom. Premises dealing with large quantities of valuables will have the workroom offices and strongroom behind a security door so as to provide a secure barrier between them and the sales floor.

Office

Private interview rooms may be required where customers can discuss discount, credit, etc.

2.63 Jones, jewellers, London, designed by Antony Sully. Three types of display cases for a small jewellers: spherical, cylindrical and circular under the worktop

2.64 Hooper Bolton, jewellers, London, designed by G. H. and G. P. Grima. The modern glazed windows are set in a classical frame which is painted black with letters and ornaments picked up in gold

2.64

.65

2.65 *Grima, jewellers, Zurich, designed by G.H. and G.P. Grima. Four large steel plates salvaged from a scrapped sailing ship were used on this exterior. The outside was left in its original rusty state after treating with a rust inhibitor*

2.66 *Same. View of the display counter behind the shopfront. Here the steel plates were sandblasted and painted black*

2.67 *Same. Plan*

2.68 *Same. Interior view. The manager's table is a travertine slab on a steel support at one end, the other bracketted to the wall. The steel plated walls were treated with matt lacquer*

.66

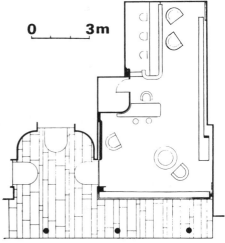

0 3m

2.67

2.68

2.7 BOOKS

Categories
Bookshops may be one of the following categories:

Shop type	Location	Merchandise
Amenity	Railway stations, airport terminals, street kiosks, hotels	Mostly light paperbacks, some popular hardbacks; may also sell magazines, newspapers, gifts
General	Main streets	A wide range of books; may also include magazines, newspapers, stationery, cards, gifts and records
Discount	Main streets	Mostly publishers' old stock at low prices; may also sell general books at normal prices
Children's	Main streets	Children's books: educational and general; may include games, and toys
Specialist	Select areas eg near universities	Specialise mainly in one subject eg architecture, medicine or law
Old books	Select areas with established reputation for bookselling	Old books, first editions, maps, prints and general collector's items

Sectioning
The architect should consult his client about the range of goods to be sold and the section headings required. For general bookshops covering a comprehensive range of merchandise, this might be as follows:

Subject heading	Classification	Display
Fiction: Adventure, Classics, Crime, Horror, Humour, Romance, Science fiction, Sex, War, Westerns	Impulse/demand	Shelves
Non-fiction (general): Antiques, Animals, Art, Biographies, Crafts, Cinema, Cookery, Do-it-yourself, Gardening, Games, Hobbies, Horoscope/Oecult, Military, Sports	Demand	Tables, cabinets or shelving
Non-fiction (specialist): Archaeology, Architecture, Law, Literature, Medical, Music, Plays, Poetry, Politics, Religion	Demand	Shelves or cabinets
New titles and bestsellers	Impulse/demand	Tables, stands
Others:		
Children's books	Impulse/demand	Shelves
Discount books	Impulse	Tables, binning
Maps and atlases	Demand	Cabinets, shelves

Books are usually separated between hardbacks and softbacks because of different book sizes. Where softbacks are displayed these may be grouped in the following ways:
1 In alphabetical order under author's name
2 Under subject headings
3 Under publishing company
4 At random.

Book sizes
Book thicknesses vary considerably, but the following dimensions may be taken as a guideline:

Type of book	Spacing per article (mm)	Number of books per metre run of shelf	Recommended shelf depth (mm)
Paperbacks	20-25	40	175
Children's books	15-30	40	200-300
General fiction	30-45	24	200
Non-fiction	30-50	22	250
Technical books	45-60	18	250

Traditional book sizes are:
Folio: 300 mm deep × over 300 mm high
Quarto: 250 mm deep × 250 to 300 mm high
Octavo: 200 mm deep × 150 to 250 mm high

Books based on the International A-series are:
A4: 210 mm deep × 297 mm high
A5: 148 mm deep × 210 mm high
A6: 105 mm deep × 148 mm high

Other goods
Other types of goods which are commonly stocked with books include:

Type of merchandise	Display	Comments
Newspapers	Racks, lower shelf platform, or counter top	On racks newspapers are arranged vertically; otherwise they are laid horizontally; allow enough shelf space for the complete copy to be displayed without overlapping
Magazines	Racks, shelves	Arranged on overlapping vertical display; shelves are inclined 15° to 25° and have a front lip
Stationery	Shelves	Standard shelves as for supermarket 'dry goods'
Gifts	Shelves, binning	Standard shelves as for supermarket 'dry goods'
Cards	Cabinet or wired stand	Usually in two sections: top section consists of display trays and lower section of a drawer for storage
Posters	Stand or hinged hanging rail for display; cabinet for storage (see Fig **2.69**)	Posters are kept in clear cellophane envelopes for protection against damage by browsing customers; on selection the assistant collects a new poster from the storage cabinet
Records and cassettes (see also section 2.8 below)	Cabinets	Usually only the jacket is displayed for security purposes and to avoid scratching; records are kept with their inner sleeves in a storage cabinet behind the record counter

Service
Service is mostly by self-selection although assistants may be close at hand to help customers find books.

Planning and layout
General principles for planning the sales floor are covered in section 3.2 below. The following points should however be mentioned here:

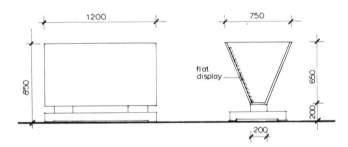

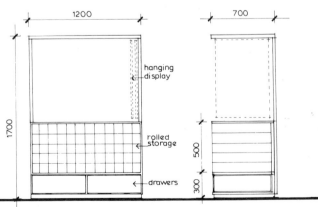

2.69 *Poster display and storage racks*

2.70 *Peter Eaton, antiquarian booksellers, London, designed by Rick Mather Architects. Plan*

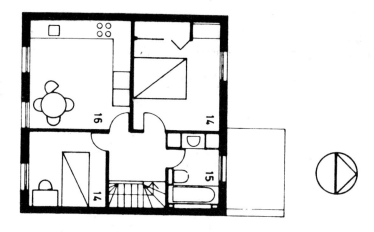

Second floor

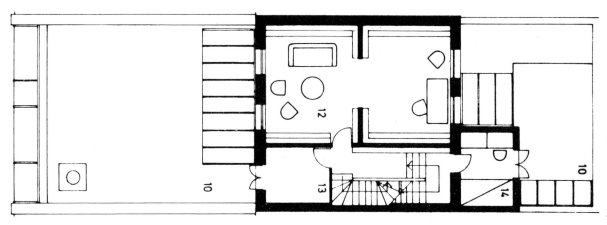

First floor

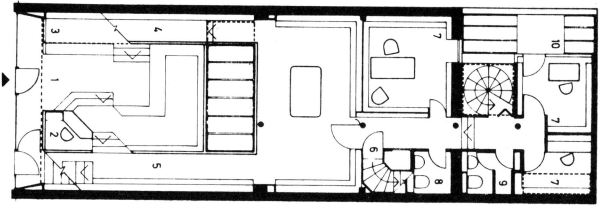

Ground level

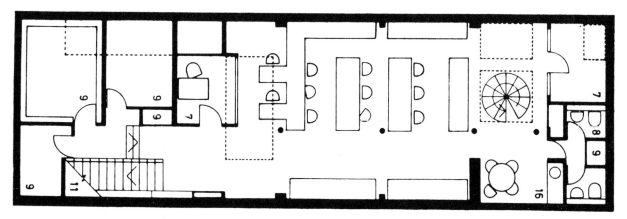

Basement

1 *shop entrance* **2** *cashier* **3** *lower gallery* **4** *upper gallery*
5 *intermediate gallery* **6** *maisonette entrance* **7** *office* **8** *W.C.*

9 *store* **10** *terrace* **11** *plant room* **12** *lounge/library* **13** *study*
14 *bedroom* **15** *bathroom* **16** *kitchen/dining*

Peter Eaton

2.71 *Same. Sections and axonometric. The building comprises a shop on the ground floor, a workroom for library suppliers on the lower ground floor and the owners' maisonette on the upper two floors.*

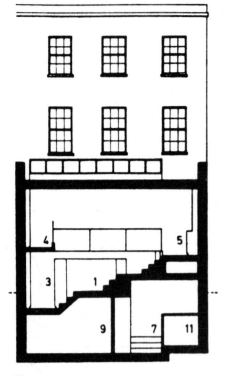

Shop front

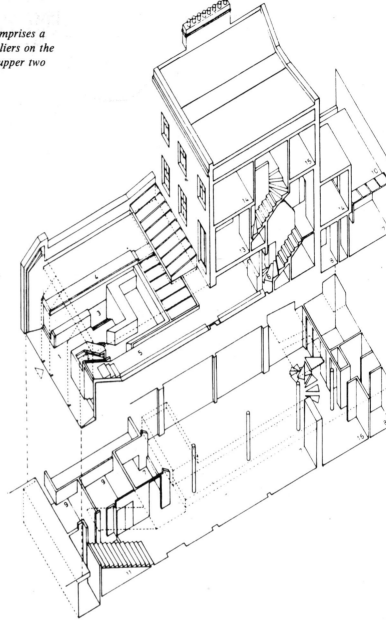

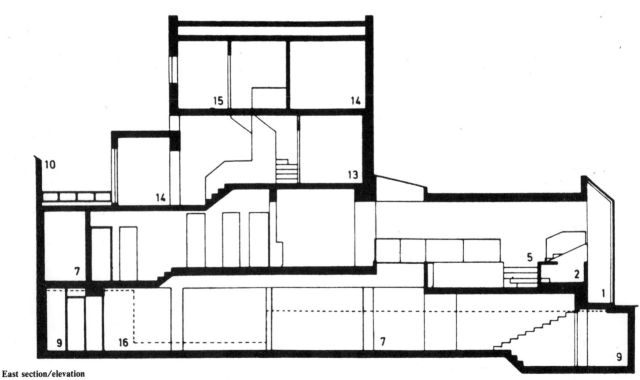

East section/elevation

.72

73

2.72 Same. Inside the shop, maximum shelving has been provided along the five different levels. The cashier's counter is located at the front with a view of all the bookshelves, thus requiring only one person to run the shop

2.73 Same. To achieve maximum light into the shop, the glass facade extends a metre forwards from the solid elements

2.74 Above. Same. Internal view of the upper gallery. In order to achieve maximum light large skylights are provided. The shop has an internal skylight opening to the basement workroom

Windows

Window display is not usually important and shops only require small window beds to display the latest titles and bestsellers. Open back windows are preferred because these allow the customer outside a complete view of the interior and give it a more natural light.

Interior

The interior should be planned as simply as possible to allow for customers to browse and at the same time to allow others to pass through the aisles without congestion. The general plan usually consists of tall units along the perimeter walls with the central space subdivided by low level cabinets, tables, stands, or shelving. Alleyways or cul-de-sacs are sometimes welcome: here are stocked the specialised categories which enthusiasts like to browse over; they are best situated at the back of the shop so that impulse sales can be stimulated by forcing the customers to pass through other goods on the way in and out. Whenever possible, this should be planned with an open view to other sales areas to allow for supervision by staff.

Finishes

Finishes are usually simple in subdued colours so as not to compete with the brightly illustrated book jackets.

Lighting

Good lighting is essential to allow for the reading of small print. Special displays such as that of the 'book of the month' may require additional highlighting with reflectors.

Stockroom

A good sized storage and sorting out room is required for receiving, checking, unpacking and pricing new books.

Office

Architects should find out if the ordering of one-off books for customers is to be done in an office or at a counter on the sales floor.

2.8 RECORDS

Categories

Record shops cannot be distinctly grouped under any clear category except by the type and range of goods held in stock. Premises may hold just a small selection or a comprehensive range of goods.

Type of goods

Main grouping	Classification
Popular LPs	Budget records, vocal, instrumental, nostalgia, humour, country and western, folk, spoken word, films/shows, TV/radio, jazz, sound effects, children's records
Classical LPs	Budget records, chamber music, opera and vocal, symphonies and concertos, and boxed sets
Rock LPs	Rock groups, solo artists, reggae, soul, rock and roll
Singles	Top thirty and latest releases
Cassettes	As for above groups
Cartridges	As for above groups
Accessories	Record cleaning kits, protective sleeves, music books, catalogues, posters and cards, blank tapes
Service	Bureau de change, theatre bookings

Service

Personal service may be provided for singles, accessories, bureau de change and theatre bookings. Other items are sold on a self service basis.

Sizes

Sizes of records, cassettes and cartridges are as follows:

Type	Dimensions (mm)	No. per 100 mm of storage shelf space
LPs	310 × 310 × 3	20-25
Singles	182 × 182 × 2	30-35
Cassettes	110 × 70 × 17	5·8
Cartridges	136 × 102 × 23	4·3

Planning and layout

General principles for planning the sales floor are set out in section 3.2 below but the following points should be mentioned here:

Windows

Window display is not important and shops only require small windows to display the latest releases and top selling albums. Architects should ascertain whether audio visual displays are required eg television sets with video recorders. Open shopfronts are preferred because they allow a large flow of customers and open the shop interior up to the pavement.

Interior

Interiors are usually open planned to allow staff and customers a complete view of the sales floor. Large shops may have special areas for each type of goods: classical records, popular records, rock records, singles counter, cassettes, cartridges, as well as service counters (bureau de change and theatre bookings). Accessories are considered impulse goods and are kept near the cash/wrap counters or checkout counters.

Singles counter

Unlike records, cassettes and cartridges, singles are not displayed to the customer but sold from behind a counter. This is usually located at the rear of the shop because singles are considered to be demand goods. Architects should ascertain how many staff will be required to man this counter and also find out what other facilities will be needed there (such as storage for records, charts, forms, stationery, wrapping paper/bags, telephones, cash registers and impulse goods). It is also necessary to determine the method of displaying the Top Thirty chart and its position.

Records

There are three ways in which records are displayed and stored (see Fig **2.75**):

1 The first mainly concerns shops which expect a large turnover of top selling albums: the record and jacket are wrapped in a clear cellophane film and placed on cabinets for display along with many other copies of the same record; on selection, the customer takes the record for payment to the nearest cash counter or checkout unit.

2 The second also applies to top selling albums but for shops with a lower turnover: for security reasons and to avoid scratching of records only the record jacket is displayed; this is inserted in a protective sleeve made out of clear plastic; on selection, the customer takes this to the cash counter where the assistant gives him a new record and returns the jacket to the display cabinet.

3 The third applies to other albums for shops with a low turnover: the jacket only is displayed as described above; on selection by the customer, the assistant collects the record protected in the inner sleeve and inserts it in the same jacket that was on display; he then removes the outer protecting sleeve, makes the sale and notes down the record number so as to place a new order with the manufacturer or wholesaler.

Cassettes and cartridges

For security reasons only the outer box is displayed. On selection, the customer takes it to the counter and is given a complete unit with the tape inside.

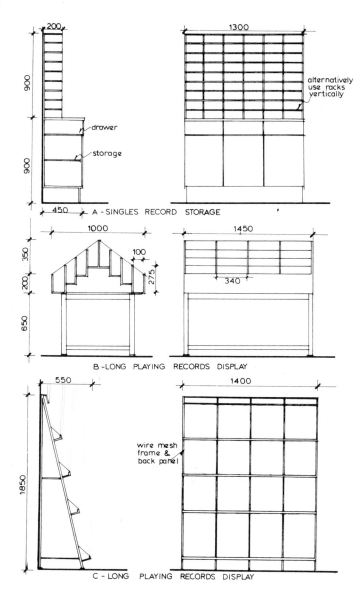

2.75 *Record racks*

(within figure labels:)
200 / 1300 / 900 / drawer / storage / 900 / 450 / A - SINGLES RECORD STORAGE / alternatively use racks vertically

1000 / 100 / 350 / 200 / 275 / 650 / 1450 / 340 / B -LONG PLAYING RECORDS DISPLAY

550 / 1850 / wire mesh frame & back panel / 1400 / C - LONG PLAYING RECORDS DISPLAY

Bureau de change counter

This facility is only suitable where there is a large influx of tourists: for security purposes the counter should not be located near the entrance, but its existence in the shop should be well advertised to inform casual pedestrians walking by who would not otherwise enter the premises. Architects should ask their clients what is needed in the way of security screens, a security door, ventilation to the enclosed area and ancillary equipment (the latter may include an operator's stool, a safe, a cash drawer or register, calculating machines and a rate of exchange board).

Theatre agency

This deals with bookings for theatres, opera, cinema, ballet, pop, jazz and classical concerts. The counter should be secluded from the sales floor in a quiet area where conversation may take place in comfort. Architects should find out what facilities are required for:
1 Display of events: this may be in the form of posters or brochures; determine the size and position of poster boards and brochure stands or racks.
2 Telephones: determine the number of lines and if they are to be separate lines from the shop or extensions; establish method of communication with other sections (manager and administration offices, bureau de change, sales counters, storerooms and so on).
3 Chairs: allow one chair for staff and two for customers for each member of the staff who will be on duty.
4 Storage: find out what storage should be provided for forms, stationery, brochures and so on.

5 Cash: ascertain whether a cash pedestal or a cash register is required for payment for the services given.

Audio system

The internal environment of record shops always needs an effective audio system. This consists of:
1 Control: establish the point of control where the equipment is to be located (this may be visible from the sales floor or be in another position of the building); determine if the person at the control point is to have other duties when not required to operate equipment.
2 Equipment: establish details of the equipment required which may include record players, tape deck, cassette deck, desk microphone, programme selector, pre-amplifier, and amplifier.
3 Distribution: determine the number and position of speakers (which may be freestanding, wall mounted or ceiling mounted).
4 Audio booths: establish if audio booths are required for customers' use and the number to be provided. General booth requirements are a minimum enclosed space of 1.0×1.2 m, with ceiling, walls and floors lined with sound absorbing materials; an entrance door fitted with a glass panel at eye level to avoid claustrophobia (750 mm to 1800 mm high $\times$ 600 mm wide); and a speaker unit mounted on wall or ceiling; the furniture should include a chair, an ashtray or 'No smoking' sign and a coat hook. Where audio booths are not possible for economic reasons an alternative is to provide seating facilities with attached audio sockets for headphones.

Lighting

In sections selling classical, popular, cassettes and cartridges the lighting is generally even and subdued. In sections selling singles and rock records it is usually low and designed to produce a special effect, perhaps emulating the discotheque environment.

Stockroom

A fairly large room is needed for storage and for receiving, checking, unpacking, sorting out and pricing new merchandise.

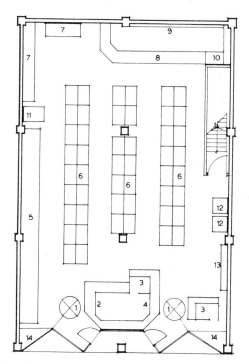

2.76 *Virgin Records, record shop, Milton Keynes, designed by Cox, Mandy and Andrews. This unit is in the Milton Keynes shopping centre and is one branch of a multiple selling popular records. Plan.* 1 *turnstiles* 2 *bags collection* 3 *checkout counter* 4 *bags return* 5 *top 30 L.P.s* 6 *catalogue L.P.s* 7 *casette display* 8 *singles/casettes counter* 9 *single/casette storage* 10 *record player* 11 *electronic games machine* 12 *poster racks* 13 *books* 14 *window display*

2.77

2.78

2.79

Virgin Records

2.77 *Same. Facade viewed from the mall. Glazing is brown tinted glass with aluminium framing finished the house brown colour. The sloping triangular mirror glass soffits match the developers panels above*

2.78 *Same. View from the entrance turnstiles. On the left are the top sellers displayed for instant recognition. The island racks are categorised in alphabetical order*

2.79 *Same. Standing racks and wire stands on the foreground display some of the impulse lines*

2.9 SHOWROOMS

Categories
Showrooms fall into the following categories:

Type of showroom	Comments
Manufacturer	Only displays the manufacturer's own brand of goods; may be for a single manufacturer or a group of manufacturers wishing to display their products together and share facilities; goods may be sold directly but more commonly prospective customers are referred to dealers (eg for motor cars, cameras, typewriters, stereo equipment and so on)
Dealer	May stock various manufacturers' brands for direct sale (eg bathroom and kitchen fittings and accessories, ceramic tiles, office and domestic furniture, carpets and so on)
Nationalised industry (Gas, Electricity or Post Office)	Offers direct sales and also service facilities: sections to be included are cashier for payment of bills, reception for enquiries and service and sales floor
Art gallery	For the display and sale of art objects, oil paintings, watercolours, prints, sculpture and so on

Planning and layout
The following items should receive the architect's attention:

Windows
Showrooms require large windows so that goods can be properly seen from the pavement. Non-reflective windows are ideal because they provide a totally clear view of the interior. In motor car showrooms large sliding glass doors may be required to allow cars to be driven out through the shopfront.

Reception desk
Establish if sales are to be centred from this position or if additional salesmen's desks are to be provided. The reception desk should be seen immediately on entering and should command the interior so as to give adequate supervision. Find out the number of staff who will man the desk and the precise requirements for its design.

Salesmen's desks
Salesmen's desks should reflect the goods they sell in quality, design and colour. Two chairs for customers should usually be provided. Establish the other functions salesmen have to perform when not attending customers (eg clerical work, designing, ordering etc).

Reception area
Establish if a more informal arrangement for reception is required. There should be provision for customers to deposit coats, umbrellas, bags and other personal belongings. Decide the needs for seating, tables, ashtrays, brochure stands and so on. Where reception areas are provided they replace the need for salesmen's desks.

Display
The way in which goods should be displayed is very much dependent on the type of goods concerned. The layout should be planned on exhibition lines following a natural sequence of movement. Determine if an open plan is required with all the merchandise visible at once, or whether low partitions are required to separate the items on display and enhance group or individual compositions.

Drawing stands
Find out if draughting facilities requiring a drawing stand are to be provided. These are commonly required where a design service is provided (eg for fitted kitchens) and may be situated in the showroom, a screened area or a separate room. Ease of access by customers is essential. Suitable equipment would include a drawing board and stand, a draughtsman's stool and trolley, shelving

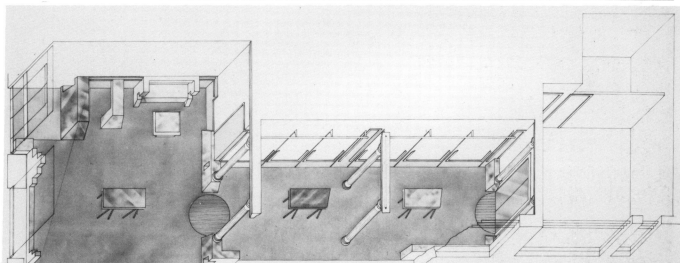

2.80 *Atlantis, fashion wholesaler, London, designed by Doug Patterson and Jerry Hewitt. Interior perspective*

2.81 *Same. Axonometric*

2.82 *Same. The stylised 'A' frame protrudes very slightly from the main facade and the upper section neatly houses the shop's name*

2.83 *Above. Same. Interior view towards the offices at the rear*

for catalogues and reference books and a plan-chest for storing materials and finished designs.

Telephones

Decide on the number of lines and extensions required and the method of communication between reception, sales staff, designers and office staff. If customers are to have access to telephones establish whether these need to be separate lines or whether extensions will do.

Indoor plants

Ascertain whether indoor plants are required on the premises and if so their number, types and the sort of containers they will need. (Plants may be bought outright or hired from specialist florists who will maintain them in healthy condition.)

Lighting

Lighting layouts must be most flexible to allow for changes in displays. Fluorescents give good background illumination with little shadow but incandescent lamps are preferable because they give better colour rendering and more sparkle.

Finishes

Finishes should suit the type of merchandise on display. (Car showrooms should have impervious, hard wearing floors and may also require trays to be placed under models to prevent staining the floor.)

Fixtures and fittings

Establish the numbers and types of general fittings that will be needed such as tables, hangers, filing cabinets and chairs (the latter will be required by waiting customers and by reception, office and sales staff, and draughtsmen will need stools). Find out also what special equipment should be provided, for example:

Turntables: these may be either permanent installations or portable models; they allow prospective customers to view goods from every angle and attract their attention by movement; they may also be needed in car showrooms for access where turning space is limited. Some examples of turntables are shown in Fig **4.13** below. Merchandise stands: it is necessary to know the types required and their sizes, numbers, loading capacity and special requirements for lighting.

Stands or racks to store and display brochures: these are usually provided so that customers may help themselves.

Ancillary accommodation

It will be necessary to know the total numbers of male and female staff that must be accommodated and their needs for rest rooms, lockers, lavatories, tea-making facilities and offices. It is also necessary to establish what space will be required for a workroom where exhibit stands can be prepared and for storage of packaging for merchandise on display, stationery, directories, brochures, catalogues, samples etc.

2.10 HAIRDRESSING

Categories

Hairdressers' shops are of the following kinds:

Type of customer	Comments
Male	Additional services include shaving and manicure; may have merchandise for sale which includes allied accessories, fashion clothing, toiletries and decorative jewellery
Female	Additional services include beauty treatments; may have the same classes of items for impulse sales as men's hairdressers
Male and female	As for the above; male and female customers are segregated at the reception desk or enter the premises through different entrances

The type of service to be provided affects the kind of design, finishes and degree of customer comfort that will be appropriate. These may be classified as:

1 Exclusive: high class establishment offering exceptional attention to customers but catering only for a small number
2 Popular: for the general public; the degree of finishes, customer comfort and design to be provided varies widely according to the location of the salon, the type of customer and the cost and quality of service intended.
3 Amenity: part of service offered within a commercial organisation for members of the staff.

Location of salon

Hairdressing salons may be located in the following types of premises:

Type of premises	Comments
Individual shop	Most popular type; may be on the ground floor plus basement and/or first floor; relatively few restrictions are found on this type of site affecting operation procedures (such as opening hours)
In a commercial building	First floor locations with direct access from the ground are preferred; salons may require larger than average signs to advertise their position; ground floor signs may have to be elaborate to give instructions indicating entrance routes
In a department store, hotel, or aboard a ship	May have various restrictive covenants affecting design, materials, and operation procedures
In an airport, or railway station	As above, but becoming relatively unpopular

Reception area

Male and female customers must be segregated on entering. Check whether one common reception point is required or whether there should be separate reception arrangements for male and female customers. The reception area should be visible from the street so as to give the salon some publicity value but consideration should be given to balancing this need with customers' desire for privacy. Requirements for reception areas are:

Staff requirements

1 Reception desk: this should be located in a prominent position so as to be seen immediately on entering, and it should command supervision of customers' waiting and cloakroom areas; establish the number of staff manning the desk eg whether one person will deal with all functions or whether two are required (one for appointments and reception and one for clerical work, sales and billing); ascertain the system for booking and precise requirements for desk design.
2 Telephones: establish the number of lines and extensions needed and the method of internal communication with the salon floor staff.
3 Clerical work: this may be done at the reception desk or it may be screened from the customer; facilities include entering records, cashing up, filing and so on.
4 Storage: find out what facilities and space are needed for storing stock, stationery and other office supplies (particularly record cards which give details of special work on regular customers such as permanent waving, tinting and beauty treatments).
5 Customer payment: ascertain the system used for billing and payment for services (cash control is normally centred on the reception desk).
6 Goods display and sales: find out the types and quantities of stock which is to be held and the ways in which this will be displayed and sold.

Customers' requirements

1 Checking-in: a bag shelf may be needed together with spaces for

writing and for customers to discuss services in comparative privacy.

2 Cloakroom: facilities must be provided for storing customers' coats, bags, umbrellas and other belongings and it is essential that they should be under the control and supervision of reception or salon staff; they may consist of a simple hanging rail, a cupboard, a screened area or a separate room and may also be used for storing protective gowns for the customers' use.

3 Waiting: seating facilities, tables, magazine racks and ashtrays are usually needed.

4 Telephones: ascertain how many are required and where they should be placed, also if separate lines or extensions or coinboxes are needed and whether space will be necessary for directories.

5 Lavatories: it is not necessary for these to have direct access to the reception area but they ought to be within easy reach.

Salon floor

Services provided by hairdressing salons include shampooing, cutting, styling, drying, setting, colouring, bleaching, highlighting and permanent waving. Additional services that may be included are manicure, eyebrow shaping and various beauty treatments.

Work positions (open planning)

All the above hairdressing services may be carried out at one single station but they are usually segregated according to function and require three basic positions:

(a) Dressing table: the services carried out here are cutting, styling, setting, colouring, bleaching, highlighting and permanent waving; the accommodation required consists of an upright chair in front of a mirror and dressing table; there should be ample space for the manoeuvering of trolleys, operator and assistant; allow a minimum space of 1·5 m wide × 2·0 m deep per station.

(b) Shampoo basin: where hair is washed, shampooed and rinsed; basins may be front wash or back wash types with hot and cold water supply, anti-splash rim and spray attachment; one chair should be supplied with each basin; allow a minimum space of 1·25 m wide × 1·5 m deep per station.

(c) Drier: besides drying hair, other services provided here may include manicure and the supply of refreshments; allow a minimum space of 0·9 m wide × 1·25 m deep per station. Architects should ask their clients how many work positions are needed of each of the three kinds: the usual ratio is one shampoo basin for every three dressing tables and four drying positions. Details of a hairdressing work station are shown in Fig **2.128**.

Work positions (cubicles)

The salon may be planned as a series of cubicles which combine dressing table, shampoo basin and drier in which case there is no need to move the customer about. This arrangement is primarily confined to high class establishments where privacy and customer comfort are specially desirable. It may also be provided in popular salons provided that cubicles are combined with open plan facilities so as to give customers a choice (ie whether they wish to be served in sociable surroundings or in private).

Beauty rooms

If beauty treatments are to be provided they should be given in private rooms: architects should ask their clients what special facilities are needed (these include dressing table, mirror, chairs for customer and operator, wash basin, trolleys, trays and stands).

Salon staff

The number and classification of salon staff should be established in order to determine the layout positions. A qualified operator will work on customers at about three dressing tables, assisted by junior staff. It may be necessary to group dressing tables and driers so that they are under the surveillance of a particular member of the staff.

Storage

The facilities needed for storing equipment, preparations and tools of the trade on the salon floor should be established.

Ancillary accommodation

Dispensary

A room or floor space immediately adjacent to the salon floor should accommodate facilities for storing preparations and utensils for preparing materials. Impervious hard wearing finishes capable of withstanding mild forms of chemical attacks are desirable. A sink is usually provided with storage shelves, cupboards, refuse bin and worktop.

Linen room

Establish the requirements for the storage, distribution and collection of clean and soiled towels, customer and staff protective gowns, etc. These may be kept in a cupboard or linen room. Also find out whether linen is to be washed, dried and pressed on the premises or to be sent out to specialised linen service contractors.

Staff facilities

Establish the total numbers of male and female staff and their requirements concerning rest rooms, lockers, lavatories, tea-making facilities and offices.

Furniture and equipment

The contract under which furniture is supplied should specify that it is capable of standing up to hard wear. All materials should in fact be hard wearing and should be selected in particular for their resistance to the effects of water and trade products.

Chairs: different kinds may be required for waiting, dressing, shampooing, drying-seat units, children, beauty treatment, reception staff and for the staff rest room; stools may be needed for operators in the salon.

Allied equipment: this may include shampoo basin units, driers (hand-held and standing units), steriliser cabinets, towel steamers, permanent waving trolleys, trays or stands, tint stands and manicure stands.

Special fittings: basic items would be a reception desk, dressing tables and display cabinets for goods on sale.

General fittings: the usual essentials are magazine racks, tables, ashtrays, hangers and filing cabinets.

2:11 AGENCIES

Categories

The various types of agencies which use shop type units for their trading may be classified as follows:

Type	Comments
Airline company	Primarily concerned with travel in the company's aircraft; may incorporate facilities for tourist information offices; vulnerability to terrorist attacks may require special consideration
Boat, coach, or railway	May belong to an independent company or be part of a national transport company; usually, but not necessarily, attached to a transport terminal
Tour operator	Major company primarily dealing with packaged holidays; may have facilities to deal with travel only
Travel agent	Independent operator or part of a chain of operators booking tickets for all three types of agency above; as travel agents deal with a large number of companies they need more display space for brochures
Theatre	Deal with tickets for entertainment (opera, ballet, cinema, pop and classical concerts and sporting events); usually require only a very limited amount of space
Bureau de change	May be an independent unit or attached to one of the above types; for exchanging foreign currencies and travellers' cheques.
Car hire	Hires out chauffeur-driven or self-drive cars; must be attached to its own garage and car parking facilities

Premises

Type of premises	Type of agency
Individual shops	All types but mostly airline companies and travel agencies; the ideal site from which to sell services directly to the public
In an office building	Tour operators; site suitable only for administrative procedures to which the public has restricted access
Transport terminal	Coach or railway company, car hire company, and bureau de change
Shared premises ('shop-in-a-shop')	Travel agent, theatre agent and bureau de change

Planning and layout

Customers' requirements

1 Waiting: provision for seating, tables, magazine racks and ashtrays.

2 Brochure stand: for the comprehensive range of brochures, catalogues, pamphlets etc which are usually on open display for self service.

3 telephones: it is necessary to know how many will be needed, where to put them and whether separate lines or extensions are required; coinboxes or booths may be needed together with space for directories.

4 Checking-in: a bag shelf, writing counter, and space to discuss services in comparative privacy may be needed; find out whether seats are required for customers and, if so, the number, types and sizes.

Operators' requirements

1 Reception desks or counters: purpose-built counters may have one level or two and it is necessary to know which type is required;

they should be located in a prominent position which can be seen immediately on entry and command supervision of the waiting area for customers; find out the number of staff serving customers, the number of desks or counters required and whether there will be separate sections for different functions, eg enquiries, national travel, international travel, hotels, car hire, etc.

2 Telephones: ascertain the number of lines and extensions required per desk or counter and the method of internal communication with other staff.

3 Display terminal: establish whether a computer display terminal is required for booking operators and if so the method of connecting this to the central computer.

4 Storage: find out what provisions are required for storing stationery, forms, booking slips, directories, timetables and so on.

5 Customer payment: ascertain what system will be used for billing and payment for services; this may be direct to operator or to a separate payment counter; if payment is direct to operator there must be provision for a cash drawer.

6 Bureau de change counter: for security reasons this should not be located near the entrance; establish whether security screens, a security door, audio grilles and ventilation to the enclosed area are required and what ancillary equipment will be needed (this may include operator's stool, safe, cash drawer or cash register, calculating machines and rate of exchange boards).

Ancillary accommodation

It is necessary to know the total numbers of male and female staff and their requirements concerning restrooms, lockers, lavatories and tea-making facilities. Architects should also find out what accommodation is required for offices and how much space is needed for the storage of brochures, displays, stationery, directories, catalogues, timetables and other items.

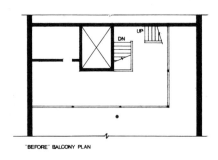

"BEFORE" BALCONY PLAN

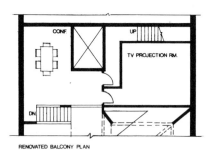

RENOVATED BALCONY PLAN

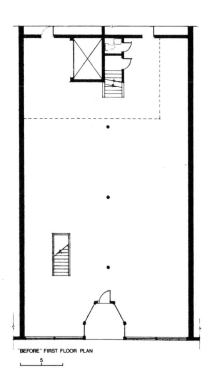

2.84

"BEFORE" FIRST FLOOR PLAN

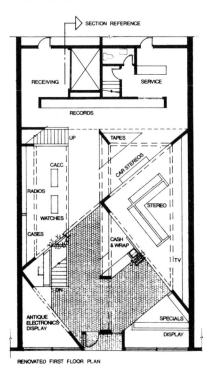

RENOVATED FIRST FLOOR PLAN

.85

2.87

.86

2ND FL.	STOR.			
BALCONY	CONF.			RETAIL
1ST FL.	RECEIVING			
BASEMENT	STOR.	SOUND RM.	RETAIL	SOUND RM.

BUILDING SECTION

2.84 *Leisure World Electronics, records and stereo goods, Baraboo, Wisconsin, designed by Jack Fleig, AIA. Plans, section*

2.85 *Same. Shop interior before renovation*

2.86 *Same. After renovation the clients ended with an interior with reduced problems of inventory, display and security. The working environment is now a pleasant one*

2.87 *Above. The new ceiling is pine; countertops, handrail and joinery trimmings are red oak sealed. Walls are painted white and flooring is quarry tiles and red carpet*

2.88

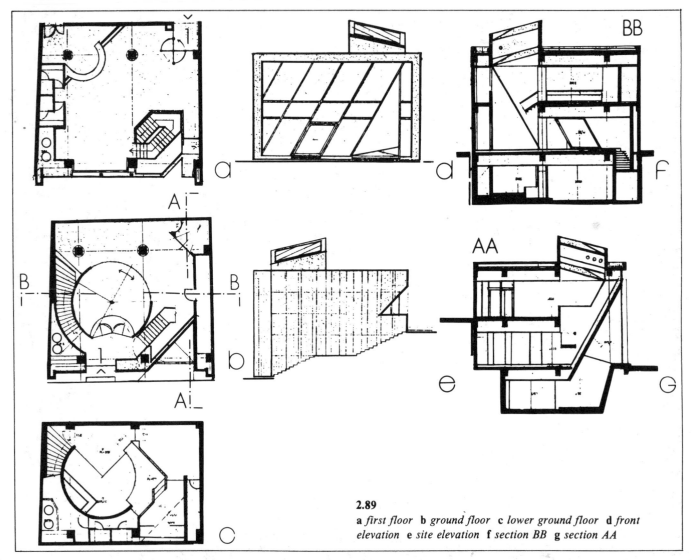

2.89
a *first floor* b *ground floor* c *lower ground floor* d *front elevation* e *site elevation* f *section BB* g *section AA*

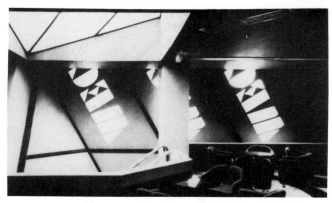

2.88 *MEC, furniture showroom, Tokyo, designed by Paolo Riani Associates with Junko Enomoto. The mirrored glazing with inclined chrome mullions is framed by a band of concrete painted black. The entrance door is set back at the centre of the facade and the void at the right drops down to the basement*

2.89 *Same. Plans and sections*

2.90 *Same. Open tread sculptured stairways connect the three floors creating a very fluid space*

2.91 *Above: Same. The company's name seen on the external facade in* **2.88** *is now viewed in reverse from the interior*

2.92 *Same. Interior view of entrance at ground floor level. The materials are stainless steel, marble and dark grey carpet and paint*

90

92

2.93

2.94

2.95

96

2.97

2.93 *Furniture showroom, Vienna, designed by Hans Hollein.*
External facade with original arched window left intact. The
metal frames are painted green matching the windows above

2.94 *Same. Internal view over entrance door. The shop logo was*
designed by the architect

2.95 *Same. Entrance doors viewed from the mezzanine gallery.*
The steel lattice work is painted green and the beads are polished
brass

2.96 *Same. Ground floor level showroom with diagonally set*
lighting

2.97 *Same. Night view*

2.98 *Same. Staircase to mezzanine with handrail set flush in the*
plastered wall

2.98

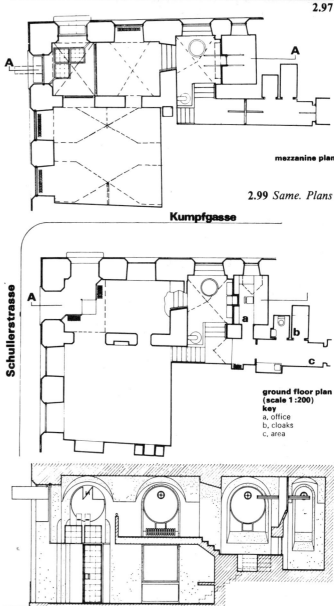

mezzanine plan

2.99 *Same. Plans*

Kumpfgasse

Schullerstrasse

ground floor plan
(scale 1:200)
key
a, office
b, cloaks
c, area

section A-A (scale 1:100)

2.100 *Same. Section*

Key
a *entrance zone*   **d** *sample display*
b *reception*   **e** *office*
c *central exhibition area* **f** *conference*

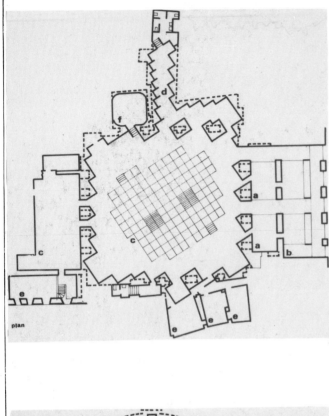

plan

section

2.101

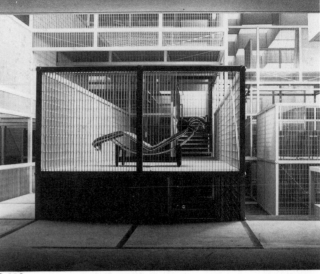

2.102

2.103

2.101 *Cassina, furniture showroom, Milan, designed by Mario Bellini. Plans and section*

2.102 *Same. The furniture is displayed inside metal cages*

2.103 *Same. Prefabricated modules allow a wide variety of assemblies*

2.104 *Same. Visitors walk through the cages which are arranged to form floor levels*

2.104

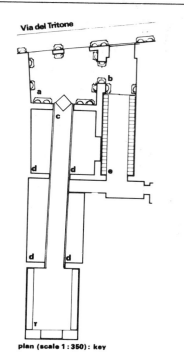

2.105 *Richard-Ginori, sanitaryware showroom, Rome, designed by Piero Sartogo. The street shopfront does not reveal what lies within, but only shows a lobby to the shop further in*

2.106 *Same. Doorway between lobby and shop interior. Black columns made from rubber mirror the street elevation outside. Coloured toughened glass doors rise out of the marble flooring*

2.107 *Same. Plan*

plan (scale 1 : 350): key

a *entrance area* b *display window* c *corridor designed in perspective* d *showrooms* e *samples* f *technical display*

2.108

2.109

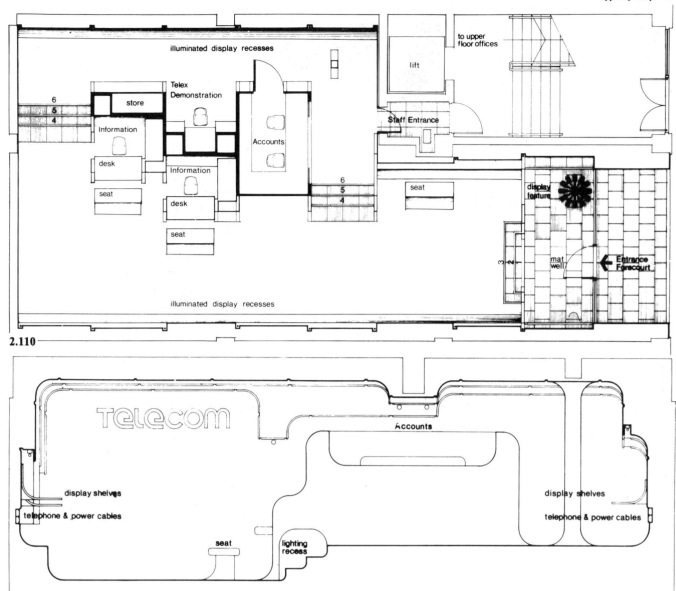

2.110

2.111

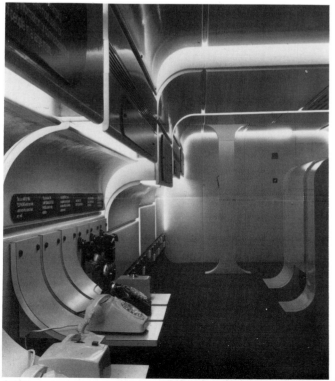

2.112

2.108 *Telecom, telephone showroom, Belfast, designed by Ian Campbell and Partners with Max Glendinning. Shopfront in silver laminate. The glazing is set back and the entrance forecourt is paved with ribbed rubber tiles*

2.109 *Same. Interior view. The brown/grey striped carpet runs up to the underside of seats, counters and worktops. Ceilings and walls are yellow postformed laminate*

2.110 *Same. Floor plan*

2.111 *Same. Section*

2.112 *Same. Detail of display worktop with concealed lighting*

2.113

2.114

2.113 *Olivetti, typewriter showroom, Brussels, designed by Hans von Klier. The 'V'-shaped typewriter stands are finished in polished stainless steel and have socket outlets built in for plugging into electrical machines*

2.114 *Same. The stands are arranged in groups and lie on a brown carpet*

2.115 *Retti, candle shop, Vienna, designed by Hans Hollein (see also **5.4** and **5.5** below). Interior view of tiny showroom which measures less than 3·7m wide: to compensate for this, floor to ceiling mirrors are used on opposing walls.*

2.115

11

2.117

2.118

2.116 *Poster Originals, poster gallery, New York, designed by Gwathmey Siegel and Associates. Ceiling is finished in polished aluminium ceiling panels, walls are mirrored at the entrance and painted white elsewhere. The carpet is grey*

2.117 *Same. Foreign posters are displayed in portfolios on the right. Contemporary American posters are pinned to wall and inclined display base. Photos: Norman McGrath*

2.118 *View towards the framing table on the right and the control desk with poster storage behind*

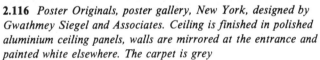

FLOOR PLAN

1   ENTRY
2   FOREIGN POSTER BOOKS
3   SLOPED DISPLAY
4   PERMANENT AMERICAN COLLECTION GALLERY
5   FRAMING TABLE
6   CONTROL DESK
7   FILES / STORAGE / WORK COUNTER
8   FRAMED POSTER DISPLAY
9   OFFICE
10 TOILET

1.119 *Same. Plan. This gallery deals with posters as an art form and accommodates a large number of American and foreign posters. In addition to sales there are framing facilities*

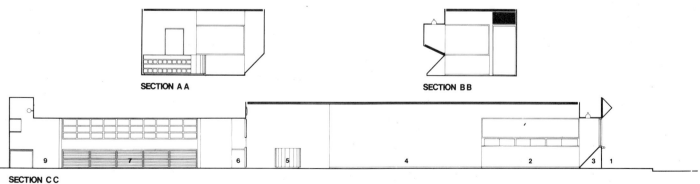

SECTION A A

SECTION B B

SECTION C C

2.120 *Same. Section*

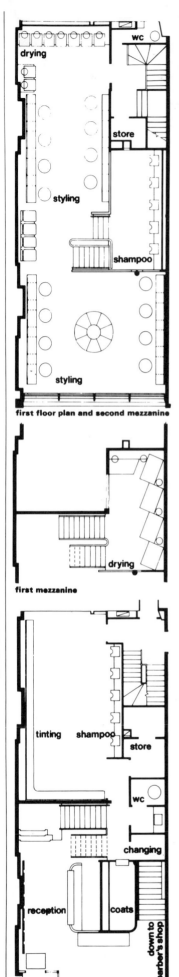

drying

wc

store

styling

shampoo

styling

first floor plan and second mezzanine

drying

first mezzanine

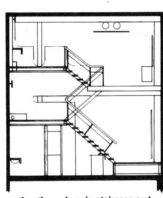

section through main staircase and mezzanines

tinting   **shampoo**

store

wc

changing

reception   **coats**

down to barber's shop

ground floor plan (scale 1/12in = 1ft)

2.121

2.122

2.123

2.121 *Vidal Sassoon, hairdresser, Manchester, designed by Gordon Bowyer and Partners with the Serventi Design Group. Plans. (While in smaller establishments the same person may still perform all the hair treatment jobs, here these tasks are performed by different persons in different areas)*

2.122 *Same. Night time view of the shopfront set into an existing Victorian facade. The central core on the ground floor is the reception counter with a seat bench in the front for waiting for friends*

2.123 *Same. View of the work stations with exposed services*

2.124 *Vidal Sassoon, hairdressers, Beverly Hills, California, designed by Gwathmey Siegel and Associates. This is one of a series of hairdressing saloons designed by the architects for the same client. Customers are divided at the reception with men directed to the ground floor and women to the first floor*

SECOND FLOOR

FLOOR PLANS

1	ENTRY	13	VIP	25	PUBLIC TELEPHONES
2	GALLERY	14	CUTTING (WOMEN)	26	MECHANICAL
3	WAITING	15	DRYING		
4	RECEPTION	16	TRICOLOGY		
5	DISPLAY	17	HAIR TEST		
6	COATS	18	MANAGER		
7	DRESSING	19	STAFF		
8	WASHING	20	DISPENSARY		
9	CUTTING (MEN)	21	STORAGE		
10	LAUNDRY	22	STREET DISPLAY		
11	TOILETS	23	OPEN		
12	APPOINTMENTS	24	LAUNDRY CHUTE		

GROUND FLOOR

2.124

2.126

2.125 *Same. Men's washing area. The floor mirrors the lowered ceiling. Photos: Norman McGrath*

2.126 *Same. The facade at night*

Continued

2.125

2.127

2.127 *Same. The women's salon appears much larger than in reality due to station wall mirrors on all sides*

2.128 *Hairdressing work station details*

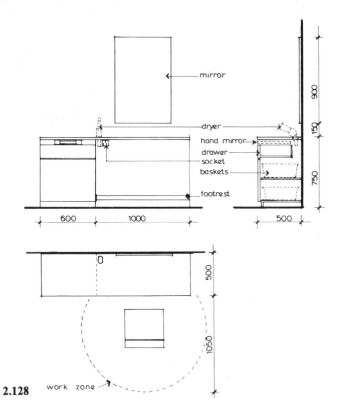

2.128

3
PLANNING AND LAYOUT

3.1 CONTROLLING DIMENSIONS

Horizontal and vertical dimensions

British Standard 4330:1968 gives the controlling horizontal and vertical metric dimensions on which the design of new shop buildings should be based; these are set out in tables I and II below. The horizontal dimension given under the heading 'Spacing' in table I may be measured between the central lines or between the faces of columns or structural walls. The term 'Zone' refers to the thickness of columns and walls with allowance for tolerances.

Space allocation

The internal layout planned for most shops may be subdivided according to the amount of space required respectively for the sales floor, for goods handling and storage, and for staff, offices and other accommodation. The relative proportion of each will vary according to type of business accommodated, type of service provided and size of the turnover. Architects should consult their clients to establish the precise amount of space to be allocated to each of these sections. As an illustration the average percentage of space allocated in food shops is as follows:

Table III Typical space allocation for foodshops

Size of shop	Sales floor (%)	Handling and storage (%)	Staff and office accommodation (%)
Small (specialist type eg delicatessen)	65	25	10
Medium (grocer)	55	30	15
Large (supermarket)	50	30	20

3.2 THE SALES FLOOR

Selling methods

Selling methods define shop layouts and are essential in determining the internal design. The methods can be classified by the type of service provided.

Personalised service

Traditionally, customers are served from behind a counter with the goods being displayed on the counter, on shelves behind it and to a small extent on display units on the sales floor. On completion of sale the assistant wraps the goods on the counter and takes the cash to the till or cashier point. This type of service is suitable for shops dealing with:

1 expensive goods eg jewellery
2 technical goods eg cameras and stereo equipment
3 goods to order eg small specialist foodshops

Table I Horizontal controlling dimensions

Spacing (mm)	Zone (mm)
2700	100
3000	200
3300	300
3600	400
3900	500
4200	600
4500	
4800	
5100	
5400	
5700	
6000	
6300	
6600	
6900	
7200	
7500	
9000	
10500	
12000	
18000	

Table II Vertical controlling dimensions

Floor to floor heights (mm)	Floor to ceiling heights (mm)	Floor to roof thickness (mm)	Window sill heights (mm)	Window head heights (mm)	Floor or ceiling changes in level (mm)
2700	2400	300	0	same as	300
3000	2500	400	300	ceiling height	600
3300	2600	500	600	or	900
3600	2700	600		2100	1200
3900	2800	900			1500
4200	2900	1200			1800
4500	3000				2100
4800	3300				2400
5100	3600				
5400	3900				
5700	4200				
6000	4500				
6600	4800				
7200	5400				
7800	6000				
	6600				
	7200				

4 exclusive goods (exclusive clothing and footwear).
The layout invariably calls for the extensive use of counters arranged along one or more perimeter walls with wall storage behind and island units in the middle of the sales floor. The exception is the exclusive shop which only serves a small clientele and may therefore be planned for maximum customer comfort.

Assisted service

Customers may select and inspect the goods openly displayed on wall and island units. Sales staff are at hand for providing general information, service and sales. On completion of a sale the assistant takes the goods and cash to a cash counter for packing and payment. This type of service suits shops dealing with low to middle cost comparison goods where customers must personally inspect the goods at leisure to check quality, variety and value. Typical examples are shops dealing with clothing and footwear. Layouts are generally open plan with wall units fitted along perimeter walls and island units plus internal displays on the sales floor. A general requirement is that the cash counter should take a prominent central position which commands good supervision of all areas.

Self service

Here customers pick the goods from open shelves and take them for packing and payment to a checking out point without any contact with shop staff. This arrangement suits many of the convenience goods such as foodshops, bookstores, stationers and so on. In shops offering personal service customers are influenced to buy what the assistants advise and show to them but here sales talk is replaced by comprehensive display. The basic plan calls for perimeter walls to be fitted with tall units with the central floor area subdivided by island units known as 'gondolas'. Generally customers prefer the perimeter fittings and fewer numbers visit the central aisles which should run lengthwise from shopfront to rear. Ideally customers should traverse a continuous route from entrance to exit covering the greatest possible amount of display. Entrances have to be wider than for other types as space must be made for wire baskets and trolleys.

Value classification

Goods sold in any type of shop may be broken down into demand, semi-demand and impulse. This classification helps to determine where each category should be located on the sales floor.

3.2 Below. Dimensions for fixtures and aisles

Demand goods

These are the basic goods which customers mainly visit the shop for. In food shops they would include staple foods such as meat and greengroceries, bread and dairy products. In men's wear shops they would be suits, coats, trousers and jackets. Demand goods are usually used to draw customers deep into the shop and may be safely relegated to positions that are relatively inconvenient to reach and not particularly obvious to see.

Semi-demand goods

This category falls between demand and impulse goods in value and should also be located between the two. In men's wear it would include shirts, woollens and sportswear.

Impulse goods

Goods in this category are usually cheap or small and are usually purchased on the spur of the moment. In food shops they would include confectionery, crisps and toiletries; in men's wear ties, underwear, umbrellas and jewellery (cuff links, tie pins). Impulse goods are usually located in a prominent position at eye level or lower and are displayed in bulk containers such as dump baskets, carousels, rack stands and so on. In relation to the floor plan they are invariably located near entrances or exits and near cash counters where customers have to queue for service.

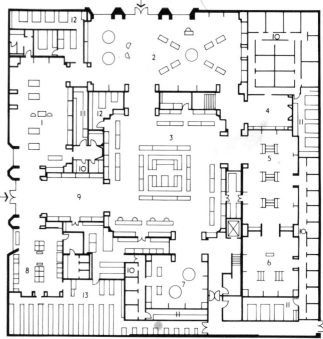

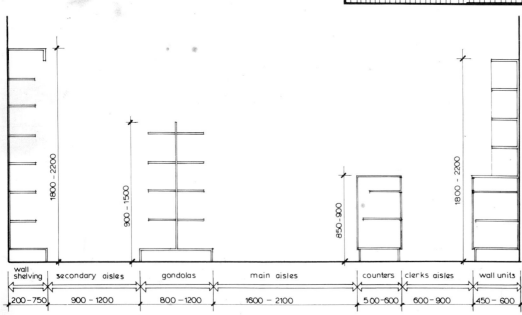

3.1 (Above) Sectional planning in a large shop: Saks at Monterey, California

1 *men's store*
2 *women's sportswear*
3 *women's accessories*
4 *salon*
5 *young dimensions*
6 *young dimensions sportswear*
7 *lingerie*
8 *women's shoes*
9 *gifts*
10 *Fitting rooms*
11 *Workrooms*
12
13 *Stockroom*

wall shelving	secondary aisles	gondolas	main aisles	counters	clerks aisles	wall units
200-750	900-1200	800-1200	1600-2100	500-600	600-900	450-600

Commodity classification

All types of goods may be broadly subdivided into various commodity headings so as to determine their location on the sales floor. This is particularly important where built-in or specialist display equipment is being installed because repositioning is often expensive and difficult. From a breakdown of commodity headings, a percentage allocation of total space can be established.

Layout

The following principles may be relevant when planning the layout of the sales floor:

1 Customers should be induced to visit all parts of the shop by the way in which demand goods or bargains are set out.

2 Areas in the rear may require special lighting with higher levels of illumination or special displays to attract customers.

3 'Dead ends' or 'cul-de-sacs' caused by fixtures in plan should generally be avoided.

4 Commodities should be classified in such a way that it is clear where they will be put.

5 Similar goods or related goods should be placed together or adjacent to each other.

6 Products with incompatible associations or a deleterious effect on each other must be separated (eg meat and toiletries).

7 Small and relatively expensive items should be placed near cash counters where they can be under constant supervision.

9 Flexibility in layout and services is essential to allow for alterations and changes in seasonal variation.

10 Shapes that look well on the drawing board do not necessarily translate to the sales floor.

Figures **3.1**, **3.2** and **3.3** illustrate various aspects of shop floor planning and layout.

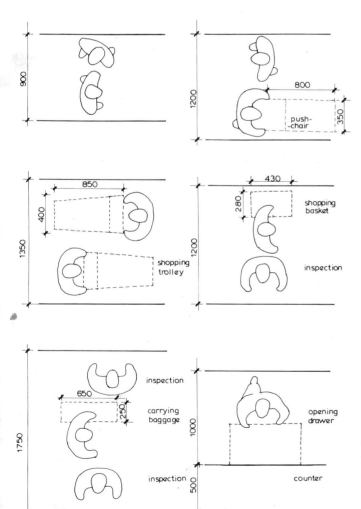

3.3 *Circulation space required for various types of functions*

Colour

Colour is used extensively in interiors to produce variations in atmosphere, character and space. It is not possible to lay down rules for the use of colour which are capable of universal application. Each scheme must however take into consideration the kind of shop, the scope of the intended design, the type of goods on display and the direction and quality of daylight and artificial light. General guidelines which may be taken into consideration regarding the selection of colours are as follows:

1 In selecting the colour scheme consideration should be given to three factors:

(a) Hue (commonly referred to as 'colour'): eg red, yellow, blue, green.

(b) Value (reflectance or lightness): a measure of the amount of light reflected irrespective of hue and chroma.

(c) Chroma (saturation or intensity): the saturation of a particular hue compared with that of neutral grey of similar lightness.

2 The psychology of colours essentially associates them with particular experiences, for example blue is cold and receding (sea and sky); beige and brown are wholesome and earthy (nature and soil); green is cool and fresh (plants and vegetation); yellow and red are warm and dominating (sun and fire).

3 Colours are prone to changes in fashion. At present there is a move towards nature (hence the current preference for buttermilk, browns and buffs).

4 The selected colour must be closely related to the type of merchandise on display; for example vibrant colours may be suitable in fashion shops but will not suit food shops.

5 Shops on more than one floor should have vertical zones such as staircases, escalators and elevator cores connected by the use of the same colour so as to provide a continuity between floors.

6 Proportions can be emphasised or corrected by the right choice of shade. Ceilings which are too high can be made to appear lower with dark shades and narrow areas made to appear wider with brighter shades.

7 Concealment can be achieved by painting exposed ducts and pipes in a dark colour so as to camouflage the shadows which they cast. Where it is essential to prevent light reaching such services the use of bright open grid ceilings greatly improves the degree to which they can be hidden.

8 Artificial light produces a distorted colour rendering compared to natural light and fluorescent sources give a rendering which differs from that given by incandescent sources: fluorescent lamps are deficient in reds and yellows and favour schemes in the blue-green range; incandescent lamps have opposite properties, rendering blues and greens poorly but favouring reds and yellows.

9 Reflectors used to highlight goods are most efficient against dark backgrounds which absorb light and reflect little back. It is better for background surfaces to be matt because glossy surfaces produce more reflections and reveal unevenness in finishes.

Planning for the disabled

The movement of disabled people (or babies in prams) requires adequate space and planning. Small differences in floor levels should be avoided. Steps less than 80 mm high are dangerous. Single or double steps should always be avoided. Where ramps are provided specially for the disabled the inclination should not exceed $4\frac{1}{2}°$ (1:12) and the length should not exceed 9 m with a preferred maximum length of 6 m. For short ramps not exceeding 2·5 m in length the inclination may be in the order of $5\frac{1}{2}°$ (1:10). Vertical movement in multi-storey buildings requires the provision of at least one lift because escalators are considered to be too dangerous. (Table IV.)

The minimum dimension through which a wheelchair can negotiate a 90° turn is 910 mm. Special provisions may have to be made for parking large prams.

Table IV Average sizes of vehicles used by disabled persons and infants

User	Type of vehicle	L (mm)	W (mm)	H (mm)	Folded Dimensions (mm)
Disabled	Wheel chair	910	660	1020	—
	Folding chair	1020	690	860	1020 × 250
	Electric chair	640	530	890	—
Babies and toddlers	Large pram	1370	710	910	—
	Folding pram	840	530	910	530 × 530
	Push buggy	900	370	890	230 × 200

3.3 STAFF FACILITIES

The facilities which should be provided for staff vary widely depending on the type and size of shop. The minimum would comprise a single lavatory plus tea-making facilities but more comprehensive accommodation might consist of a separate staff entry, cloakrooms, lavatories, restrooms and a first aid room.

Staff entry

It is necessary to establish whether a separate entry is required for staff independently of customers and goods and if so to decide on the method of controlling entry and exit. Where space permits parking for staff cars and cycles should be included in the plans. If other figures are not available 235 m² of the gross area available should be allotted for each car. Staff entry lobbies may house the following items:

Rack storage: for staff to deposit shopping bags before entry and to hold goods bought from the shop for collection at the end of the day. This equipment helps to prevent pilfering and is used for that reason by the larger stores. The racks may be labelled according to staff seniority and staff categories, in alphabetical order (staff categories include management, buyers, sales, office, maintenance and cleaners).

Notice board: for the display of announcements, statutory regulations and so on.

Checking-in machines: an adjoining space for storing cards should be provided for each machine to hold 50 to 80 cards.

Porter: a desk or separate office from which a porter can control entry and exit: this is also the usual position for switches, meters and fuse boards.

Cloakroom

If a cloakroom is provided it should be able to handle the extreme loads during peak use at opening and closing times. When it is not provided arrangements must be made elsewhere for the storage of clothing not used during opening hours and for working clothes not taken home; adequate ventilation is essential. Open storage racks may be used for such storage but these require supervision by designated staff to avoid theft. An alternative provision is to have personal lockers. These may be full height (with a top shelf, hook to hang coats and space for umbrellas, shoes and parcels), half height (to take a jacket, shoes and parcels) or quarter height (to take parcels and folded clothing).

Table V Types and sizes of personal lockers

Type of locker	Height (mm)	Width (mm)	Depth (mm)	Area per user (m²)
Full height	1800	400	300	0·36
Half height	900	400	300	0·18
Quarter height	450	400	300	0·09

Lavatories

Sanitary conveniences and washing facilities (which must be adequately maintained, lighted and ventilated) are required by the Offices, Shops and Railway Premises Act 1963.

One closet and basin is sufficient where the number of staff does not regularly exceed five at any one time, whether or not both men and women are employed. If the number exceeds five separate accommodation must be provided and marked to indicate which sex it is provided for. The following numbers of conveniences are required by the Schedule to the Regulations of the above Act:

Table VI Sanitary accommodation for males (no urinals provided) and females

Nos. regularly employed at any one time	No. of water closets	No. of wash-basins
1 to 15	1	1
16 to 30	2	2
31 to 50	3	3
51 to 75	4	4
76 to 100	5	5
over 100	5 + 1 closet for every additional 25 persons	5 + 1 wash-basin for every additional 25 persons

Table VII Sanitary accommodation for males (urinals provided)

Nos. regularly employed at any one time	No. of water closets	No. of urinals	No. of wash-basins
1 to 15	1	0	1
16 to 20	1	1	2
21 to 30	2	1	2
31 to 45	2	2	3
46 to 60	3	2	4
61 to 75	3	3	4
76 to 90	4	3	5
91 to 100	4	4	5
over 100	4 + 1 closet for every additional 25 persons. Every 4th additional closet may be replaced by a urinal		5 + 1 wash-basin for every additional 25 persons

Washing facilities must include a supply of running cold and hot, or at least warm, water. Soap and drying facilities must also be provided. For females there should be sanitary bins or incinerators. The architect should establish if separate accommodation is required for senior staff (management) and general staff. If customers are to use the same conveniences as staff an additional closet and basin should be added to the number required by the Regulations. For females a handbag shelf should be provided adjacent to the wash-basins and water closets.

Restrooms

A restroom may be used for the following purposes:

For accommodating social functions in large premises after business hours: these may be quiet or noisy in nature (eg staff meetings, parties, dances and so on); the architect should establish the quality and quantity of furniture to be provided.

For refreshments: facilities needed may be a supply of fresh drinking water, tea-making equipment, and, if there is no canteen, provision for preparing food and eating it; a sink, refrigerator, cooker and refreshments dispenser may have to be accommodated.

For first-aid: if there is no separate first-aid room a separate first-aid cupboard must be provided and be readily accessible; each first-aid point must be placed under the charge of one responsible person.

As a cloakroom: for the storage of clothing if there is no separate cloakroom.

Additional facilities

A client may ask for the following special facilities to be provided:

Sick room: a visiting doctor and/or a permanent on-duty nurse may require an office, waiting space, an examination cubicle, washing facilities and a WC.

Canteen: this should be large enough to accommodate all staff at not more than two sittings. Kitchens should be sited near vertical transportation with adequate storage and preparation areas. There may be separate facilities for senior and general staff. A separate ventilation system is essential to prevent smells reaching other parts of the building. Allow 0.75 m^2 to 1.4 m^2 per person.

3.4 OFFICES AND OTHER ACCOMMODATION

Administrative offices
Provision for the following administrative functions must be allowed for regardless of the size of shop, whether they are all contained in one room or carried out in a number of rooms and whether all of them are carried out by one person (the manager) or by a number of persons.

Management
Marketing, buying, sales management, interviewing staff and customers.

Accounts
(a) Hire purchase and credit control: the office should be readily accessible to customers, possibly adjoining the sales floor.
(b) Sales accounts: recording all sales receipts and sending bills to customers.
(c) Wages: paying staff and looking after petty cash and other day to day expenses.
(d) Ledger department: recording and paying for all purchases and orders placed by buyers (space should be allowed for accountants to audit the books and for settling all money matters).

Administration
(a) Secretarial and typing: reception, correspondence, advertising and stationery control.
(b) Communications: telephone switchboard and telex facilities.
(c) Computer: this should be centrally placed so as to be as accessible as possible for all the functions included in its program (eg administration, stock control, accounts etc).

Personnel
Recruiting and training staff: the office should be easily accessible to staff and provide space for interviewing applicants for jobs.

Security
Monitoring the position on the sales floor shown by the closed circuit television console: dealing with shoplifters and other matters (the office may be used by night patrol officers after shopping hours).

Conference
A general meeting room for private discussions.

Private room
Facilities may have to be provided (mainly in exclusive shops) for customers to inspect goods and discuss prices and credit facilities with the sales staff in private. They must be easily accessible (adjoining the sales floor if possible).

Catering facilities
Where a self service cafeteria or a restaurant is to be provided for customers it should be sited so as to command a good view of the premises. The space to be allocated should be 1.0 to 1.4 m^2 per person. Between 45 and 60 per cent of the total area allocated for the purpose of catering for customers should be used for the kitchen which should be sited near vertical transportation and provided with proper ventilation to prevent smells reaching the sales floor. Half the total kitchen area should provide facilities for preparing, cooking and serving food, washing-up and an office for the chef. The other half should be used for storage (larder, vegetables, refrigeration equipment, cutlery, crockery and bottles).

Workshop
A workshop may be required either for servicing and maintaining the premises or for the repair and/or alteration of goods. The size and type needed will of course vary according to the size of the premises and the goods sold there. Typical layouts are shown in Fig 3.4. Architects should establish exactly what is needed with their clients at the stage when their brief is in the process of being formulated. Workshops for the repair and alteration of goods have already been discussed or touched on in sections 2.2, 2.3, 2.4 and 2.6 above. Requirements for workshops concerned with the servicing of shop premises are as follows:
(a) Use: design, preparation and construction of window displays, display stands, ticketing, showcards and general artwork.
(b) Storage: space should be allocated for the storage of displays, models and props when not in use; servicing and repair equipment such as ladders, lighting equipment and so on must also be accommodated.
(c) Planning: workshops must be conveniently placed in relation to display windows so that displays can be easily set up and removed.
(d) Equipment: some typical requirements are a designer's drawing board or bench with plan drawers underneath it; high level shelves for storing manufacturers' catalogues and samples of material; a deep workbench with drawers underneath it and a tool rack on an adjacent wall.
(e) Lighting: the interior should be well lighted preferably by natural daylight; any fluorescent lighting used should give a good rendering of colours; directional spotlights simulating window conditions may be worth considering; ample provision should be made for electricity points.

Storage
Architects should check with their clients on the percentage of total space which is to be allocated for stockrooms. This is closely related to the anticipated turnover, the type of service provided, and the amount of goods on display on the sales floor. Storage methods depend on whether goods are perishable or nonperishable. Perishable goods may be taken to cold stores, special stores, or directly to display cabinets on the sales floor. Nonperishable goods are usually taken to a receiving room for checking and distribution where they are generally stored in racks or open shelving. Some space must also be allocated for goods for dispatch to clients and for the storage of clean packaging for return to manufacturers.

3.5 GOODS HANDLING
All shops require some provision for the handling of goods. These may vary from off-pavement deliveries for small units to the comprehensive range of operations undertaken by large retail concerns.

Taking in
Unloading operations are relatively simple in small shops and may be done in one of the following ways:
1 Unloading off the front pavement and carrying the goods through the sales floor to a receiving area usually at the rear.
2 Unloading off the front pavement and lowering goods through pavement access doors down to basement storerooms.
3 Unloading in a protected yard and delivering through rear or side access doors.
4 Unloading and delivering in fully recessed and sheltered loading docks.

Delivery and dispatch
The architect should establish the size, frequency and number of deliveries and dispatches with his client at the outset so that the entry position and delivery route may be suitably planned. Delivery may be done by the client's own fleet of vehicles which may be

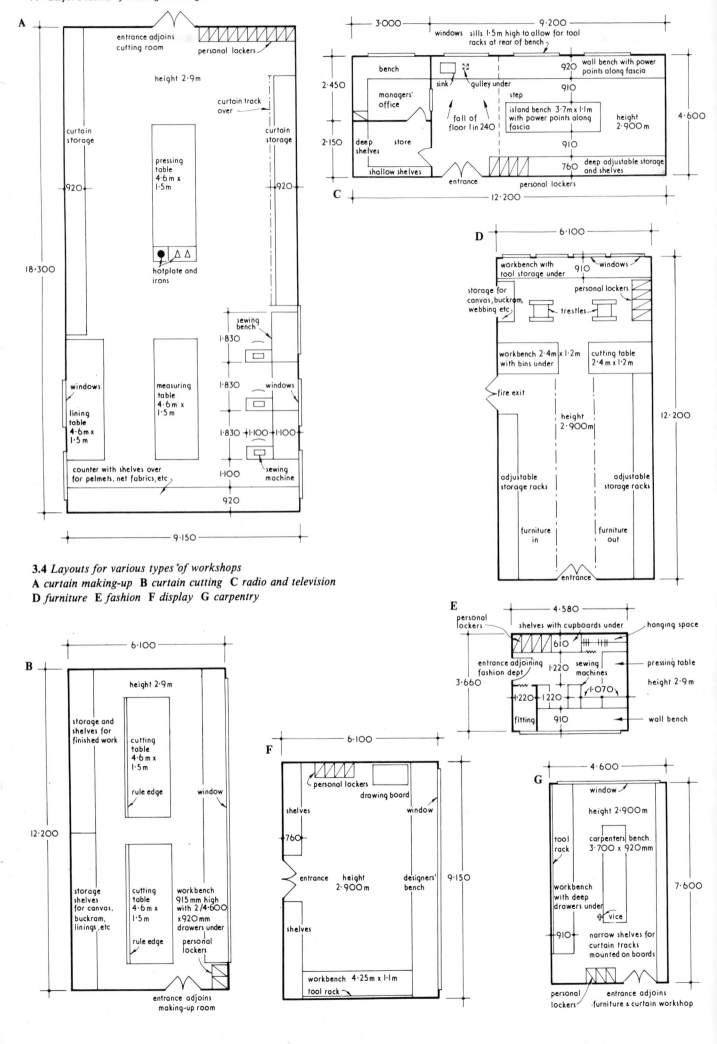

3.4 *Layouts for various types of workshops*
A *curtain making-up* **B** *curtain cutting* **C** *radio and television*
D *furniture* **E** *fashion* **F** *display* **G** *carpentry*

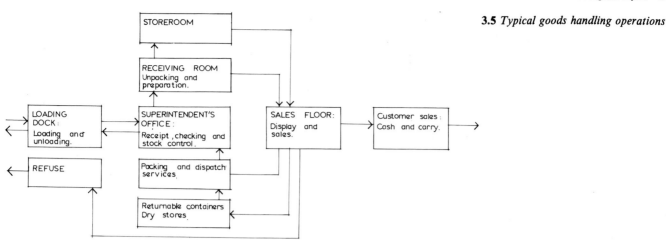

3.5 *Typical goods handling operations*

of standard make, type or size. Alternatively it may be carried out by a varied selection of vehicles provided by haulage contractors. Goods coming in must be unloaded, received, checked, stored and distributed to the sales floor. Outward movements include packing and dispatch to customers, return of stock or packing materials to factories or warehouses and waste disposal. Typical goods handling operations are shown in Fig **3.5**. It is not necessary to provide separate facilities for loading and unloading provided the two operations can be programmed for different times. A common procedure would be for vans to be loaded early in the morning (say by 9.30 a.m.) and for incoming goods to be received from then onwards until mid afternoon when the store vans return from the day's delivery rounds; vans returning early enough can then be loaded for the following day's round.

Loading docks
Trucking ways should have a minimum width of 3·37 m and ideally this should be 3·85 m. If the trucking way is restricted buffer strips should be fixed to side walls at about 0·75 m above the road level to prevent damage to wall surfaces. The maximum gradient should not exceed 1:15. Minimum turning circles for commercial vehicles measure 14·05 m in diameter. There may be provision for an unloading platform on to which the vehicles back and unload. This should have a minimum depth of 2·2 m and be raised about 0·85 m above the yard. The nosing can be covered with a protective material such as timber so as to prevent damage. If the yard is protected with a canopy the normal Ministry of Transport requirement in Great Britain is for it to have a minimum headroom of 5·03 m. Lavatories for van drivers must be provided at some accessible position if the drivers are not permitted to use the store lavatories. The refuse yard (discussed in more detail in section 9.3 below) is usually incorporated with the loading dock. Figure **3.6**, an example from a department store, illustrates the principles involved in goods handling at loading docks.

Security
A transport superintendent is usually appointed for the purposes of supervising and co-ordinating handling operations. His office should overlook the whole loading dock area including all entries and exits so as to control loss of stock from vans or from the shop. Loading yards should be capable of being shut off from the street when not in use. Roller shutters are preferable to sliding folding doors for this purpose because they can be easily operated by remote control.

Handling equipment
For dealing with the horizontal movement of goods the handling equipment may include carts, trolleys and conveyor belts. Inclined movement requires rollers, belts and chutes. Vertical movement necessitates the installation of lifts and hoists. Distribution trolleys are shown in Fig **3.7**.

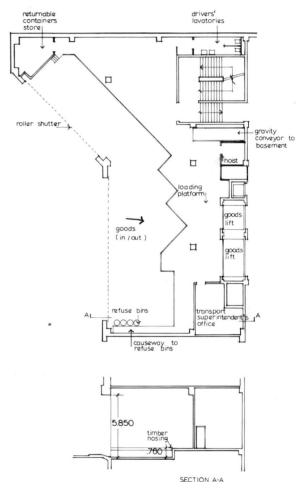

3.6 *Typical loading dock*

Service areas in shopping centres
The following recommendations are derived from the guidelines prepared by the British Multiple Retailers Association. They apply only to large scale developments in the region of 10,000 m² of gross floor area.

Traffic flow
A continuous traffic system is preferable to a system using cul-de-sacs. This is because more space is required for the satisfactory turning of vehicles to relieve the congestion caused by manoeuvering procedures. A one-way system is preferable to a two-way system.

Vehicles
It is realised that the range of vehicles may be very wide and recommendations are therefore made which cater for most types of vehicles. They cover rigid goods vehicles of up to 11 m in length and

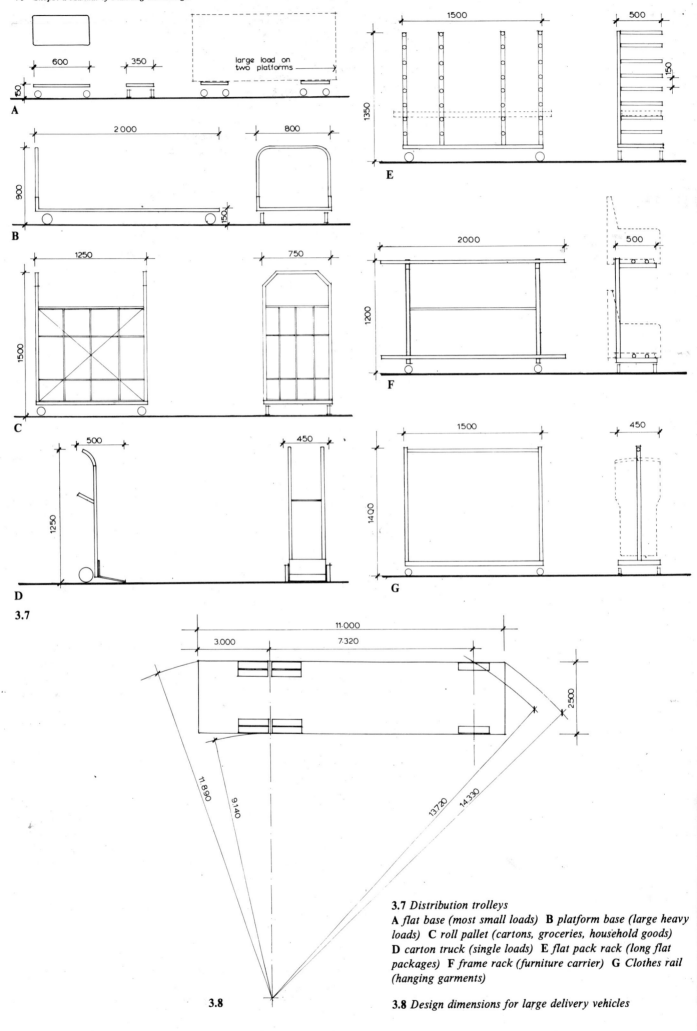

3.7

3.7 *Distribution trolleys*
A *flat base (most small loads)* **B** *platform base (large heavy loads)* **C** *roll pallet (cartons, groceries, household goods)* **D** *carton truck (single loads)* **E** *flat pack rack (long flat packages)* **F** *frame rack (furniture carrier)* **G** *Clothes rail (hanging garments)*

3.8 *Design dimensions for large delivery vehicles*

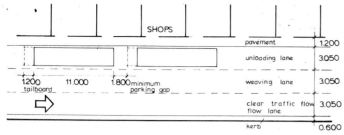

A - ONE WAY SERVICE ROAD WITH SHOPS ON ONE SIDE ONLY

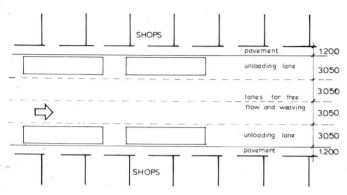

B - ONE WAY SERVICE ROAD WITH SHOPS ON BOTH SIDES

3.9 *Service roads*

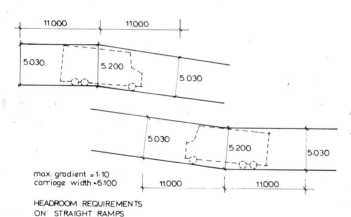

max. gradient = 1:10
carriage width = 6.100

HEADROOM REQUIREMENTS
ON STRAIGHT RAMPS

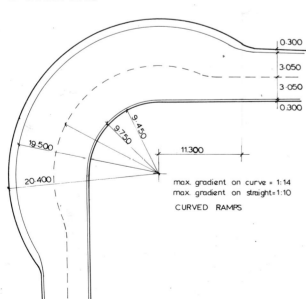

max. gradient on curve = 1:14
max. gradient on straight = 1:10
CURVED RAMPS

3.10 *Ramps*

2·5 m width (Fig **3.8** gives design dimensions for large delivery vehicles).

Service roads

The dimensions for a one-way road serving premises on one side only should be as follows:

1·2 m for footpath between shop and carriageway (this serves as a buffer strip and also as a means of escape in emergencies).

10·15 m for carriageway (consisting of a 3·05 m loading and unloading lane, a 3·05 m weaving lane and a 3·05 m traffic flow land — see Fig **3.9** (*A*)).

0·6 m for buffer strip.

Where the service road serves both sides of the road, the measurements should be:

1·2 m for each of two footpaths, one on each side

12·2 m for carriageway (consisting of two loading and unloading lanes and two weaving and traffic flow lanes — see Fig **3.9** (*B*)).

Headroom

This should be 5·03 m (the normal Ministry of Transport requirement).

Ramps

Ramps serving multi-storey buildings should adhere to the following recommendations:

(a) Straight ramps: one-way traffic — carriage width should be 6·10 m (to permit passing of stalled vehicles)

two-way traffic — carriage width should be 7·32 m

gradient — maximum of 1:10

headroom — 5·03 on level sections; where the ramp changes gradient the headroom should be increased to 5·20 m (as shown in Fig **3.10**).

(b) Curved ramps: one-way traffic — 0·6 m buffer strip on outer curve, 9·75 m carriageway (to permit passing of stalled vehicles) and 0·3 m buffer strip on inner curve (as shown in Fig **3.9**).

two-way traffic — not recommended because it requires very wide carriageways.

gradient — 1:14 maximum.

(c) External ramps: it is recommended that all external ramps should be provided with electrical heating elements in order to prevent icing on the carriageway.

Turning points

Where cul-de-sacs are unavoidable a minimum T-turning point should be provided. Carriage width should measure 3·65 m and buffer strips of 0·6 m should be provided at either side. Alternative means of turning include vehicular turntables. These should measure approximately 9 m in diameter with a sweep diameter of approximately 13·5 m. Turntable pits should be 0·3 to 1·8 m deep.

3.6 MEANS OF ESCAPE IN CASE OF FIRE

Small shops

In Great Britain shops with a floor area of less than 280 m² are excluded from the compulsory provisions relating to fire escape arrangements contained in the Building Regulations 1976. However non-mandatory recommendations relating to small shops are made in CP 3: Chapter IV: part II: 1968 (Shops and Department Stores).

These define a 'small shop' as one which has not more than three floors with a maximum area of 280 m² per floor. Their main points are summarised below.

Single storey small shops

Where the entire floor of a single storey small shop is on one level with exits direct to the open air no specific limitation is suggested of its size provided that the width of the exit or exits is adequate for the density of persons anticipated.

Table VIII Anticipated density of persons per gross floor area for various types of shops

Density (m²/person)	Type of shop
1·9	Shops trading in common consumer goods: food, hardware, clothing, footwear, cosmetics, household goods etc
7·0	Specialist shops in expensive trades: bespoke tailoring, furs, furniture, jewellery, art galleries etc

An aperture 535 mm in width allows the passage of 100 people in 2½ minutes. Each additional 152 mm allows for the passage of 30 more persons in that time. It should be noted however that a minimum of 765 mm clear opening is recommended and an opening of 1070 mm preferred. If the shop is long and narrow with the ratio of greatest length to smallest width exceeding 4:1 there should be a secondary exit at the end opposite to the main front entrance.

Multi-storey small shops
A single open staircase is acceptable provided:
(a) Each floor does not exceed 280 m² in area.
(b) The distance from the furthest point on any floor to the final point of exit does not exceed 30·5 m.
(c) The distance from the staircase at ground floor level to the exit (where the route is through the ground floor sales area) does not exceed 15·2 m; the exit door should be clearly visible from the stairs and there should be no obstructions.
(d) The minimum width of the staircase is 765 mm for a stair serving a floor area of up to 230 m² and 1070 mm above this.
(e) There is a secondary exit in narrow long shops.
(f) No part of the upper floor served by an open staircase is at a greater distance from an enclosed staircase or exit door than 9·1 m plus the least distance between the staircase opening and the opposite wall.
Other recommendations are:

1 Sales floor at second floor level: this may be permitted provided a fire resistant screen and door separate it from the lower floors and a second means of excape is provided for the second floor.
2 Fire alarm system: this must be provided throughout the shop.
3 Exit doors to street: when shops have 'in' and 'out' doors, both should be able to open outwards unless there are sufficient 'out' doors; if it is intended that only 'out' doors should be used for escape they must have 'Exit' signs over the doorway.
4 Common passageway: shops in development schemes should have a common passageway at the rear to provide mutual escape routes for all of them, especially at basement and upper floor levels.

Large shops
Shop premises having an area greater than 280 m² per floor are controlled in Great Britain by Part E of the Building Regulations 1976. The main provisions are summarised in Appendix 2 below. It is therefore only necessary to give brief particulars here. Section E is divided into two parts. Section I which is concerned with structural fire precautions adopts the concept of limiting the spread of flame by compartmentation. A shop must not exceed 2,000 m² in area or 7,000 m³ in volume. If it does so it must be subdivided into compartments bounded by 'compartment floors' and 'compartment walls' as defined in regulation E1. Section II deals with means of escape and its objectives are to safeguard the lives of employees and customers in the event of fire and to facilitate fire fighting in tall buildings where the upper floors are beyond the reach of mobile fighting appliances. This section lays down rules regarding horizontal routes to staircase enclosures, vertical routes (staircase enclosures themselves) and escape routes from the base of stairs to the final exit. In London, under the London Building Acts (Amendment) Act 1939, floor areas up to 4,000 m² may be permitted as well as greater volumes of compartmentation provided that special provisions are observed relating to fire escapes and fire precautions. The Act permits buildings up to 30 m high on favourable sites but no floor over 24 m can be used for sales purposes.

4
FIXTURES AND FITTINGS

4.1 SELECTION

Most types of fixtures and fittings used for the purposes of display and storage are widely available from a large number of manufacturers. These are however mainly intended for popular grades of shops and may have similar features. For this reason it may be desirable for architects to design their own equipment when commissioned to design any relatively exclusive shop. The main types of storage and display equipment generally available are set out below.

4.2 CABINETS

Cabinets are used for storing and displaying small items and for housing items which require special security storage. There are three basic types, wall units, counters and gondolas.

Wall units

Wall units have a normal height of between 1900 and 2100 mm. They may be full sized cabinets or split cabinets where the lower half is of different type from the top half (for example the lower part may consist of a series of drawers and the upper half may be fitted with shelves). Units may incorporate a canopy with concealed lighting to highlight the goods: if space becomes limited goods may be displayed on top of the canopy which then acts as a top shelf. One very adaptable system is shown in Figs **4.1** and **4.2**.

Counters

Counters are usually provided with a glass top and with display shelves below. Part or whole of the front, back and sides may also be made of glass. They vary in width from 525 to 650 mm wide and in height from 700 to 900 mm. When counters are to hold cash registers they should be of sturdy construction to take the load and stresses caused by the mechanical movements of the till. The cash register base should have a minimum flat surface area of 550 × 550 mm square. The space under the register pedestal can be used to store paper bags and stationery. Adjoining the cash register there should be space allocated for packing or wrapping. Shops which do not use a cash register require a till drawer which must be incorporated in a special counter. Electrical equipment is often demonstrated on counter tops. If there is such a requirement, built-in sockets may be desirable to avoid trailing flexes. Other outputs requiring electrical power are electric registers and integral counter lighting. Figure **4.3** illustrates two types of counter.
4.3 illustrates two types of counter.

Gondolas

Island units, termed 'gondolas' should be kept below eye level to allow for supervision against theft and to afford a greater sense of spaciousness. This factor limits the gondola heights to 1400 mm.

Type of fitting	Comments	Use
Cabinets	Covers a wide range of fittings; may be wall unit, island unit, display counter, or cash/wrapping counter; may be open, closed with sliding or hinged doors, with wooden or glass flaps, fitted with drawers, trays, or racks or in any combination of the above	Most types of goods which require some protection against dust or pilferage (clothing, jewellery, cameras, electrical goods, china, etc)
Clothes rails	May be independent units or built-in; types may be straight rails, circular rails or special designs; they may be freestanding, fitted to walls, or hung from ceilings	Men's wear, women's wear, and children's wear (trousers, shirts, skirts, coats, etc)
Shelving systems	May be classed as light, medium, or heavy duty depending on the loading requirements; many types of brackets are available which enable them to be used without the conventional shelves	All types of 'dry goods' (books, food, household goods, hardware, stationery, accessories, etc)
Perforated panels	There are two basic types of panels: pegboards and louvred panels; pegboards are more suitable for lightweight goods and may be used as a backing panel for shelving systems; louvred panels made from sheet steel may be used for heavy goods and are more durable	Mainly for display of small items; prepacked goods are displayed with a range of accessories including hoods, loops, hangers, and tool holders
Dump baskets	Usually circular in plan; may be single or multi-deck	Mainly for 'throw-away' lines; suitable also for cheap impulse items
Display models	Models may be full size male, female, boy or girl; part models include head and shoulders, busts, hand and arm, leg and foot	For the display of clothing; also used to attract attention by giving display of any goods a human scale
Stands	May be individually designed and built to display a selection of articles, or specially supplied by a manufacturer to display his products	Individual stands are suitable for the display of a few selected items, almost elevating them to the status of 'objets d'art' (eg typewriters, cameras, stereo equipment; manufacturers' stands serve for mass display (eg cosmetics, sunglasses)
Turntables	Platforms may be flush base, raised base, tiered or framed; turntable units may also be ceiling hung	Turntables provide movement which attracts the eye: suitable for window or special internal displays
Safes	Locking may be with keylocks, combination locks or a combination of both; small safes may be anchored to walls or floors; larger safes may be protected by timelocks and a range of intruder detection devices; may be built into walls or floors or freestanding	For storing cash and valuables
Refrigerated cabinets	Types are distinguishable by their required storage temperatures: eg deep frozen or quick frozen or chilled foods Cabinets may be open, closed, single-deck or multi-deck	Storage of perishable foods; used in most foodshops and also by florists for the display of flowers in hot weather

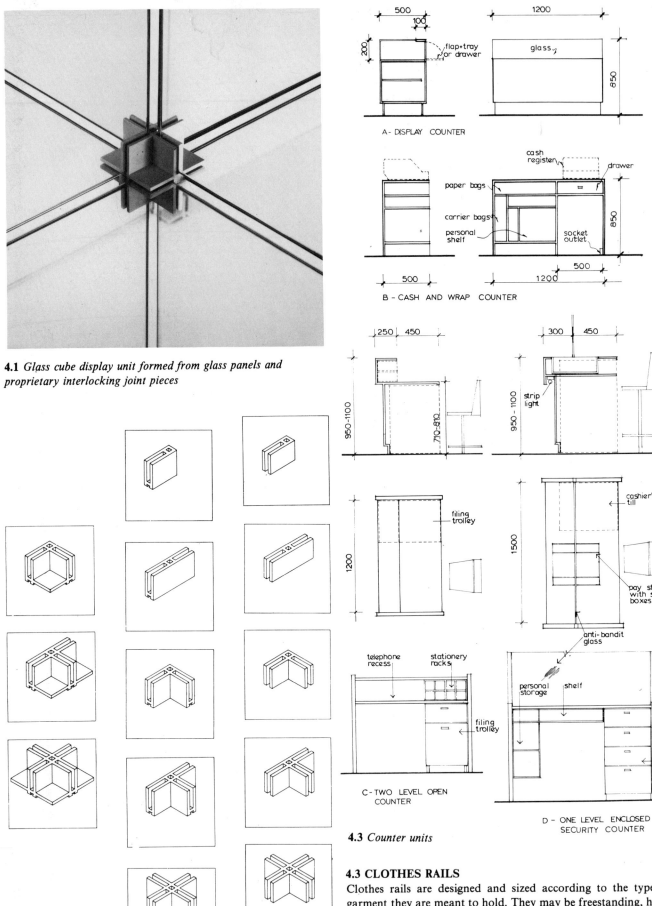

4.1 *Glass cube display unit formed from glass panels and proprietary interlocking joint pieces*

4.2 *Same. Many permutations are possible from the range of pieces manufactured (R. T. Display System)*

4.3 *Counter units*

4.3 CLOTHES RAILS

Clothes rails are designed and sized according to the type of garment they are meant to hold. They may be freestanding, hung from the ceiling or incorporated in a wall cabinet.

Freestanding units

These incorporate stands which may be provided with castors to allow for ease of movement within the sales floor. Limitation to under 1400 mm high (as for other gondola units) does not obstruct the interior and allows for adequate supervision against shoplifting. The main types of freestanding units, illustrated in Fig **4.4**, are as follows:

Straight rail: this can be single or double; if it is double the second rail is attached adjacent to the first rail or above it; standard lengths are 900, 1200, 1500, 1800 mm; the height varies from 1100 to 1500 mm.

Circular rail: this type is very popular because it fits into most awkward plan shapes and allows customers to gather and inspect the merchandise from all angles; however one disadvantage of this system is 'bunching' caused by the restricted space on the inner side of the circular rail which creates some difficulty in inspecting goods and limits the amount on display (this is avoided in the more recently developed use of cross or double bar rails); circular rails can be single or double tiered; double tiered rails may have both rails in the same diameter or the upper rail with a smaller diameter; total diameters range from 700 to 1100 mm and heights from 1100 to 1500 mm.

Cross bar rail: this can be a double or a triple bar unit; it consists of T-bar hanging rails fixed to a common base frame (the bars are adjustable in height and direction); the overall base width varies from 600 to 1200 mm and the height from 1100 to 1500 mm.

Double Z rail: this can be single or double tiered; the unit is a cross between the straight rail and the circular rail; it allows customers to inspect a range of garments from one position (as in circular rails) but without the problem of 'bunching' associated with them; it consists of four short bars arranged at right angles to each other cantilevered from a central pole; the hanging bar length may be 300 to 450 mm and the overall base width from 600 to 900 mm.

Projecting rail: hanging rails are cantilevered from a central pole: they may be standard rails or 'waterfall' rails (which are arms set at an angle with notches to take the hangers); each rail holds 8 to 12 garments and up to four arms can be fixed to each pole.

Spiral rail: this is circular in plan but on a spiralling form which resembles a 'waterfall' arm with notches to hold a pre-set number of hangers; diameters 700 to 1100 mm; heights 1750 to 2000 mm; number of garments held 50 to 65.

Hanging units
Clothes rails hung from the ceiling are of the straight type. They leave the floor unobstructed but may require bracing to prevent the rail bar from swinging.

Wall units
Wall units have a permanent condition which rather restricts the alterations which can be made to floor layout. To allow for some flexibility they can be dimensioned on a module designed to make it possible to move them with the minimum of disturbance. Wall units usually take long garments such as coats and ladies' dresses. If they are required to take short garments these are invariably hung on two-tiered rails so as to take up most of the wall space available. It is normal to incorporate the rails within some sort of cabinet which may include recessed lighting and a canopy which acts as an element of protection against dust and serves as a high level storage shelf.

Proprietary coathangers with security elements such as lockable chains that thread through the arm sleeves of garments can be incorporated with any type of clothes rail. These are mainly for expensive garments such as furs and winter coats in high turnover shops where the staff cannot afford adequate supervision.

Table I Space requirement for men's garments

Type of garment	Average spacing per article (mm)	No. of articles per metre of rail*
Casual shirts	25 to 30	36
Trousers	35	28
Raincoats, dressing gowns	50	20
Coats, jackets and suits	90	11
Winter coats	110	9

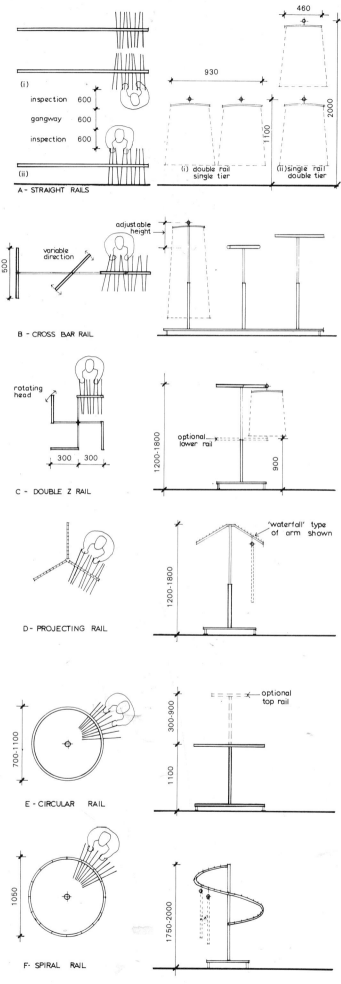

4.4 *Clothes rails*

Table II Space requirement for women's garments

Type of garment	Average spacing per article (mm)	No. of articles per metre of rail*
Skirts, light shirts, trousers	25 to 30	35
Night dresses	40	25
Day dresses, evening and bridal wear	50	20
Coats, jackets, suits	80	12
Winter coats	100	10
Fur coats	150	7

*An allowance of 150 mm should be given at the end of the rail for movement of hangers.

4.4 SHELVING SYSTEMS

Shelving systems provide a cheap and most adaptable way of displaying goods. They are ideal for the display of 'dry goods' (all goods that do not require specialised storage conditions eg merchandise in cartons, tins, bags, bottles, pots or unpacked). Since the goods to be displayed are so diverse in shape, size and weight the system must be versatile enough to suit all requirements.

Selecting a system
Considerations affecting the selection of equipment are:
(a) Assembly: each shelf must be independently adjustable without interference to the adjoining shelves; it should be possible to perform this work easily without the use of skilled labour or specialist equipment; it should also be easy to assemble or disassemble the system so as to permit changes in layout.
(b) Adaptability: the system must relate to other shopfitting elements such as cabinets, counters, partitions etc and be suitable for incorporation with them if necessary; it must also be backed by a range of accessories so as to give greater versatility for display.
(c) Cleanliness: the finishes must be easy to keep clean and must withstand rough treatment from cleaners which might make shelves look worn or unhygienic.
(d) Robustness: the units must adequately accept heavy unbalanced loads without becoming insecure.
Figure **4.5** illustrates dimensions for shelving units. The relationship between the height of a unit and the number of shelves it can accommodate varies with the size of merchandise on display. Table III provides a guide for general use.

Table III Shelving units: numbers of shelves for different heights

Height of unit (mm)	Wall unit with base shelf	Gondola unit with base shelf	Wall unit with cabinet base
900	3	3	0
1200	4	4	1
1500	5	Not suitable	2
1800	6	Not suitable	3
2100	6 + canopy	Not suitable	3 + canopy

Shelving systems are generally classified as light, medium or heavy depending on the loading requirements. They comprise uprights or standards, back panels, brackets, accessories and shelves (see Fig **4.6**).

Uprights
Uprights can be fixed to the wall, fixed between floor and ceiling or freestanding (see Fig **4.7**). They are usually made from aluminium alloy with anodised, chromed or enamelled finish. Open channel sections are fixed by screwing on timber grounds and serve wall units. Closed channel sections when used for partitioning are fixed on the floor and ceiling with adjusters and may be braced with metal rods and stays. When used as freestanding units they require supporting legs which may or may not have foot levellers. The main types of upright sections are as follows:

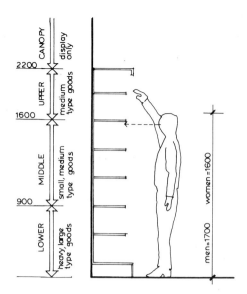

4.5 *Shelving unit dimensions*

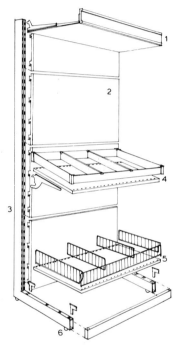

4.6 *Typical shelving unit assembly*
1 *bracket with soffit panel and grooved pelmet to take commodity label* **2** *back panel* **3** *upright* **4** *bracket with metal shelf and glass binning components* **5** *base shelf with wire binning components* **6** *leg supports with screw adjusters and front plinth cover*

Section type	No. of slotted grooves*	Application
'U' shaped (open channel)	1 or 2	For wall fixing with or without back panels; may be surface or flush fixed; lightweight sections are suitable for cabinet fittings
Square or rectangular (closed channel)	1, 2 or 4	For freestanding units or partitioning; brackets may be fixed on one or two sides of uprights
Circular or oval (closed channel)	2 or 4	As for square sections but in round form; suitable for fashion displays and finishes are usually to a higher standard, often chromed
Triangular hexagonal or octagonal	3 6 4	For freestanding display or single pole display; octagonal uprights also serve in the construction of cubicles or partitions

*The number of slotted grooves determines the number of brackets the uprights may take at the same level. Double slotted uprights are used for continuous shelving as they allow shelves on either side to be adjusted without interference to the others.

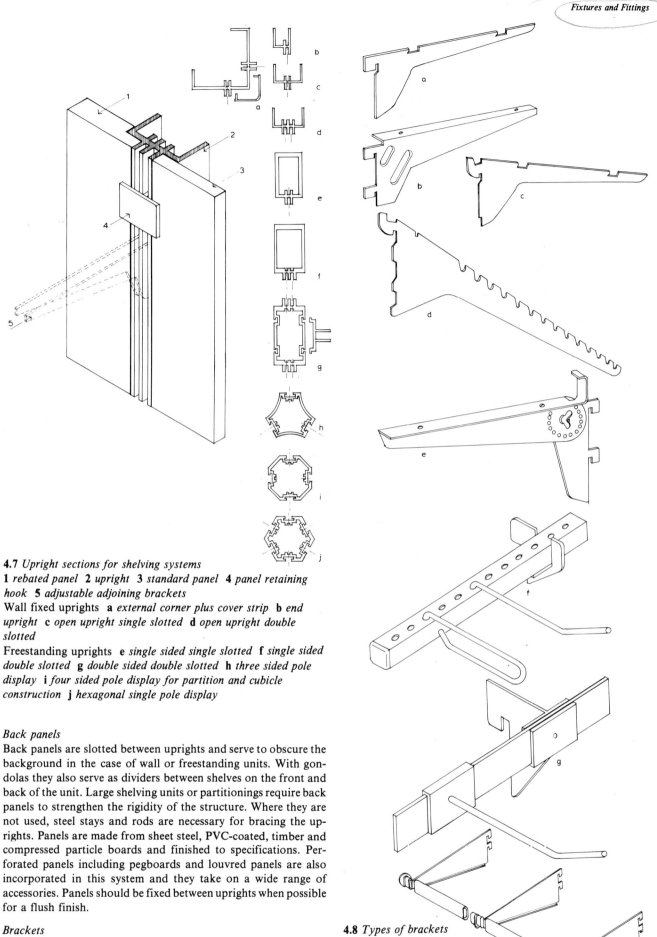

4.7 *Upright sections for shelving systems*
1 *rebated panel* **2** *upright* **3** *standard panel* **4** *panel retaining hook* **5** *adjustable adjoining brackets*
Wall fixed uprights **a** *external corner plus cover strip* **b** *end upright* **c** *open upright single slotted* **d** *open upright double slotted*
Freestanding uprights **e** *single sided single slotted* **f** *single sided double slotted* **g** *double sided double slotted* **h** *three sided pole display* **i** *four sided pole display for partition and cubicle construction* **j** *hexagonal single pole display*

Back panels

Back panels are slotted between uprights and serve to obscure the background in the case of wall or freestanding units. With gondolas they also serve as dividers between shelves on the front and back of the unit. Large shelving units or partitionings require back panels to strengthen the rigidity of the structure. Where they are not used, steel stays and rods are necessary for bracing the uprights. Panels are made from sheet steel, PVC-coated, timber and compressed particle boards and finished to specifications. Perforated panels including pegboards and louvred panels are also incorporated in this system and they take on a wide range of accessories. Panels should be fixed between uprights when possible for a flush finish.

Brackets

Brackets range from 75 to 600 mm in projection and some of the many forms available are shown in Fig **4.8**.
1 Straight: this is the simplest type which takes on most types of shelves and is used for light to medium loads.
2 Inclined: similar to straight brackets but sloping up or down; downward inclination of 6 to 15° will accommodate large displays;

4.8 *Types of brackets for shelving systems*
a *straight* **b** *flanged*
c *inclined* **d** *serrated* **e** *adjustable inclination* **f** *piccolo bar plus mounting and attachments* **g** *flat wall bar plus mounting and attachments* **h** *hanging rail plus mounting and attachments*

continued

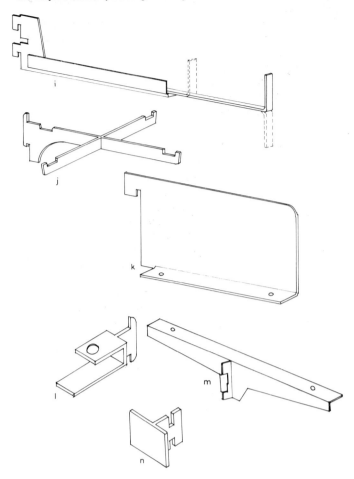

Types of bracket for shelving systems
i *adjustable bracket for pelmets* **j** *display bracket* **k** *bookshelf bracket* **l** *bracket for glass shelves* **m** *centre bracket*
n *panel retaining hook*

bookshelf brackets have an upward inclination of 15 to 25° to hold books securely so that they do not drop easily on browsing customers.

3 Serrated: long brackets with an inclination of 35 to 45° and a number of teeth for holding display accessories.

4 Flanged: similar to straight brackets but with a flange so that the shelves may be screwed; suitable for heavy loads.

5 Telescopic: amount of projection adjustable; fitted with front lipping for fixing to a canopy.

6 Cross-plan: a special type used with central pole stands for the display of small prepacked items.

7 Clip bracket: a very small projecting bracket for taking glass shelves.

8 Piccolo bar mounting: a special bracket which takes on the piccolo bar: this is a square section bar perforated with holes on to which a large number of attachments may be hooked.

Accessories
The following devices may be used to complement shelves to provide greater variety and flexibility:

Retaining rail: this is made from chromed steel wire and prevents goods from rolling off the front edge of the shelf; the normal height is 25 mm.

Binning risers: these are similar in construction to retaining rails but higher (standard heights 75, 130, 180 and 300 mm); used for the separation and display of loose goods they comprise front and side risers and internal partitioning; front risers may be straight or inclined.

Glass binning holders: where shelf binning is made from glass these holders are used for holding the glass; they are normally 75 mm high to hold 6 mm glass.

Racks: these are made of mild steel wire with a chromed or plastic coated finish; they are used for displaying a wide range of goods including magazines (where racks may be single, double or treble), shoes, wine and small packages; they may be designed either to rest on shelves or to fit directly to uprights by the use of locating brackets.

Wire holders: these are steel rods of varying profiles which hold a number of large objects including hats, shoes and sports equipment; they hook on to a Picolo bar or pegboards.

Wire hangers: similar to wire holders but either straight or looped; used for hanging up small pre-packed packages.

Sign-holders: these hold cards identifying goods and are fixed by clips or bolts; gondola sign holders are two sided.

Shelves
Shelves can be made of plywood or blockboard and covered with veneer, laminate or fabric, of glass (6 mm thick if not loadbearing, 10 mm thick and toughened if loadbearing), or of metal (plastic coated sheet steel or chrome plated steel wire). If they span a long distance they can be fitted with a shelf stiffener, a metal open square section member which can also serve as front lipping and as a label rail. They are normally fixed on a horizontal plane but deep shelves may be inclined upwards or downwards (see remarks on inclined brackets above).

4.5 PERFORATED PANELS

Perforated panels provide a cheap and versatile system for storing and displaying small items of merchandise. There are basically two types: pegboards and louvred panels.

Pegboards
Pegboards are often used in conjunction with shelving systems and frequently as a backing panel between the vertical uprights. This panel is made from 6 mm hardboard perforated with 63 mm circular holes in a grid of 254 mm centres. Finishes are available in a wide range of colours. A range of accessories are available for fitting on to the pegboard as desired: they include a range of hooks, rails, holders, clips and wire trays. The pegboard system is only suitable for light items because it cannot accommodate heavy loads.

Louvred panels
Louvred panels are made from cold rolled mild steel sheets with press moulded angular brackets. The stronger material permits heavier loads. A typical load for a well-fixed panel is 70 kg per 300 mm of vertical run of standard width panel. In gondola units the loading depends on the strength and construction of the panel supports. A typical panel comes in a standard width of 450 mm and in varying lengths of 450, 900 and 1800 mm. Panels normally have a stove enamelled finish and can be single sided for wall use or double sided for gondola use. This system is illustrated in Fig **4.9**. It can take a series of attachments including bins, single, double and closed loop hooks, shelf trays, rails and tool holders. Bins are designed to clip on to the panels or to stack when not in use. Usually they have a front recess for holding identification labels. They are also available in a range of colours for easy classification. Larger bins have internal dividers.

Table IV Typical bin characteristics

Load (kg)	Internal Capacity (ml)	Bin density*
2	426	16·0
5	917	10·7
9	2458	6·0
14	6550	3·2
18	13530	1·6

*Number of bins per 300 mm run of a standard 450 mm deep panel.

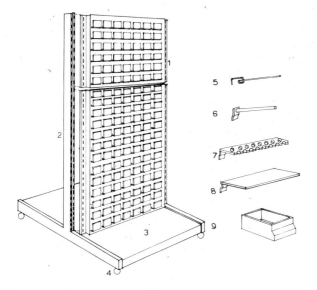

4.9 *Perforated panel system*
1 *back panel* **2** *freestanding upright* **3** *base plate* **4** *castor wheel*
5 *display rail* **6** *hanging rail* **7** *tool shelf* **8** *display shelf*
9 *container*

4.6 DUMP BASKETS

Dump baskets are used for 'binning' ie the bulk display of cheap small merchandise considered to be impulse goods or 'throw-away' lines; see Fig **4.10**. They may be freestanding single deck units (which are usually circular, but sometimes square, in plan), multi-deck units, or single units fitted against the wall or to the end of a gondola (which may be square, semi-circular or circular in plan); circular types include carousel units which revolve round a central post. They are mostly made from welded or woven wire mesh in aluminium or steel, chromium plated, plastic coated or anodised. All-plastic models are used for the display of lightweight goods: these may be clear or opaque; one popular model is spherical in shape with an opening to take in and remove the goods. Sizes vary widely according to manufacturer and model but most models are between 600 and 900 mm in diameter. Single deck units are about 700 mm high, and multi deck units up to 1800 mm high.

4.7 DISPLAY MODELS

Display models may depict the whole or just part of the figure of a man, woman or child. Full sized models are articulated to allow for posing and made up in sections which disassemble to allow for dressing. Because of their relative instability, they require a base to stand on. Most types are manufactured with a housing under one heel which connects to a spigot on the base plate: this is available in two sizes. Small bases measure approximately 75 × 50 mm and can be concealed by the feet: they require screwing into the window bed. Large bases measure approximately 450 mm square and can be decorated in the same finish as the window bed so as to become inconspicuous. Models are usually about 1650 mm high and a minimum floor space of about 950 × 700 mm should be allowed for displaying each one. They are supplied with a range of accessories such as wigs, heads, tools etc to allow for variation in display. Their display value is enhanced when a number of models are grouped to form balanced compositions and when they are highlighted by oblique spotlighting. Part models have recently become unpopular. Where still in use they generally consist of the following parts: head and shoulders (for the display of wigs, hats, furs and jackets), bust (for shirts, sweaters, scarves and underwear), hips (for underwear), hand and arm (for gloves and jewellery) or leg and foot (for stockings and shoes).

4.8 STANDS

Stands are extensively used in shops for the display of goods. Types for mass display of items such as posters, records, cassettes etc have already been mentioned in chapter 2 above. Two groups should be specially noted here:
Manufacturers' stands: many manufacturers of small goods provide their own stands and supply them to retailers at no extra cost; the kinds of goods displayed on these include such items as cosmetics, sunglasses, toiletries, tools, sweets, and optical or electrical goods; this sort of stand is mostly used in showrooms. .
Specially commissioned stands: no rules can be laid down for designing or building these because each commission has to be considered individually.

4.9 TURNTABLES

Movement in a window display attracts attention to it: the most economical way of producing this effect is to revolve goods on a turntable. In this way the effectiveness of a given window frontage can be increased by a process of simple mathematics: for example a turntable 2500 mm in diameter fitted in a window 2500 mm wide gives a display perimeter of over 7500 mm; obviously the larger the turntable the more goods it can show. Other advantages in the field of display are that the back of goods can be shown as well as the front and that goods can be seen simultaneously inside a shop as well as outside. Turntables are also useful for the purpose of bringing in large objects such as motor cars and revolving them within a limited area. Different types are shown in Fig **4.11**. In choosing a turntable the main features to look for are its load capacity and diameter. Table IV below gives typical dimensions and characteristics. Special fittings which should be noted are:
Hesitation control: this provides the facility for automatic stopping any number of times per revolution; after a variable pause of up to 60 seconds the turntable will re-start automatically.
Static centre: this gives the effect of contra-rotation by having a static disc surmounted by a static boss fitted to the centre of the

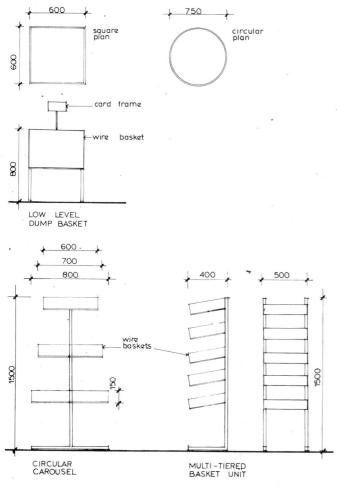

4.10 *Three types of wire dump baskets*

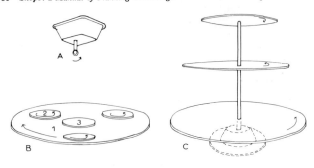

4.11 *Types of turntable*
A *ceiling unit for ceiling mounting and taking suspended loads*
B *turntable base (***1** *platform* **2** *secondary discs* **3** *static centre which may have counter rotation)* **C** *multi-tiered turntable*
D *framework turntable*

turntable (contra-rotation can also be provided by fitting a smaller turntable rotating in the opposite direction).
Slip ring: this provides a power take-off (normally between 2 and 5 amps) on the rotating platform for decorative lighting.
Turntables may be ceiling mounted or floor mounted. Ceiling mounted models take suspended loads off a rigid shaft pole. They are used either for direct display of merchandise or for supporting decorative window fixtures such as kites, fans, globes etc while the window bed is used for the main display. Floor mounted units can be in any of the following forms:
(a) Flush base: the turntable platform is flush with the floor and finished with the same decoration; the drive unit is recessed and out of view.
(b) Raised base: the platform is higher than the floor; the drive unit is surface fixed on the floor and can be removed when not required; usually applicable to the smaller turntables.
(c) Tiered platform: three or four platforms are placed concentrically on one drive unit, one above the other; this system can also be installed on ceiling models.
(d) Framed platform: instead of being in the usual circular form the platform consists of a metal frame on which a particular type of merchandise can be displayed (Fig **4.11** (*D*) shows a frame for supporting a motor car).
(e) Ceiling mounted unit: used for taking suspended displays.

Table IV Typical dimensions and characteristics of display turntables

Type	Diameter (mm)	Height (mm)	Load capacity (kg)	Speed (rpm)	Weight of unit (kg)
Ceiling units	125	100	20	2	2·5
	175	120	100	2	3·4
	290	140	130	2	4·2
Floor units	165	50	7	4	0·45
	200	75	20	2	1·35
	900–1500	165	230	1·5	16·32
	1800–3000	200–300	820	1	127–364

4.10 SECURITY SAFES

Types
There are three basic types of safes:
(a) Wall safes: these provide limited protection for cash and small valuables and can be easily concealed, but are ideally suitable for domestic use or for shops with low to medium risks.
(b) Underfloor safes: like the above type this will deter the casual burglar but not the professional; it is suitable for low to medium risk shops.
(c) Freestanding safes: because of their bulk these are not easy to conceal; they are built to withstand severe forms of attack; the smaller types may be anchored to structural points of the building to prevent carting away; they are suitable for medium to high risk shops.
If required, security can be increased by using any of the intruder detection devices discussed in chapter 7 below.

Construction
Doors: these are rectangular in shape and constructed from an outer layer of steel plate, an internal lining material and an inner steel plate welded to the outer plate; their overall thickness is of the order of 100 to 200 mm; the lining material possesses qualities of toughness which will resist all forms of oxygen cutting apparatus as well as drills and other forcing tools.
Body: built in similar materials to the door but usually thinner.
Bolts: the front door is fitted with heavy sliding bolts on all four sides which when extended lock into receptors on the safe body; the number of bolts provided varies with manufacturer, model and safe size, normally between one and two are provided at the top and bottom edges, and three to five at the sides; the greater the number of bolts, the better the resistance provided against explosive attacks.
Locks: these may be operated by a key, by a combination or by a time device. In key-operated types eight-mortice locks are normally used. Combination locks can be fitted instead of or in addition to key-operated ones; they are controlled by a code number which has the advantage that (unlike keys) it cannot be copied: the code can also be changed easily so that no security problems are caused by changes of staff. Time locks operate independently of any other kinds used in addition to them; they can be pre-set to go off guard only at selected times and so prevent the safe from being opened until the correct time has been reached even if the other locks have been forced or unlocked.
Fittings: large safes are usually supplied with a number of removable drawers constructed of steel plates and secured with additional keylocks; shelves made of sheet steel flanged and secured to the supports by clips may also be fitted: these may be fixed or adjustable.
Finishes: standard safes are usually finished in light or dark grey but other colours can be specified; control mounting panels, handles, bolt throwing handwheels, escutcheons and combination lock dials are stainless steel or chrome plated.
Dimensions: there are no standard dimensions for safes and each manufacturer produces his own models and sizes. Some guidance can however be gathered from the following table:

Siting
The following points should be taken into consideration when deciding where to put a safe:
1 The floor should be strong enough to take the imposed load: existing floors may therefore have to be strengthened.
2 Access routes should be investigated before the safe is delivered: check that doorways have sufficient clearance and survey any other obstacles which have to be negotiated.
3 Consideration should be given to the fact that goods may have to be moved from the sales floor or display window to the safe for night storage.
4 The safe should be easily accessible to the manager or other persons authorised to open it.
5 The safe should be as inaccessible as possible to burglars so as to give them the longest travelling route: this is an apparent contradiction of considerations 3 and 4: a balanced solution has to be established.

Table V Freestanding safes: typical sizes, weight and capacity

Internal cubic capacity (m³)	External dimensions (mm)			Internal dimensions (mm)			Gross weight (kg)
	Height	Width	Depth	Height	Width	Depth	
0·21	1092	750	775	863	508	482	1278
0·29	1397	750	775	1168	508	482	1647
0·34	1626	750	775	1397	508	482	1907
0·50	1855	953	724	1625	711	432	2489
0·62	1855	953	826	1625	711	533	2616

6 If possible the safe should be kept out of view but at the same time in an easily surveyable position (eg within a cupboard in the manager's or security officer's office).

4.11 REFRIGERATED CABINETS

Types of cabinet
Refrigerated cabinets may be single deck (giving only one level of display) or multi-deck (fitted with a number of internal display shelves). They may, in either case, also be open or closed. Open cabinets are preferred by supermarkets because they allow the customer direct and easy access. Closed cabinets suit circumstances where the need for access is only occasional (eg in a frozen food store) or where goods are on display to customers but only accessible to staff (eg at a delicatessen counter); they may be designed either for access at the rear but with a glass panel in front, for access at the front through a glass or opaque door, or for access from the top through a glass or opaque lid. Different types of cabinet are shown in Fig **4.12**.

Cooling systems
Systems available for keeping temperatures down are either
(a) conduction: products are cooled by being laid down on a cold surface which removes heat by conduction; this principle is also used on built-in slabs such as the fishmonger's slab and the butcher's window display slab; or

(b) convection: products are cooled by being enveloped in a moving layer of cold air circulated by convection; this may be achieved naturally by gravity or mechanically with fans; pre-packed foods may be stored either in gravity cooled systems or in fan assisted systems; unwrapped foods should however only be stored in gravity cooled systems.

Refrigeration temperatures
Most cabinets are designed to operate on a small variable range of temperatures to suit varying environmental conditions. They can however broadly be distinguished by the type of goods they are meant to store. This aspect has already been dealt with above under Supermarkets (section 2.1, tables II and III).

Finishes
External finishes may be stove enamelled mild steel, stainless steel, plastic or metal laminates. Internal finishes may be enamelled galvanised mild steel or glass fibre reinforced plastic.

Dimensions
The dimensions for refrigerated cabinets vary a great deal. Overall dimensions are generally of the following order: length 1800, 2400, 2700, or 3600 mm, depth 800 to 1100 mm, height 900 to 1800 mm. The overall dimensions of refrigerated cabinets are however no indication of their storage capacity. This is related to the efficiency ratio of shelf area over floor area; and to the capacity of the 'refrigerated zone' (ie the volume enclosed by a boundary within which all stored products are maintained at the specified temperature). It may be seen from table VI below that the most efficient type of cabinet is the wall unit with multi-decks and that the least efficient is the gondola with a single deck.

Table VI Comparative net storage volumes for refrigerated cabinets

Cabinet type	Cabinet length (mm)	Net storage volume (m³)	Shelf area (m²)	Occupied floor area (m²)	Efficiency ratio % shelf area to floor area
Wall unit (single deck)	1800	0·42	1·18	1·45	81·3
	2700	0·60	1·79	2·17	82·5
Wall unit (multi-deck)	1800	0·62	2·37	1·79	132·4
	2700	0·93	3·56	2·70	131·9
Gondola (single deck)	1800	0·40	1·20	1·86	64·5
	2700	0·60	1·79	2·80	63·9

Installation
Refrigerated cabinets incorporate compressors, motor assembly condensing units, evaporators, valves and circulation pipes. A considerable amount of heat is produced which has to be got rid of. Each cabinet must be planned with electricity outlets that are accurately located and able to sustain sufficient power load. An alternative solution is for the refrigerant to be piped to the display cabinet from a remote plant room. This ensures that operation is silent. It also stops any heat (which might otherwise be considerable) being produced next to the display cabinets. The refrigerant

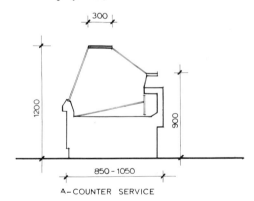

A—COUNTER SERVICE

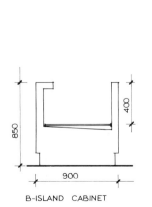

B—ISLAND CABINET

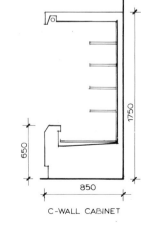

C—WALL CABINET

4.12 *Refrigerated cabinets*

must however be taken along floor ducts under high or low pressure and the outlet points must be accurately located for connection to the cabinets. Condensing units in the plant room may be air cooled or water cooled. Air cooled systems are dependable and efficient provided that the plant room is properly planned and ventilated. With water cooled units ventilation is less important, but still necessary. Cold water is provided for cooling purposes by circulating heated water through a cooling tower usually sited externally and on a roof. This involves some maintenance costs both for the tower and for the feed pipes. Manufacturers should be consulted on the planning of installations and on points of detail when plans are being carried out.

Siting

The following points are relevant to the siting of refrigerated cabinets:

1 To ensure economy and constant temperature cabinets should not be exposed to direct sunlight, excessive draughts or radiant heating from lighting equipment or other sources.

2 Open cabinets should be provided with covers which can be fitted after closing hours (they require storage space during opening hours and they can be quite bulky).

3 In small installations incompatible foods such as fish and fruit may be stored in the same cabinet provided that they are properly packed in vapour-proof material.

5
THE SHOPFRONT

5.1 FACTORS WHICH INFLUENCE DESIGN

The shopfront is the exposed transparent surface of the shop which attracts passers by. To produce a good shopfront is therefore one of the most important tasks of the designer, who has to make sure that it catches the eye, satisfactorily identifies the shop, displays the merchandise on sale to best advantage and entices potential customers inside. The factors which influence shopfront design may be divided into general considerations and particular considerations.

General considerations

The site

1 Exclusive, ordinary or poor neighbourhood: this influences materials, standard of finishes and design considerations (eg traditional period shopfronts in hardwood framing or large glazed areas in aluminium framing); the likely incidence of vandalism and litter determines the need for roller grilles or collapsible shutters.

2 Prominent or sheltered location: is the shopfront to be viewed from a distance or from close up? this may determine sizes for lettering, framing sections and glazing panels.

Nature of business

1 Convenience or comparison goods: comparison goods (unlike convenience goods) demand to be shown in competitive surroundings: the more luxurious the goods the more important the shopfront becomes.

2 Size of goods: small goods, like jewellery, are viewed very closely and only require small glazed areas so as to focus attention and high sills are usually provided; large goods (in contrast) are viewed from a distance and are best shown in fronts with large glazed areas; sills are low or non-existant.

The environment

Exposure: the shopfront acts as a shelter from the elements.

(a) Solar radiation: if a window is under severe exposure consider the use of canopies, blinds or solar control glass.

(b) Wind: deep lobbies protect entrances against prevailing winds.

(d) Near seaside: premises require finishes which weather well and are resistant to salt air corrosion.

(c) Traffic: lobbies protect the interior against noise, dust and smells from vehicular traffic.

Shop character

1 Neighbourhood: in high class shopping areas new shops should keep in line with the standards and designs set (eg traditional period, modern or stylishly individual); in middle and middle to low areas there is the option of producing complementary or contrasting designs.

2 Type of goods: the design should invariably relate to the goods being sold (eg bright and cheerful for toy shops, conservative and subdued for gentlemen's outfitters).

continued

5.2 TYPES OF SHOPFRONT

There are four basic types of shopfront from which many combinations are possible (see Fig **5.7**):

Type of shopfront	Type of goods	Objectives
1 Flat front		
Shopfront glazing is projected as far forward as possible and built in a straight line; the entrance door may be aligned or set back from this line	Mostly 'convenience' goods eg foodshops, chemists, florists, newsagents	Allows for the maximum use of internal floor space; goods are displayed near the pedestrian; cheap form of construction, maximising internal floor space
2 Arcaded front		
A lobby is formed on the shopfront providing a transient space between pavement and shop; types may be plain, splayed, staggered, modelled; wide arcades may include island showcases	Mostly 'comparison' goods eg clothing and footwear, household goods, photographic and electrical goods	Allows for a better inspection of goods by sheltering customers from pedestrian traffic; more window display space is possible; allows browsers to inspect merchandise without committing themselves to enter the shop and provides the opportunity for inspection at leisure after closing hours; provides shelter from inclement weather and is not subject to glare problems; loss of internal floor space is compensated for by increased display value including possible use of island showcases
3 Enclosed front		
Shopfront is mostly solid with small display windows	Mostly luxury goods eg jewellery, leather-goods, tailored fashions, gifts	Only suitable for exclusive shops in high class shopping areas; relies more on service provided and exclusiveness of merchandise than on display; minimal display serves to focus maximum attention on what is displayed
4 Open front		
Part or whole of the shopfront glazing opens to the pavement	Mostly large goods, or shops with a large flow of customers eg motor car showrooms, greengrocers, supermarkets	Allows uninterrupted large flow of customers; useful for the movement of large merchandise such as motor cars; flexibility in controlling size of entrance opening according to need and weather conditions; the whole interior becomes the display as traditional window displays are not possible

5.1 *Mary Farrin, boutique, London, designed by Wilkinson, Calvert and Gough. Gold grp lettering and decorative frame on tinted glass*

5.2 *Above. Schulin, jewellers, Vienna, designed by Hans Hollein. The facade in the form of a burnt flame is constructed from layers of marble: this interlayer relationship repeats on the door frame*

5.3 *Retti, candle shop, Vienna, designed by Hans Hollein. Renowned prizewinning shopfront in polished aluminium sheeting bent round the corners to produce a wrapped round effect. The facade gives no indication of the shop's name or trade (see also **2.115** above)*

5.4 *Same. The shop's name can in fact only be seen from a sideways angle or on entering. The illustration shows the detail for the minute display window*

5.5 *Jewellers in Barcelona. This 'cracked' facade is clad with a highly polished granite facing. The glazed window and door are well set back at the end of an inclined grooved tunnel entry in grey rubber*

5.6 *Contact Lenses, London, designed by Trevor Banchero Associates with Peter Beaven. This narrow facade is the front for a much larger interior consisting of reception area, shop floor, consulting rooms and technical workrooms. The canopy is bronze acrylic on metal frame*

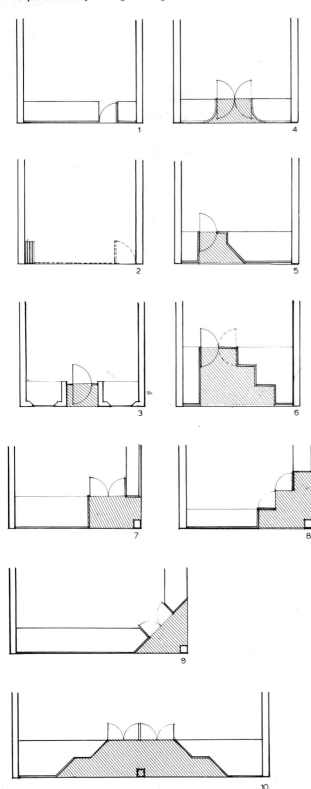

5.7 *Types of shopfront*
1 flat glazed *suitable for small shops in local shopping areas.*
Note that in the position drawn the door cannot open outwards
over the pavement **2** open *suitable for displaying the interior of*
the shop where windows are not possible; also suitable for moving
in bulky goods and for allowing a large flow of customers
3 enclosed *only suitable for high class shops in exclusive areas;*
minimal windows attract greater attention to the goods displayed
4, 5, 6 recessed *suitable for most shops in shopping centre*
developments and high streets. The arcades shelter customers
from pedestrian traffic and permit inspection of goods from all
angles. Types shown here are curved **(4)**, splayed **(5)** *and*
modelled **(6)** **7, 8, 9** corner *sites with entrance at corner*
10 double unit *with entrance at centre*

Particular considerations

Access
Select the best locations for the main customers' entrance and for
staff and goods entrances; determine the number or exits required
to meet expected pedestrian traffic in normal and emergency
situations.

Glazed areas
Glazed areas may be in large panes of glass with minimal exposed
framing down to small areas of glass with a high degree of sub-
divisioning by framing; a correct balance is achieved by assessing
the type of goods to be displayed, neighbouring shops and design
criteria.

Fascia
Fascias may be large or small, internal or external, plain or signwritten; investigate adjoining fascias and determine the need if any
for matching them in material, colour, size and height.

Lettering
The type of lettering used should suit the sort of goods sold and the
overall design for the shop: it may be conventional or out of the
ordinary, flat or solid, illuminated or not illuminated; where
possible include associated logos and corporate graphics; the size
of lettering should be determined by the distance of the viewpoint
(ie small letters are adequate when they need only be read from
close-by).

Illumination
Intensity for the illumination of windows and signs is determined
by the neighbourhood (eg a major shopping centre is more brightly
lit than a semi-residential area; lighting to windows may be
general for 'convenience' goods or localised for 'comparison'
goods; note that the colour of lighting sources may affect the
apparent colour of displays.

Colour
Select a predominant colour which suits the goods to be sold eg
bright for toys and 'wholesome' (brown or beige) for health food
shops.

Finishes
The quality of finishes should be appropriate for the neighbourhood and the cost of goods to be sold; in certain developments
there may be lease covenants specifying what materials may or may
not be used.

5.3 ELEMENTS OF THE SHOPFRONT
Figures **5.8** and **5.9** illustrate the basic elements of traditional and
all glass shopfronts.

Fascia
The fascia serves to mask the structural members supporting
structures above the shop or the framing to the shopfront. Although normally a background to the main sign, fascias can be
treated as an advertising trade mark and their design should be
carefully considered in relation to adjoining properties, shop signs,
blind box, canopy and shopfront.

Canopy
Canopies are permanent fixtures and are normally provided by the
developer as an integral part of the building to visually distinguish
shops on the ground floor from premises on the upper floors. If
new canopies are to be provided, they must have adequate means
of rainwater drainage and should conform to statutory requirements concerning minimum height from pavement and maximum
projection.

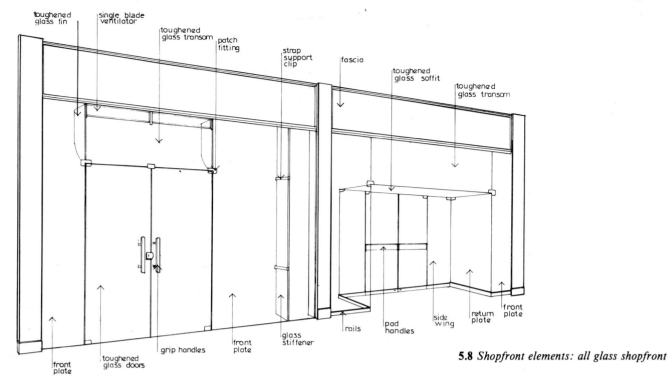

5.8 *Shopfront elements: all glass shopfront*

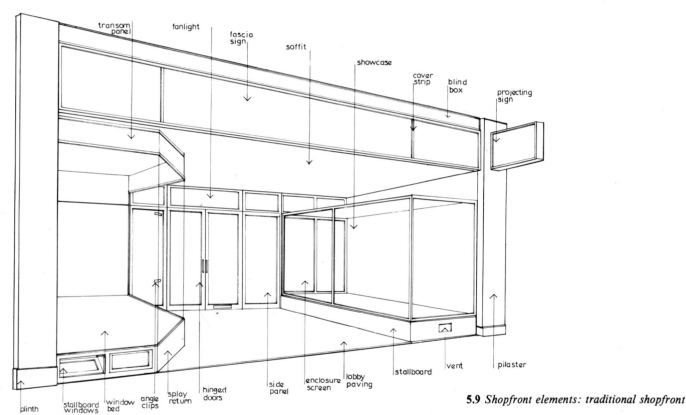

5.9 *Shopfront elements: traditional shopfront*

Blinds

Blinds may be fitted above or below the fascia. Dutch blinds, collapsible arms or telescopic arms may for example be provided. When not in use the blind retracts into a blind box which may be exposed or set into the fascia: however the blind lath always remains exposed. Like canopies, blinds have to conform to statutory requirements.

Signs

A sign is essential for the identification of the shop. It may be illuminated or non-illuminated, flat or built-up. Signs may be placed on the blinds, the fascia, pilaster, the window surface, the stallboard, the shopfront paving or internally. Projecting signs at right angles to the fascia or pilaster are easier to view from a distance but tend to cover each other when used by various adjoining premises; they have to conform to statutory regulations concerning minimum height from pavement and maximum projection. Illuminated signs also have to conform to such regulations in the light of their possible effect on traffic safety and general amenity: the main considerations here are the overall size of a sign, its colour, its brightness and whether it is flashing or animated.

Pilasters

A client's legal position relating to pilasters may be one of the matters under which his status under any leasehold agreement has to be clarified (eg either the tenant or the landlord may be responsible for the whole frontage or each may be responsible for half of it). Responsibilities for pilasters may affect the way they are used (eg to support projecting signs, alarm bells or fire switches), their finish in relation to the rest of the shopfront or how they should be maintained.

Display windows

The design of display windows plays an important role in the design of a shopfront because its main purpose is to attract and bring in the casual shopper. Window sizes are largely determined by the type and size of goods on display. Generally they are between 1·5 and 2·5 m in depth, glazed to the floor or with a raised window bed and stallboard. The internal lining on walls and bed may be permanently integrated with the shopfront design (eg stainless steel throughout), permanent but as an independent element (eg soft linings to take pinning displays), or in removable sections for service access and changes of display (eg housing built-in turntables or intermediate display levels). Deeply recessed lobbies may use island showcases for additional display. For security purposes it may be necessary to use night gates to enclose the lobby.

Stallboards

Stallboards may be desirable for design purposes (as with high display windows) or for functional purposes (to take smoke outlets, basement or window ventilators and changes in pavement level).

Entrances

The number of entrances to be provided should be related to the number of frontages, the size of the sales floor area and the number of persons in the premises at peak trading times. Door exit widths should not be less than 1070 mm for the first 200 people in the store plus 150 mm for each additional 30 people. To estimate the number of persons in the store at peak times allow 1 person for every 1·9 m² of the sales floor. In Great Britain the Building Regulations are very strict regarding means of escape in case of fire: relevant provisions are outlined in Appendix 2. Entrances should be sited in relation to the main pedestrian traffic flow, adjoining shops and access to car parking or public transport facilities. If the plan is long and narrow with the ratio of greatest length over shortest width exceeding 4:1 there should be a secondary exit at the opposite end to the main front entrance.

Shopfront paving

The client's legal position regarding areas in front of the shopfront should be ascertained with regard to usage (pavement lights, escape hatches, goods delivery and so on), standards of finish and maintenance. Pavings to recessed lobbies should be of reasonable standard and should relate to the internal finishes. Some considerations affecting the choice of finishes are cost, colour, texture, resistance to impact, corrosion and wear, slipperiness and ease of maintenance. Pavings must be laid to fall away from the entrance door and step-ups between pavement and lobby paving should be avoided. The inclusion of signs on shopfront pavings may be worth considering.

Mats and mat wells

Mats can be made from rubber, sisal, plastic or metal and made solid or with open mesh. Usually they are set into a mat well and are removable for cleaning or replacement. The minimum width should be equivalent to the width of the entrance opening and the depth should not be less than 900 mm. Striped mats made from fibre-reinforced rubber strips separated by extruded aluminium strips should be laid with the strips at right angles to the direction of pedestrian flow so as to provide the maximum scraping edges.

Multi-storey shopfronts

Multi-storey shops or shops which have the use of an upper storey or basement may wish to open up a floor so that customers can view the extended sales area. In such cases shopfronts can take the form of any of the types described previously but they should also make use of the extended height (see Fig 5.10). It should be noted however that in Great Britain the Building Regulations require that the total internal interconnected spaces shall not exceed certain limits (a maximum of 2,000 m² in area or 7,000 m³ in volume).

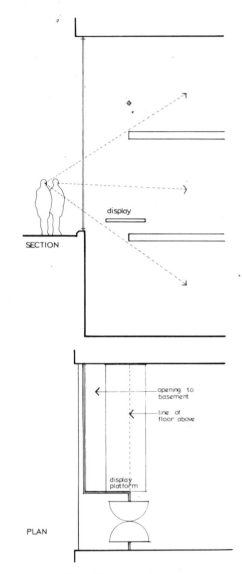

5.10 *Tall shopfront for multi-storey shop*

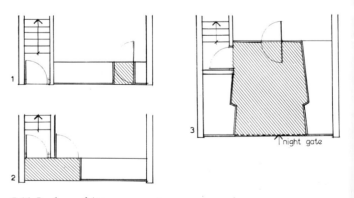

5.11 *Lock-up shops*
1, 2 *these are two commonly used methods* **3** *where deep lobbies are formed local authorities may require gates which are closed at night. This is unsuitable where there is domestic accommodation above the shop unless there is some alternative means of access*

Table I Typical window sizes for various types of shops

Viewpoint	Type of shop	Window depth (mm) A	Window height (mm) B	Sill height (mm) C	Length
Very close	Jewellery, spectacles, stamps, pictures, books, wines	450 to 950	up to 850	750 to 900	Varies; small windows are accepted in exclusive shops
Close	Toys, footwear, electrical and optical goods, records, gifts	750 to 1500	up to 2100	450 to 750	Varies according to frontage dimensions
Medium	Clothing, china and glass, sports equipment, household appliances	1000 to 2500	up to 2400	300 to 450	Varies according to frontage dimensions
Distant	Furniture, floor coverings, cycles, motor vehicles	2000 to 3200	As ceiling height	0 to 100	Wide frontages may be subdivided

Lock-up shops

Lock-up shops with separate accommodation above them require separate means of access to the upper floors. Where the accommodation on upper floors is in office use (ie daytime hours) a shared night gate may be accommodated; but if this accommodation is in residential use (ie day and night) night gates may only be erected to protect the shop lobby (see Fig. **5.11**).

5.4 SHOPFRONT DIMENSIONS

This section should be read in conjunction with the dimensions given in section 3.1 above.

Window depth

Dimensions for display windows are generally determined by:
(a) Type and size of goods on display: large articles like furniture require a minimum depth of about 3·0 m which includes provision for handling space; small articles requiring close inspection need only about 0·45 m; general display windows are usually 1·5 to 2·5 m in depth.
(b) Access: this must be simple and quick if the goods on display are required for sale; window beds may have a window back, enclosed or glazed, or be backless; window backs are not popular in small shops because they obscure the interior and are only used for security (as in jewellers) or for hygienic control (as in some types of foodshop); they also require adequately located access doors and if the merchandise on display is heavy or bulky adequate space must be allowed for manoeuvering.

Sill height

The sill height or base level on which goods are placed on display is determined by:
(a) Type and size of goods on display: articles requiring close inspection by virtue of their small size, fine detail, or concentration of display (such as jewellery or stamps) require high window beds up to 900 mm high; large items such as furniture do not require raised beds at all and consequently shopfronts may be glazed down to the ground.
(b) Stall risers: stallboards housing smoke outlets to basements or ventilation facilities needed to stop condensation on shopfront windows will affect sill heights.
(c) Equipment: some equipment which has to be placed out of sight may be recessed under the window bed (eg motor drives for turntables).
(d) Intermediate display levels: these may be required as built-in fixtures or to be removable.

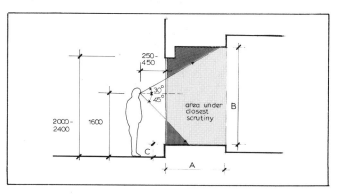

5.12 *Window dimensions (letters refer to table I)*

Soffit height

Window soffit heights are determined by:
(a) the height of items to be displayed.
(b) the provisions which have to be made in soffits or pelmets for window lighting.
(c) the scale on which the shopfront is designed.

Recessed lobby

Recessed lobbies may be designed to provide a simple and direct entrance to a shop or planned in a more complex way so as to create a staggered effect presenting the maximum number of displays to customers before they enter the shop floor. Their width and depth depend entirely on the nature of the particular design proposed, for example on the way in which a client wants his merchandise to be displayed and on the desirability of sheltering potential customers from the general flow of pedestrian traffic along the pavement outside. As stated in section 3.6 above the minimum width of openings which provide means of escape from large shops in the case of fire is subject to statutory control in Great Britain (see also Appendix 2).

Typical window sizes

Table I should be read in conjunction with Fig **5.12**.

5.5 SHOPFRONT GLAZING

Types of glass

Glazing is the major component of any shopfront. Different types of glass are designed to suit a range of varying needs. These may be classified as follows:

Type of glass	Manufacture	Characteristics	Application
Float plate glass	Manufactured with flat parallel surfaces which produce very little distortion	May be clear or coloured green grey and bronze; coloured glass is used for decorative effects and does not have heat absorbing or reflecting qualities	Suitable for all shopfronts, showcases, counter tops and load bearing shelves; cheapest type of glass for the above uses
Toughened glass	Subjected to heating and cooling treatment which greatly increases its strength	Will withstand loads four to five times greater than untreated glass; once treated it cannot be worked on ie all notching, cutting, drilling and surface work must be carried out before the toughening process	Suitable for all-glass shopfronts, entrance doors, display cases, partitioning and all situations where use of conventional glass might be considered hazardous

continued

Type of glass	Manufacture	Characteristics	Application
Laminated safety glass	Consists of two or more layers of glass bonded by interlayers of plastic film	The elasticity and adhesive qualities of the plastic give the glass strength and prevent a shattered plate from collapsing	Used as anti-bandit glass in shopfronts and security screens
Solar control glass	Float plate glass types reduce heat gain by absorption and re-radiation; laminated glass types reduce solar gain by reflection	Various colours are available which include green, grey, bronze, blue green, and gold	Only suitable for service shops such as hairdressers or travel agents where a clear view of the interior is not required; cannot be used for shops which display goods in the window, as the tinting causes colour distortion
Opaque coloured glass	There are two types: one has the colour integral with the thickness of the glass, the other has the colour ceramic-fired into one surface; the latter is normally supplied as a toughened glass	This is a finishing material with all the best qualities of glass: weathers, easily cleaned, resistant to dirt and chemical attack; almost any colour can be specified	Suitable for fascias, pilaster and stallboard cladding

Float plate glass

Float plate glass is made by running a continuous ribbon of molten glass over the surface of liquid metal (tin) at controlled temperatures. This produces glass which is remarkably flat with parallel surfaces and very little distortion. For normal shopfronts glass 6 mm thick is adequate but large shopfronts require 10 or 12 mm.

Table II   Clear plate glass: sizes and applications

Nominal substance (mm)	Approx. weight (kg/m²)	Normal maximum sizes of manufacture (mm)	Application
4	9·7	2760 × 1220	Small areas only
5	12·2	3180 × 2100	
6	15·9	4600 × 3180	Normal shopfronts, showcases and lightweight display shelves
10	24·4	6000 × 3300	Large shopfronts, counter tops and loadbearing shelves
12	31·8	6000 × 3300	Extra large all glass shopfronts and in exposed conditions
15	36·6	3050 × 3000	Glazing where strength and high quality are required; application for decorative purposes
19	48·8	3000 × 2900	
25	64·7	3000 × 2900	
29	73·5	2280 × 1820	
38	95·2	2280 × 1820	

It should be noted that normal manufactured sizes cannot be automatically considered as suitable sizes for glazing: safe glazing sizes must take into consideration construction details, wind loads and vibration from vehicular traffic.

Table III   Recommended maximum sizes for use of 6 mm glass in shopfronts

Construction method	Sheltered position (mm)	Exposed position (mm)
Clean cut plates glazed into frames on all four sides	1500 to 1800 × 4500 1900 to 2100 × 4350 2200 to 2700 × 4200	1500 to 1800 × 4050 1900 to 2100 × 3550 2200 to 2500 × 3050 2600 × 2700 × 2900
Clean cut plates on three edges, top edge fixed to metal brackets and mitred plates fixed in pin bars without holes	1500 to 1800 × 3650 1900 to 2100 × 3500 2200 to 2550 × 3050	1500 to 1800 × 4050 1900 to 2100 × 2750 2200 to 2550 × 2650
Mitred and polished edge plates with plates drilled and clipped at angles or pin bars used with holes for clips	1500 to 1800 × 3550 1900 to 2100 × 3300 2200 to 2350 × 3050	1500 to 1800 × 3050 1900 to 2100 × 2800 2200 to 2550 × 2650
Cement glazed plates and all plates fixed sloping inwards about 8 to 9°	6 mm substance is not suitable for this unless in small sizes not exceeding 2·5 m² or 1500 mm in length	

It should be noted that glass becomes very expensive if a window is over 10 m² in area, over 4000 mm long or over 2400 mm in both length and width. This factor should be watched by designers because it may make a particular design uneconomical.

Plate glass may be coloured green, grey or bronze during manufacture. Coloured plate glass does not however have the same properties of heat absorption or reflection as solar control glass and is therefore used mainly for decoration. It should be noted that it is only suitable for service shops such as hairdressers or travel agents and that it cannot be used for display windows because the tint causes colour distortion in goods exposed to it.

Toughened glass

Toughened glass is an annealed glass which has been subjected to a heating and cooling treatment that greatly increases its strength. In general a toughened glass will withstand a load four to five times greater than a similar untreated glass and will therefore tolerate higher degrees of deflection or twisting. Toughened glass cannot be worked on. All drilling, notching, cutting and surface work must be specified and carried out before the toughening process. If broken, it will fracture into granular pieces so as to minimise damage. Normally the ratio of length to width should not exceed 1:7. Dimensions in excess of this ratio are not recommended and it may be essential to ask the manufacturer for his advice. Exact sizes and requirements must be quoted on ordering. Toughened glass is used where safety or protection are the main considerations, for example for shopfronts, entrance doors, display cases, loadbearing shelves, partitions or balustrades and in any other cases where conventional glass might be considered hazardous.

Table IV   Toughened glass types and sizes

Type	Nominal substance (mm)	Maximum size (mm)
Clear glass	5	1520 × 915
	6	2600 × 1500
	10	3100 × 2500
	12	3100 × 2500
	15	3100 × 2500 (max. 6·7 m²)
	19	3100 × 2500 (max. 5·6 m²)
Spectrafloat bronze	6	2600 × 1350
	10	2700 × 2000
	12	2700 × 2000
Antisun grey and bronze	6	2600 × 1350
	10	2700 × 2000
	12	3100 × 2410
Antisun green	6	2300 × 1300
	10	2300 × 1300
Cast glass	6	2600 × 1350
	10	3050 × 1800
Patterned (patchwork, pinhead, morocco, cotswold)	5	750 × 600
	6	1520 × 915
	10	2600 × 1350

Laminated glass

Laminated glass consists of two or more layers of glass bonded by layers of polyvinal butyral. Its strength and safety lie in the elasticity and adhesive qualities of the plastic membrane which prevents a plate from collapsing if shattered. It is available in the following forms:

Safety laminated

(a) General use: in substances ranging from 4·4 to 6·8 mm, this is used for glazing entrance doors and for situations where there is the risk of people falling against glass; it may be clear or tinted to match side panels and transoms.

(b) Anti-bandit use: in substances ranging from 7·5 to 11·5 mm, this is used for glazing entrance doors, windows and display cases where there is the risk of vandalism or attempted breakage (see table II in chapter 7 below).

(c) Bullet resistant: in substances ranging from 25 to 64 mm, this is used indoors only to provide protective screens against attack by firearms.

Tinted greys

These are known commercially as 'Shadowlite' and 'Deeplite'. The plates are bonded by interlayers of different shades of neutral grey which give varying degrees of light transmission. The main application is for one-way vision panels where a higher level of light prevails on one side. Light grey tint density gives a light transmission of 55 per cent, mid grey of 28 per cent, dark grey of 9 per cent and extra dark grey of 2 per cent.

'Solarshield'

In this type one of the plates has a thin film vacuum deposited on the inner surface which acts as a reflector of solar heat. It is used on shopfronts and is available in bronze or gold tints.

Solar control glass

Solar control glass may be used to reduce solar heat gain or internal glare and also for decorative purposes. Reductions in solar gain are achieved either by absorption and re-radiation or by reflection. The main types of solar glass are 'Antisun', 'Parsolgrey', 'Parsolbronze', 'Spectrafloat', and 'Glaverbal'. Each type has several tints and differing transmission characteristics.

Table V Transmission characteristics of 'Antisun' solar control glass

Colour	Transmission of visible light (%)	Transmission of solar heat (%)	Nominal substance (mm)	Normal size of manufacture (mm)
Green	78	65	5	4550 × 2500
	75	60	6	
Grey	41	60	6	
	24	48	10	4550 × 2500
	18	44	12	
Bronze	50	60	6	
	32	48	10	4550 × 2500
	26	44	12	

Reflective tinted films may be applied in-situ to most types of clear plate glass to produce effects similar to those given by factory manufactured solar control glass. The application of such films should however only be regarded as a temporary expedient because they cannot withstand weathering or cleaning operations. Solar control glass should only be used after careful consideration. A 'heavy' tinted glass will appear to be opaque from the outside on a bright day obscuring the interior and the goods in the window display. This type of glass is mainly suitable for service shops such as travel agents, opticians, banks and so on.

Opaque glass

Opaque glass is available in two categories, with colour pigmentation chemically fired into the one surface or with colouring introduced throughout the substance of the glass. The former is normally supplied as a toughened glass and commercially known as 'Armourclad'. Because it is toughened this offers increased strength and resistance but cannot be worked on after toughening. Exact sizes must therefore be quoted when ordering from the manufacturer. A glass with the colour running right through the thickness is 'Tintopal'. This is an annealed glass and can be worked on like normal glass.

Table VI Coloured opaque glass types, sizes and colours

Type	Nominal substance (mm)	Normal maximum size of manufacture (mm)	Standard colours
'Armourclad'	6 mm float or cast	2600 × 1500 total area must not exceed 2·3 m²	Dark, mid and light greys; pale, lime and dark greens; cobalt blue, turquoise, light stone, black (non-standard colours are available to order)
	10 mm float	3950 × 1250	
	10 mm cast	2750 × 1500	
'Tintopal'	6 mm	2440 × 1220	Black and white

Both the above types of glass are unaffected by weathering and are extensively used for claddings, infill panels and fascias. As they are impervious and resistant against damp, dirt, and most chemicals they are also suitable for internal use where hygienic and decorative finishes are required.

Decorated glass

The surface of glass can be treated by several processes to achieve different decorative effects:

Acid etching

This process is suitable for permanent signwriting. The glass is treated on the surface with hydrofluoric acid. The degree of obstruction of light and the texture depend on the number of treatments applied and on the addition of mica flakes to the acid. Usually the background is left clear with the design etched in single or multiple shades and textures.

Sandblasting

This is suitable for creating decorative effects. The glass is abraded with carborundum particles, propelled by compressed air. Obstruction can be set to different densities from light to deep and to varying shades from clear to full.

Painting or gilding

This is usually applied to the back of the glass. If ceramic paints are used they can be fused permanently into the surface of the glass. Gilding is the application of gold and silver leaf as a form of decoration.

Bending

The glass is heated in an oven until sufficiently pliable to take the form of the mould upon which it is placed. (Float plate glass is normally used for shopfronts and showcases.) It may be fixed with the curve on the horizontal or vertical plane (the latter is suitable for non-reflecting windows). The minimum radius of curvature is approximately 150 mm; there is no limit on the maximum radius.

Glazing techniques

Glass may be assembled in a shopfront in the following ways:

Glazing into framed sections

This is the simplest and most popular form of assembly and involves glazing into any of the following frames:

(a) Timber: various types of hardwoods are used including afromosia, iroko, mahogany, oak, sepele and teak; components are machined and cut to length in workshops and brought to site for assembly; glazing beads may be pinned or screwed and should be on the inside for security reasons; timber frames are becoming unpopular because of their cost and the continuous maintenance which they require.

(b) Metal sections: extruded aluminium sections are the most common; these may be pre-cut to length and screw-assembled on site or factory-assembled for rapid installation; the finishes available include etched and anodised, polished and anodised and brush grained and anodised; the colours manufactured are silver, bronze, gold and black; metal frames may also be made of rolled steel, stainless steel and bronze.

(c) Metal cladding on hardwood core: any of the above metal sections may be clad over a timber core to provide a cheaper framing system.

Where laminated security glass is used the frame should be of robust construction to prevent it from being forced out when under attack. The edge cover should never be less than 12mm and preferably 19mm wide. The glazing compound should not contain any chemical which will be liable to affect the interlayer. Bent glass requires additional tolerance between the back of the rebated frame and the inner face of the glazing bead: the amount allowed will depend on the type of bend.

Channel and groove glazing

The effect of this technique is to provide a window with no visible fixing beads so that it appears to be fixed direct into concrete, marble, stone or any other building material. As it is impossible to insert glass into channels on all four sides one side must consist of a removable bead. A deep groove must be provided on the side adjacent to the one chosen for this purpose and channels of normal depth on the other two sides. The glass is inserted into the groove and then slid back into the channel opposite so as to be equally covered on both sides. It is then eased into the remaining channel, after which screwed or 'snap-in' beading can be fixed on the side opposite to this. The glazing is completed by pressing synthetic rubber or PVC into the space between glass and frame to hold the glass firmly and provide a weathertight seal.

Suspended glazing

Where very large and tall openings are to be glazed the glass may be suspended from the head of the opening thus eliminating distortions in the glass (particularly with large plates) because it hangs freely. This patented suspension system involves the use of metal pads stuck to the two faces of the glass by means of a glass adhesive and gripped by compression fittings attached to adjustable hangers. The method allows for possible movement of the head and the vertical and bottom edges must therefore be permitted movement without leakage. This is achieved by use of flexible synthetic rubber strips set into the side and bottom channels. The system particularly suits toughened 'all glass' assemblies in which structural framings are not used. Individual plates are attached to each other by means of metal patch fittings fixed at the corners of the plates and the joints between glass are sealed with suitable permanently resilient sealant. Vertical stiffeners ('fins') set at right angles to the main plates are required to provide resistance to wind pressure on the glass facade. In assemblies which are only one plate high the stiffeners are anchored at the top integrally suspended with the plates; the bottom end is housed in a slot so that, when under load, the back edge bears against the back of the slot. In tall assemblies it is common to use cantilevered stiffeners. In some cases one stiffener extends from the head to the top of the lowest plate. In others it is necessary to use two stiffeners, the second being secured to the floor. Toughened glass doors are manufactured to match panels but they should be structurally isolated from the assembly.

Glass to glass joints

(a) Corner clips: this system avoids vertical framing between the front glass and the return window; glass edges should be mitred and held together by means of metal clips bolted through holes drilled in the glass; the joint between glass is filled with a setting compound to prevent glass to glass contact and the egress of water and dust; occasionally a very thin section glazing pencil bar is introduced to seal this joint.

(b) Glass to glass adhesives: most of these adhesives are two-part materials which have to be mixed on site immediately before

application and will set in periods from 3 to 24 hours; where large areas of glass are used structural stiffeners ('fins') are stuck at right angles to give stability against wind pressure; to help them resist wind suction they may be capped with a metal clip which stops the plates being forced outwards: it should be noted that if the glass breaks it will be necessary for the cement joint to be broken down and re-made.

5.6 COMMON SHOP WINDOW PROBLEMS

All windows are subject to a certain amount of glare: clients are concerned to avoid this because it tends to obscure displays. It may emanate from the sky, the pavement surface or other sources such as adjoining illuminated signs or vehicular traffic. Figure **5.13** illustrates typical ways of treating shopfront glass to reduce glare:

1 Tilting the glass: the shopfront may be tilted forwards or backwards; glass tilted forwards gets better protection at its base and suffers less from wind-driven rain and dust, in order for this method to succeed the pavement surface must be kept clean and matt black at all times; glass tilted backwards provides more usable space because the window bed is extended but runs the risk of damage at its base; this method requires the use of a deep canopy with a matt black soffit.

2 Curved glass sections: a quite elaborate and expensive method which virtually eliminates all glare is to use two curved glass sections with matt black surfaces at the base and a canopy soffit; this gives the illusion that there is no window between the pavement and interior: in this method a considerable amount of display space is lost because of the room taken up by the curved glass and baffles.

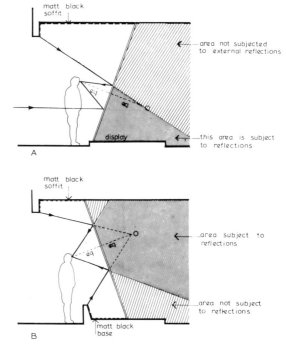

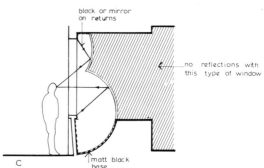

5.13 *Non-reflective windows*
A *glass tilted back* **B** *glass tilted forwards* **C** *curved glass sections*

Two alternative ways of reducing glare are to increase internal illumination levels and to use canopies or blinds. These methods are discussed respectively in sections 8.1 and 5.8 below. Tinted glass which controls reflected glare is not suitable for shop windows because it obscures the merchandise on display.

Condensation

Condensation on shopwindows is caused by the difference in air temperature and humidity on opposite sides of the glass: to avoid its occurrence conditions on either side should be kept to as nearly equal as possible and to achieve this effect heating equipment should be kept away from window enclosures; if possible ventilation should also be provided at sill and top rail levels. In places where damp internal air is unavoidable, such as launderettes and restaurants, the only satisfactory solution is to seal off the window enclosure from the shop interior. Where high humidity in the window enclosure is essential (eg florists) an alternative is to provide a water curtain where water is pumped in a fine spray at the head of the window and runs down the glass to be collected and re-circulated.

Overheating

The action of the sun on shop windows may cause such a serious build-up of heat that there is a risk of damage to displays. Another source of damage may be the heat produced by window lighting. Solutions to overheating problems like these may include the installation of shop blinds, the use of solar control glass or the extraction of heat by mechanical ventilators: if the last of these three possible solutions is adopted it may be a good idea to direct the extracted air to some other area of the shop which is too cool for comfortable use (eg the entrance lobby in winter).

5.7 ENTRANCE DOORS

Types available

Entrance doors are mostly glazed with timber or metal frames matching shopfront construction. The following are typical details for unframed all-glass toughened glass doors and framed glazed doors.

Door type (leaf, framing material)	Relevant standards	Specification of component materials	Mode of manufacture	Finishes supplied	Maintenance
Toughened glass	None	For external use minimum substance is 12mm although in internal use 10mm is adequate Doors are categorised under three groupings dependent on type of rails and patch fittings specified: A Top and bottom rails B Bottom rail and top corner patch C Corner patch fittings All holes for handles, letter plates etc must be specified before toughening process A range of 'no-gap' doors is available	Toughened glass is ordinary plate glass which has been subjected to a process of heating and sudden cooling which makes it very strong It does not require traditional metal or wood leaf framing All exposed edges are polished Door pivots are incorporated in the top and bottom rails or patch fittings	Clear glass or tinted bronze or smoke grey Metal rails, pivoting patches and furniture in a wide range of materials: anodised aluminium, stainless steel, chromed steel, bronze	Clean glass with water and detergent, finish with 'squeegee' Metals to be cleaned as described below
Aluminium	BS 1474: 1972 BS 1615: 1972 BS 3987: 1974 BS 4842: 1972	Extruded aluminium alloys in a wide range of rectangular sections Glazing should be 6mm or 10mm laminated float glass is sometimes specified Glazing may be clear or tinted to match side panels Weatherstripping is available as standard, ironmongery supplied	The extruded sections are cut to length and joined by means of torsion bars or angle cleats welded or screwed to stiles Middle rails can be fixed by screws alone Glazing is normally factory assembled with gaskets	Finishing may be etched and anodised, polished and anodised, or brush grained and anodised Main colours are silver, bronze, black and gold	If neglected finish will pit Wash down with water to which a mild detergent may be added: if grime has built up remove with non-scratching scourer When dry, polish with furniture cream with a wax content; a thin layer of lanolin may be added after the surface has been cleaned Door leaves are delivered to site with a protective film which should be removed only when all building work has been completed
Steel	BS 729: 1971 BS 1449 Part I: 1972	Rolled mild carbon steel sections to specified profiles Glazing as for aluminium doors Weathering clips into sections	The rolled sections are cut to length and welded at corners with internal members either welded or tenoned and rivetted; they are fabricated in jigs to ensure they are flat and square	Doors may be hot dip galvanised to BS 729, primed for site decoration or stove enamelled, to B.S. colours: a detailed discussion of the painting of metals is given in BRE Digest numbers 70 & 71	Regular redecoration is critical to prevent deterioration
Stainless steel	BS 1449 Part 2: 1972	Type 316 to BS 1449: Part 2 should be used externally on account of its corrosion resistance; grade 304S is suitable for internal application	Stainless steel sections are formed principally on a brake press although roll forming techniques are also used; they may be drawn as a thin cladding over steel, aluminium, timber cores, or unsupported in thicker sections	Finishes available are polished, matt, or satin and coloured finishes also available to order	Only requires regular washing down to maintain initial appearance Polish with a soft cloth dusted with whiting powder

continued

Door type (leaf, framing material)	Relevant standards	Specification of component materials	Mode of manufacture	Finishes supplied	Maintenance
Bronze	BS 2870: 1968 BS 2874: 1969 BS 1975: 1969	Sections can be extruded or cast Cast members provide for heavier and more expensive doors with a variety of designs and surface textures (normally used on prestige solid doors)	Bronze, an alloy of copper can be extruded and built as for aluminium frames	The colour of the oxide skin that forms on the surface can be varied by the addition of trace metals, in tones ranging from light gold to dark chocolate; the finish surface can be polished or etched	Apply a good wax sparingly
Timber 1971	BS 1186 Part 2: 1971 BS 459 Part 1: 1958 BS 4787 Part 1: 1972	Various types of hardwoods including afromosia, iroko, mahogany, oak, sapele, teak, walnut Mortice and tenon joints are considered superior to dowelled joints but are more expensive Timber not inherently durable should be preservative treated to PRL Technical note 24. Glazing beads should be on inside for security	Components are machined and cut to length from selected kiln-dried timber	Hardwood doors are usually clear finished	Requires yearly recoating and frequent stripping

Method of operation

The above types of doors may operate in the following ways:

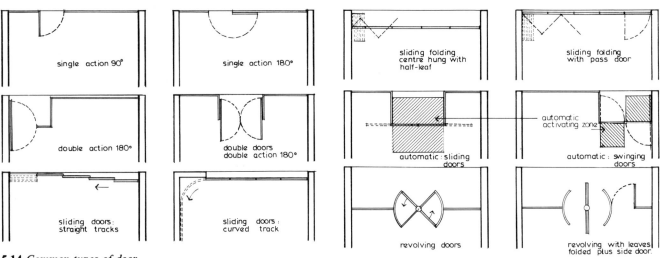

5.14 *Common types of door*

Principle	Operation	Application	Comments	Advantages	Disadvantages
Pivoted (centre pivot)	Single action 90° Double action 180°	All types of retail premises Can be incorporated with automatic control (see below) Can be used on toughened glass doors	Should not be on sites exposed to high wind pressures as doors tend to be blown open; increasing the spring tension causes difficulties to customers opening door: in such situations best solution is to fit a double bank of doors which act as an air lock Most popular type in commercial use	Full width of door rests on floor pivot allowing for easy frame preparation Spring closers may be completely concealed Permits single or double action Can be set to check open at 90°	Hardest type to weather satisfactorily Floor spring requires floor preparation
Pivoted (offset pivot)	Single action 90° Single action 180°	As above	As above	As above: can be fully weathered	Permits only single action Overhead closure cannot be concealed: floor springs must be used for full concealment
Hinged	Single action 90° Single action 135°	Smaller retail premises When applied to toughened glass doors should only be used internally		Can be fully weathered Provides greatest clear opening Permits only single action	Jambs carry total weight of door, requiring stronger frame preparation Closer spring is exposed

Principle	Operation	Application	Comments	Advantages	Disadvantages
Hinged *continued*					
					There can be no built-in check at 90°
Sliding	Straight track Curved track	Premises where large entrances are required eg car showroom Can be incorporated with automatic control (see below)	Stacking panels require one track per leaf which may restrict total number of panels		
	Top hung		Maximum weight for a top hung door is approximately 360 kg (equivalent to a door measuring 15 m²)	Little floor preparation is required Dirt on floor guide does not become critical	Support structure is required Transom glazing is difficult Pass doors are not practical
	Floor track		Maximum weight for a floor track door is determined by wind load factors	No special structural support is necessary Large doors are possible Pass doors can be accommodated Transom glazing is possible	Track cleanliness is critical
Sliding/folding		Premises where it is desirable to open the whole frontage, to induce customers or to facilitate flow of large number of persons eg pavement restaurants, retail units in enclosed shopping centres	The frontage is divided into a large number of small modules		
	End folding		Maximum weight of door leaf is approximately 65 kg	Doors can be set in line with the shopfront Require small area for stacking as compared to straight sliding doors All panels can be of equal size	Stile hinges and tracks are always subjected to torsional forces when open Floor track traps dirt
	Centre folding			Full door weight is directly suspended from overhead track resulting in no forces Doors can be slightly longer than end-folding types Toughened glass doors can be used: these do not require stiles which give a lighter visual appearance	Doors must be set back from building line Floor track traps dirt Toughened glass doors are hard to weather satisfactorily One end leaf must be half panel
Automatic	Actuating control by: Electric switch plate operated by push button, elbow switch or kick plate Microwave scanner mounted on transom Photo-electric cell Pressure mat	Commercial buildings and premises where customers are likely to be laden, handicapped, or arriving in large numbers eg jewellers, supermarkets, department stores	Automatic doors give a prestige status and speed passenger flow Use results in minimising heating and air-conditioning losses		
	Swing doors			Cheapest to install Does not require wide opening Closer spring cannot be concealed	Can strike person on wrong side of door
	Sliding doors			Safest type to use: cannot strike people Opening gear is concealed in transom Bi-parting doors permit two way flow	

Principle	Operation	Application	Comments	Advantages	Disadvantages
Revolving	Manual or motorised	Not suitable for retail premises Entrances to commercial or institutional buildings eg offices, banks, hotels	Most types have four leaves but three-leaf doors are available mainly for internal use Leaves must be collapsible or the revolving section must be flanked by ordinary swing doors	Best for draught exclusion Eliminates stack effect (suction created by differences in internal and external temperatures) Best for dust control Excludes street noise Channels flow in both directions	High cost Cannot be used by handicapped persons Manual types require some exertion Difficult to carry large items through Children can trap fingers and toes

Toughened glass doors

Toughened glass doors perform all the functions of conventional doors with the added advantage that they provide a total transparency without requiring orthodox frames. When they are used in conjunction with matching side and transom panels it is possible to fill the entire opening with glass. As toughened glass is much stronger than ordinary untreated glass it can be used without fear of its collapsing if users accidentally collide with it. Toughened glass doors are available in clear glass or tinted grey, green or bronze to match shopfront glazing. They are manufactured in 12 mm glass; float glass for clear doors and cast or tinted glass for tinted doors. Because of the greater strength of the material, doors are usually used without the orthodox wood or metal frames and are pivoted with floor or head springs. Toughened glass doors are available in four standard sizes but can also be made to measure in sizes up to 1220 × 2540 mm.

Table VII Toughened glass doors: standard sizes and required openings

Standard door sizes	Required opening sizes	
	Single doors	Double doors
(mm)	(mm)	(mm)
762 × 2134	768 × 2147	1534 × 2147
838 × 2134	844 × 2147	1686 × 2147
914 × 2134	920 × 2147	1838 × 2147
914 × 2438	920 × 2448	1838 × 2448
Maximum size up to 2540 × 1220		

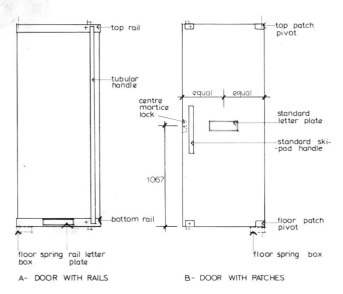

top rail
tubular handle
centre mortice lock
1067
bottom rail
floor spring box   rail letter plate

A- DOOR WITH RAILS

top patch pivot
equal   equal
standard letter plate
standard ski--pad handle
floor patch pivot
floor spring box

B- DOOR WITH PATCHES

5.15 *Armour-plated doors*

Ironmongery

Door accessories should be planned at the ordering stage as once the glass is toughened no further drillings, cuttings or notchings can be entertained other than surface decoration work.

Door springs

Door springs are contained in a metal box and may be set into the floor. Replacement can be made without disturbance to the foundation casing. Where doors are installed back to back (as in a bank of doors) they are controlled by individual springs. Overhead door springs are not recommended for heavy doors weighing more than 90 kg. The spring box can be concealed in the transom rail if required. Springs are designed to operate through a single action 90° or a single or a double action 180°. Models are available that will either hold a door open or return it automatically.

Top and bottom rails

The upper rail is used to accommodate the top pivot housing and the bottom rail accommodates the pivot housing for the floor spring spigot. Locks can be incorporated on either or both rails. Matching rails and end caps are generally available in lengths up to 1220 mm for use on glass side panels. Rails are available in the following finishes: bronze metal antique, polished bronze, satin or polished chrome, natural aluminium, black or gold anodised aluminium.

Patch fittings

Various types of patch fittings are available for use on toughened glass doors and matching toughened glass side panels; they include pivot housings, door stops, door fittings and assembly fittings. Patch fittings may be used independently or in conjunction with top or bottom rails and are available in almost the same range of finishes.

Locks

Most shops use five-lever deadlocks fitted to the top and bottom rails. Where a shopfront displays a bank of doors locks can be fitted which will accept the same key. Doors which use patch fittings instead of rails may be accommodated with a centre patch-fitting mortice lock plus additional patch-fitting locks as required. Patch fitting locks are not suitable for alarms as the electrical wiring cannot be concealed and it is prone to damage and tampering.

Handles

Handles can be designed in sympathy with the shopfront, or with the firm's established logo. All drillings for unique or unusual handles must be specified at the time of ordering before the glass is toughened. Standard grip handles or push pads are generally available from manufacturers. Horizontal push pads or handles may incorporate cylinder locks if required.

Letter plates

The normal position for letter plates is 1067 mm from the bottom of the door and equidistant from the sides. They can however be set in any reasonable position on the door or adjoining side panel. They can also be set in the bottom rail but the narrow depth strictly limits the bulk of post they can accept and the low position is unpopular with the Post Office.

Decoration

Letters, numbers and designs can be applied to all glass doors in the same way as on the main shopfront glazing. Techniques employed for this purpose include signwriting, screenprinting, acid-etching, sandblasting and gilding.

5.8 CANOPIES AND BLINDS

Uses

Where shopfronts are severely exposed to the sun they require some form of solar control. The most practical remedies are canopies or blinds. These not only control solar heat gain but also reduce glare, protect the goods in window displays, shelter pedestrians against bad weather and have decorative and advertising potential.

Canopies

Canopies are permanent fixtures and are usually provided as an integral part of the main building. When they are very high they are sometimes fitted with hanging blinds on the outer edges (but look better without them). The effect produced by a canopy is to impose a horizontal plane between the ground floor and the upper floors of a building, so giving more visual impact to the ground floor level. Architects considering installing new canopies should decide on an appropriate method of disposing of rain water.

Blinds

Blinds are temporary fittings designed to retract when not in use. If the blind box is housed under the fascia the latter will not be visible to shoppers on the near pavement and a sign identifying the shop will be required in the shop window. If the blind box is above the fascia the latter will be obstructed to shoppers on the opposite pavement and some form of sign will therefore be required on the blind itself. The main types of blind (see Fig **5.16**) are:

Sliding arms

This is the simplest type of blind where the front rail is supported at each end by an exposed arm attached to a joint that moves on a vertical metal slide fixed to the pilasters. The side arms folded up against the slides are unsightly and when in a down position project in the path of pedestrians.

Trellis arms

These are also known as lattice folding arms. They eliminate the vertical slides used for the above type and allow the blind to be on a more horizontal plane so that a longer projection is possible for a given length of material. Trellis arms are quite unsightly and the blind sometimes becomes hard to operate because of their numerous joints.

Folding arms

In this system the arms fold inwards in a knuckle joint and tuck into the blind box when the blind is not in use. The blind box must be deeper to accommodate the folding arms. With large blinds it may be heavy to operate and gearing mechanism may be required. Sometimes the heavy load may cause distortion in the arms which may result in making the blind difficult to fold back neatly into the blind box.

Telescopic arms

These require a deep recess for their withdrawal. The large housing unit has to be installed in the initial stage of shopfitting and is more expensive than other systems. However it has the advantage that it may be operated either manually or electrically. Telescopic arms may be used for blinds of any length. The front rail is made from one piece and can be reinforced to prevent sagging. Very long rollers and blinds can be built in independent sections with the gaps between blinds covered over by narrow filling pieces.

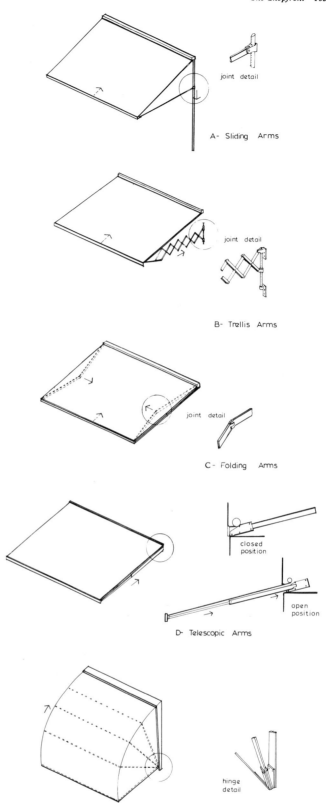

5.16 *Types of blinds (awnings)*

Dutch blinds

Dutch blinds are entirely different from the types listed above. They are quadrant-shaped in section and may have a straight or curved front rail. The front projection is usually equal to the blind height although larger projections may be obtainable. Attention should be paid to the design of the front rail so that it covers the sides as well as the top of the blind box in its drawn position. Dutch blinds can be applied to circular-headed windows and are very decorative.

5.17 *Controlling dimensions for blinds (see table VIII)*

Blind materials
Until recently blinds were traditionally made from heavy water-proof cotton fabrics but these are now complemented by man-made materials such as synthetic Dralon and PVC plastics. Natural fabrics are prone to quicker deterioration than man-made materials due to wear, fading and rotting. Another experimental material for blinds is aluminium slats: although these are very expensive to

install they require little maintenance and do not need to be replaced. The lath and blind box can be made from wood or from such metals as stainless or zinc coated steel, aluminium and bronze. Blinds may be finished in plain colours, striped, patterned or decorated with the shop's sign.

Dimensions of blinds
The most important dimensions which have to be established for blinds are size of blind box, total width, extent of projection and height of lath above pavement. The latter two dimensions are subject to statutory regulations in Great Britain where they should normally be 2200 to 2400 mm high and set back not less than 450 mm from the edge of the pavement but these figures should always be checked with the Local Authority because they vary from region to region. Table VIII, which should be read in conjunction with Fig **5.17**, sets out the controlling dimensions required in different areas.

Table VIII Controlling dimensions for blinds in different areas

Area	Dimension (see Fig. 5.17) (metres)		
	A	B	C
City of Westminster	0·60	2·13	2·30
City of London	0·60	2·30	2·44
City of Manchester	0·46	2·30	2·30
Most other areas of Great Britain	0·46	2·30	2·44

6
SIGNS

6.1 DESIGN AND POSITIONING

Primary considerations

Every shop needs some form of sign for identification. The average sign normally indicates the name of the firm owning the property, some add a further message to identify the trade, some include a graphic image such as the firm's logo. In assessing the type, size and design the following factors should be taken into consideration:

Client's requirements

The client may have a pre-established image or may be trying to establish a new one. Branches of multiple stores require design, colour, and size to conform to their corporate image.

Local characteristics

The type of locality (major shopping area, secondary street, residential) will determine the level of brightness for illuminated signs.

Site characteristics

The height and size of the fascia and the width and height of the frontage will influence the size and positioning of the signs.

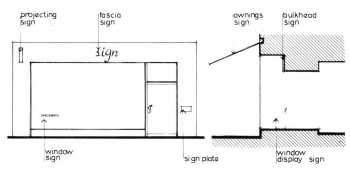

6.1 *Positioning of signs on the shopfront. They may be placed on any element*

Merchandise to be sold

The type of goods sold may influence the style of lettering used eg traditional or modern, ordinary or unusual.

Position

Shop signs may be displayed in any of the following elements of the shopfront (see Fig **6.1**):

Fascia

This has always been the traditional place for the main sign. The fascia is an imposing position which attracts the eye and is not normally obscured by pedestrians or traffic. Excessively large signs give the appearance of a billboard and should be avoided. Although normally a background to the sign the fascia can be made into an advertising trade mark by means of the colour, finishes and type of design chosen.

Blinds

Blinds fitted above the fascia obscure the extent to which signs on it can be seen from the other side of the road. If blinds are fitted below it the signs may be invisible to pedestrians on the pavement in front of the shop. In either case it may be necessary to have some form of sign reproduced on the blinds themselves. The effects of deep and shallow blinds are illustrated in Fig **6.2**.

Pilasters

Pilasters are traditionally used as fixing points for projecting signs. It should be established if they are the property of the client or the landlord; if they are the latter's his permission will be required before signs can be mounted on them. The architect should also ascertain which particular pilasters may be used for this purpose because one of them may be required for the use of the adjoining property.

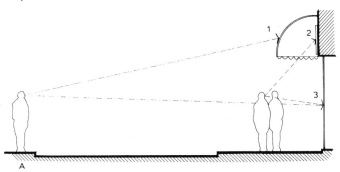

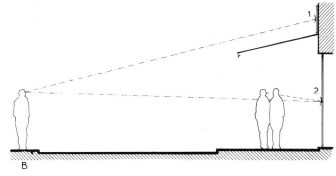

6.2 *Effect of blinds (awnings) on the positioning of signs*
A Deep type of blind over fascia **1** *sign on blind is only visible from the opposite pavement* **2** *sign on fascia is only visible from the near pavement* **3** *sign on the window is seen from both near and far pavements*

B Shallow type of blind fixed under the fascia sign
1 *sign on the fascia is only visible from the opposite pavement*
2 *sign on the door is seen from both near and far pavements*

Window

Low level signs are often desirable in addition to those mounted on the fascia. Because of their nearness to the pedestrian's eye smaller letters may be used on these. Large letters stand out well if there are only a few of them but in large quantities they confuse the viewer and obstruct the amount of daylight received and the field of visibility inside the shop. Letters displayed vertically in Chinese style are harder to read than those set out in horizontal lines and should be avoided.

Internal

Internal high level signs at bulkhead level are sometimes installed instead of the traditional fascia signs. These are applicable when:
(a) The fascia is awkwardly placed or shaped (eg too high above the pavement or too narrow to take the intended sign).
(b) Circumstances cause the unavoidable formation of a deep bulkhead in the shopwindow (eg the need for mechanical plant).
(c) The overall design is enhanced by such an expedient.
Signs displayed internally should whenever possible be in keeping with the type of lettering and graphics used externally. The shop's identity can be reflected on all sides in such items as counter signs, labelling of merchandise, price tags, carrier bags and wrapping paper.

6.2 ILLUMINATED SIGNS

Types

Illuminated signs are generally one of the following types:
(a) Individually illuminated letters and graphics
(b) Internally illuminated panel
(c) Floodlit panel.

Individually illuminated signs (letters and graphics)

Individually illuminated signs are generally lit by cold cathode tubes and may be in any of the following forms (see Fig **6.3**):
1 Visible tubing on a backing panel: the cold cathode tubes used in this technique are shaped as required and mounted on a backing panel which may be plate glass or opaque. When used with glass panels the appearance from the back face should be considered. With opaque panels the electrodes which measure about 20 mm in diameter × 65 mm in length may be concealed provided they are made accessible. Bare tubing is generally difficult to read from sharp angles or from distances. It suffers from dirt and is difficult to clean. When unlit it is illegible. This type of sign may be encased in glass or clear perspex to protect it from dust. If the encasing material is heavily tinted the tubing becomes invisible when unlit.
2 Visible tubing mounted on solid metal letters: this technique gives high surface illumination: in the daytime the metal surfaces of the letters stand out in their own right; at night the same message is made to stand out by the illuminated tubing.
3 Visible cathode tubing mounted in an open section metal trough: this technique confines the light given to the area within the outlines of the letters. The system is suitable where the sign has to be read from some distance away because it overcomes the blurring which may occur from using visible tubes. As an alternative a series of individual tungsten lamps can be mounted in the troughs to produce a different effect.
4 Concealed tubing behind solid letters: this technique is the same as the one above except that the section is reversed to give a halo effect on the background panel. As the intensity of the light given by this sign is low it should only be considered for use in areas which are dimly lighted.
5 Concealed tubing faced or encased with plastic letters: with metal sided letters the plastic face may be flat or moulded and retained by many types of flanges on the front return; with all-plastic letters a change of colour is sometimes used for the letter returns so as to avoid a distorted appearance when viewed obliquely. This type of sign has an excellent appearance whether unlighted

in the daytime or lighted at night (when the illumination is evenly distributed).

Internally illuminated panels

Internally illuminated signs may be back-lit or side-lit.
1 Back-lit: this type is used predominantly on the fascia and may be single sided, double sided or three dimensional. Its construction consists basically of a metallic box housing cathode tubes and a front acrylic panel with inscribed letters and artwork.
2 Edge-lit: signs of this type are not used externally because of their low luminosity. They use a fluorescent or tungsten lamp to illuminate the edge of a clear acrylic plastic panel on which etched letters are displayed by the refraction of light. They are mainly used for exits, telephone kiosks etc.

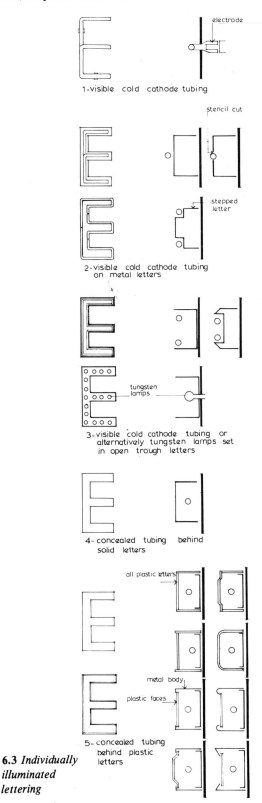

1-visible cold cathode tubing

2-visible cold cathode tubing on metal letters

3-visible cold cathode tubing or alternatively tungsten lamps set in open trough letters

4- concealed tubing behind solid letters

5- concealed tubing behind plastic letters

6.3 *Individually illuminated lettering*

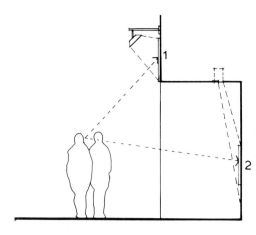

6.4 *Floodlit signs*
1 *fascia sign*
2 *low level sign
on pilaster or
side wall of
recessed entrance
lobby*

Floodlit panels

These panels do not light up. They are illuminated only from an external source. This is usually provided by an arrangement of incandescent bulbs which have a short life especially if exposed directly to rain when heated. The general effect of floodlighting is disturbed if even a single bulb is not working. Floodlit fascia and low level signs are illustrated in Fig **6.4**.

Lamps

Cold cathode

The rated life of a cold cathode tube is 25,000 hours. Tubes are made in straight lengths, in grid form or in the shape of the letter or logo. The most common tube diameters are 9, 11, 15, and 20 mm. Light output increases with tube wattage and for a tube of any diameter the higher its operating current, the greater its light output. Cold cathode tubes operate at above mains voltages and require step-up transformers. These are about 300 mm long, 225 mm wide and 125 mm deep and should be sited within 2 metres of the tubes. Tubes are available in many colours produced through the use of different gas fillings and fluorescent powders. Argon/mercury fillings are inclined to darken at the ends in cold weather unless fitted with special electrodes to counterbalance this tendency. The colour of an unlit tube seen in daylight differs from its colour when illuminated.

Hot cathode (fluorescent)

The rated life of a hot cathode fluorescent tube is 7500 hours. Tubes are manufactured in straight lengths of from 150 to 2400 mm and in diameters of 16, 26 and 38 mm. They are mainly manufactured in straight lengths but are also available in 'U' shapes and circles. They operate on mains voltage and are largely used in internally illuminated panel signs. When mixing varying tube lengths in one sign box it is essential to select tubes with similar light output per unit length and of similar colour rendering. Failure to do this results in unevenly illuminated panels.

Tungsten

The rated life of tungsten lamps is 1000 hours. They are used for floodlighting or signs of the open trough types discussed above. Their biggest disadvantage is their short life: continuous maintenance is necessary to replace every single lamp that becomes defective. In exposed positions the life cycle is further shortened if rain falls on the heated bulbs. Tungsten lamps are mainly used because of the brilliant sparkle they produce. They may also occasionally be used to give 'running effect': this is achieved by alternate brightening and dimming of each individual lamp to produce the apparent effect of movement.

Construction

Lighting box

Lighting boxes for internally illuminated signs or individually illuminated letters are usually made from anti-corrosive extruded aluminium or lead-coated steel. The face panel is retained by flanges, the returns of which may be recessed flush with the body. The cathode tubes are supported in retaining clips fixed to supports at the back which also houses the lighting control gear. Fascia sign boxes may be recessed into the fascia. If surface-mounted they require weather proof flashing on the top side.

Table I Cold cathode tubes: colours and other characteristics

Illuminated colour	Daylight colour	Lumens per 300mm length		Gas filling
		15mm diameter at 60mA	20mm diameter at 120mA	
Emerald green	White	500	680	Argon/
Dark green	Yellow	350	480	mercury
Ice blue	White	225	310	
Azure	White	130	180	
Light blue	White	85	115	
Alpine white	White	325	440	
Jasmine yellow	Yellow	240	330	
Rose	White	190	260	
Blush	Cream	85	115	
Cardinal	Red	40	55	
Normal red	Clear glass	75	75	Neon
Ruby red	Ruby red	35	35	
Magenta	White	80	85	
Amber	White	85	85	

Table II Hot cathode tube characteristics

Lamp length	Rating (watts)	Lighting design: lumens (at 2,000 hours)*							
		White	Plus White	Warm White	Daylight (cool white)	Natural	North light	De luxe natural	Artificial daylight
2400	125	8800	8350	8700	8400	6500	5300	4800	3800
	100	8000	7600	-	-	5900	-	4400	-
	85	6850	6500	6750	6500	5000	4100	3800	-
1800	85	6250	5850	6100	5800	4350	3600	3200	2600
	75	5750	5500	5650	5450	4000	3200	2900	2400
1500	80	5200	4950	5100	4950	3900	3100	2700	2300
	65	4750	4500	4600	4450	3400	2700	2500	2100
	50	3600	-	3550	-	2400	-	1900	-
1200	40	2800	2700	2700	2650	2100	1700	1500	1200
1050	40	2800	2700	2700	-	-	-	-	-
900	30	1850	-	1850	1750	1400	-	-	-
600	40	1700	-	1700	1600	1300	-	900	-
	20	1100	1050	1100	1050	800	700	600	500
450	15	750	-	750	600	600	500	-	-

*Lumen output beyond 2000 hours decreases at 2% to 3% per 1000 hours use according to the colour and loading. Light output of fluorescent tubes falls sharply after the first 100 hours and then decreases steadily at a slow rate of about 2% to 3% per 1000 hours.

Dimensions

Table III Sizes and luminance data for internally illuminated panel signs (see Fig 6.5)

Type of panel	Thickness of diffuser (T) (mm)	Depth of box (D) (mm)	Hot cathode 1200 mm 40 watts, daylight		Cold cathode 15 mm 60 mA, white	
			Lamp spacing (S) (mm)	Luminance (lux)	Lamp spacing (S) (mm)	Luminance (lux)
Single sided panel sign (fascia)	3·2	75	125	95	90	35
		150	200	60	125	25
		230	325	35	230	10
		300	450	30	-	-
	4·8	75	125	85	100	35
		150	200	50	150	20
		230	325	35	230	10
		300	450	30	-	-
	6·4	75	125	80	115	30
		150	200	45	180	20
		230	325	30	250	10
		300	450	20	-	-
Double sided panel sign (projecting)	3·2	100	65	110	65	35
		180	150	40	75	25
		230	175	30	125	20
		300	200	15	200	10
	4·8	100	65	100	65	30
		180	150	35	75	25
		230	175	30	125	15
		300	250	15	200	10
	6·4	100	75	85	65	25
		180	150	35	100	20
		230	175	30	150	10
		300	250	10	225	5

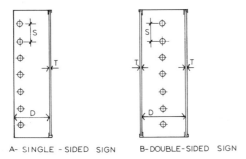

A- SINGLE - SIDED SIGN   B-DOUBLE-SIDED SIGN

6.5 *Internally illuminated sign (see table III)*

Front diffusers

The diffusing panel can be made out of a range of materials:

Glass: this has the advantage over acrylics that it does not hold a static charge causing accumulation of dirt and dust. It is however weak against impact and is only available in a limited range of opals and colours. Glass is expensive to mould or cast into relief shapes and is now rarely used in sign-making.

Cast acrylic: this is made in rigid sheets in sizes up to 3·0 × 3·7 m. It is easily moulded, shaped, cut and worked on. It is prone to scratching but resists weathering well and has a high surface reflectivity which assists light output. It has an excellent appearance in daylight when not lit. These qualities make it ideal for use as a diffusing panel. Acrylic sheets soften gradually at high temperatures: this allows for a simple vacuum to form between 150 and 160°C.

Extruded acrylic: this process allows acrylic to be produced at a lower cost than when cast while maintaining similar qualities of finish, workability and ease of forming.

Polycarbonate (glass reinforced polyester): this material is used where high strength is required and is particularly useful for areas where vandalism is likely. The polyester resin is coloured by introducing pigments into the basic resin mix. Cost is a little higher than for other materials.

CAB (Cellulose acetate butyrate): this has not the weathering qualities of acrylics but is very tough. It is used where sharp and accurate mouldings are required and allows for vacuum forming. Because the material is tough it allows for thinner substances to be used.

PVC: this is made in flexible sheets (plasticised) and rigid sheets (unplasticised). It weathers well but its colour fastness is not as good as that of acrylics. Rigid PVC is used in situations where a degree of fire resistance is required (such as pedestrian precincts). Diffusing materials are produced with standard surfaces in a high gloss finish but a range of textures can be obtained (eg matt, pinspot, stippled and reeded).

Joints

The normal thickness of front panels ranges from 3 to 6 mm according to the overall size of the sign. Standard sheet sizes are about 1·8 × 1·2 m although larger sizes are available to order. This means that large signs usually require one or more joints which ought to be planned in relation to the artwork. For a temperature range of 27°C the expansion and contraction of an acrylic sheet can be as much as 4 mm per metre and provision must be made to prevent the lighting tubes from showing through gaps between adjacent panels. There are four common types of joints: external fillet, internal fillet, scarfed and lapped (see Fig **6.6**). Allowances must be made not only for movement between panels but also at the top, bottom and sides of the frame. Diffusing panels up to 750 mm are supported at the base with movement joints at the top and sides. Large panels exceeding this size may be top hung from metal brackets with an acrylic rib cemented along the top length.

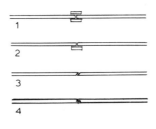

6.6 *Types of joint on diffuser panels* **1** *external fillet of panel colour* **2** *internal fillet of panel colour: this is only suitable with opaque panels or there will be a shadow line* **3** *scarfed joint* **4** *lapped joint*

Signing

There are several ways of applying the lettering and artwork to the diffusing panel:

Paint: the sprayed or screenpainted sign is applied to the front surface of opaque acrylics but unless protected by a sheet of glass it will be prone to wear and damage. With clear acrylics the signs are painted on the reverse surface and the acrylic is then given a coating of diffusing paint. Ventilation slots are required in this case to avoid condensation on the inside of the box. The sheet can be vacuum-moulded to give greater impact if required.

Fret cutting: fret cut letters and simple artwork can be applied to an opal acrylic sheet which should then be protected by a clear front sheet. This is a relatively expensive process because of the precision work involved.

Applied acrylic: letters and artwork can be applied to the diffusing panel by chemical bonding with the edges sealed to prevent water and dirt penetration. The sections may be flat with square edges, flat with metal bevelled egdes in silver, gold or stainless steel, built-up letters with plastic or metal returns or built-up with moulded letters (see Fig **6.7**).

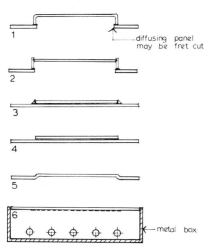

6.7 Types of applied lettering on acrylic panels **1** *built-up moulded letters* **2** *built-up letters* **3** *flat letters with bevelled metal edges* **4** *flat letters with square edges* **5** *reverse silkscreened moulded acrylic panel* **6** *reverse silkscreened flat acrylic panel*

6.3 NON-ILLUMINATED SIGNS

Cast letters
Individual letters are supplied by manufacturers from their standard set of moulds. This predetermines the typefaces and sizes available although special one-offs can be made to order at a significant cost. Letters range from 50 to 300 mm in size and can be cast from bronze, aluminium, resin and stainless steel. Aluminium letters may be stove-enamelled to selected colours and can be cast with a smooth flat face or raised outlines round the edges. Cast letters are usually fixed clear of the background surface to reduce weather staining marks and give more depth. They are supplied with grouting rods for setting into pre-drilled holes or set into rotating hollow cups.

Cut-out letters
Individual letters are cut out from sheet plastic or metal. The minimum sizes vary according to the thickness of material used. For 1·5 mm thick acrylic the smallest size is 15 mm high, for 3 mm it is 25 mm and for 6 mm it is 50 mm. There are no limitations on the larger sizes. Cut-out letters may be fixed to smooth backgrounds with impact adhesive. Where the background is irregular or a stand off effect is desired they are fixed with snap-on studs and cups.

Built-up letters
Built-up letters can be made from wood, plastic or metal (metal letters are usually made from lead-coated sheet steel and finished by stove-enamelling). Their standard height varies from 125 to 750 mm. Plastic letters higher than 750 mm come under stress and have to be braced to counteract it. Built-up letters may be surface mounted or set away from the background like cast letters.

Painted
Painted signs can be executed by hand by signwriting artists or produced by techniques such as spraying or silkscreening. The latter process is expensive but becomes economical when repeated over a number of times to recoup the cost of the screen. It is therefore particularly useful for multiple stores which have the same requirements for a number of branches.

Signplates
The principal method of making signplates is by engraving. This is applied to the reverse surface of clear plastics and on the front surface of opaque plastics and metals. The minimum size of letters is usually about 6 mm high but for bold typefaces of solid engravings this can come down to 4 mm. There is no upper size limit. The basic types of engraving shown in Fig **6.8** are:

Surface outline: each letter outline is engraved on the front surface by a deep line which is enamelled in a contrasting colour.

Surface solid: the whole letter section is engraved and enamelled.

Reverse outline: the letter outline is engraved on the reverse surface of a transparent material. Colour is applied to the engraved outline. If desired the letter face can be given a coat of contrasting colour and the whole background can also be colour-sprayed to turn the plastic opaque.

Reverse solid: the letters are engraved in outline on the reverse surface but both the engraved lines and the letter face are filled with the same colour.

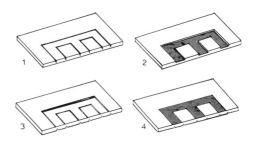

6.8 *Engraving methods on signplates*
Surface engraving **1** *outline* **2** *solid* Rear engraving (on transparent plates) **3** *outline* **4** *solid*

Crests and coats of arms
Crests and coats of arms can be produced from cast aluminium and fibreglass. In aluminium the sizes range from 77·7 cm^2 to 4500 cm^2 and the colours are stove-enamelled. In fibreglass the sizes range from 77·5 cm^2 upwards with large crests made in sectionalised parts. Colouring is by polyurethane enamel. Because of the cost involved in producing moulds crests become cheaper if produced in batches rather than singly.

Fixing methods
Fixing methods for signplates and for individual letters, respectively, are illustrated in Figs **6.9** and **6.10**.

6.4 LEGIBILITY
It is difficult to lay down rules on the legibility of illuminated or non-illuminated signs. Illuminated signs are visible at greater distances but this does not necessarily mean that they are legible. Different factors govern the legibility of signs which are designed to be read from a distance and printed signs which need only to be read at fairly close quarters. Legibility is affected by the following factors:

Letter height
It is generally accepted that 25 mm high letters will be legible at distances up to 15 m and that each additional 25 mm increase in height will extend the range of legibility by 15 m. Lower case letters generally occupy about 15 per cent less space than equivalent capitals and may be used where the amount of available horizontal space is critical.

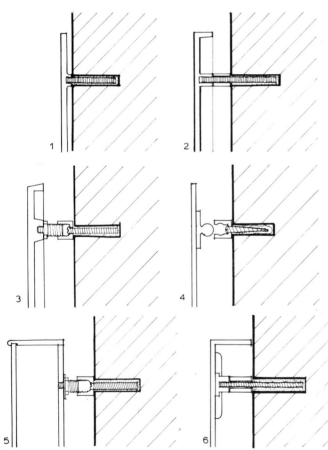

6.9 *Fixing methods for signplates*
1 face fixing *countersunk hole with countersunk screw and coverdome to rawlplug in masonry* **2** mounted plate *impact adhesive to mounting board secret screwed to fixing wall* **3** secret fixing flat to wall *tapped boss on reverse, allthread into clearance hole and boss recess* **4** secret fixing stand-off *tapped boss welded on reverse allthread nut and washer through fixing hole* **5** removable secret fixing stand-off *tapped boss on the reverse, metal threadscrew and mastic to clearance hole*

6.10 *Fixing methods for individual letters*
1 cut-out acrylic letter *applied tapped boss and allthread into clearance hole with mastic into masonry* **3** cast metal letter *tapped boss, distance piece and allthread into clearance hole* **3** cast metal letter *ditto into locator piece, woodscrew to timber or rawlplug to masonry* **4** cut-out acrylic letter *clipped into plastic cup screwed to rawlplug in masonry* **5** built-up acrylic letter *tapped hole into acrylic bridge, locator with metal thread screws, nut and washer* **6** custom made fibreglass letter *tapped boss bonded on reverse with spindle into clearance hold and mastic*

Typeface

The most legible typeface is the sans serif letter having a height/width ratio of 4 : 3 for the letter 'E' (eg Helvetica Medium). If letters have serifs they may be confused with one another (eg 'E' with 'B' or 'C' with 'O'). Extended or condensed typefaces are usually less legible than those of normal proportions, but this depends on letter spacing. With illuminated letters, particularly where bare cold cathode tubing is used, the spacing must be greater to allow for halation. These points are illustrated in Fig **6.11**.

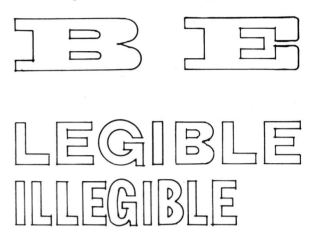

6.11 *Legibility and typeface: (top) the serifs on the letter 'E' make it look like 'B'; (bottom) the normal letters on the upper line appear less legible than the condensed letters on the lower, but taking account of halation and viewing from a distance, the reverse is true*

Colour

Mist or polluted air has a scattering and absorbing effect which varies for different colours. Red has the maximum penetration followed by yellow, green, white and blue (which is the least effective over long ranges). Figure **6.12** illustrates the differences in visibility between red and blue.

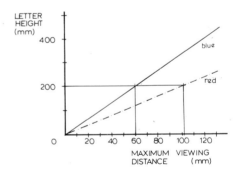

6.12 *Colour penetration: A 200 mm high letter illuminated in blue can be seen from 60 m; if a letter of this size is illuminated in red it is visible at up to 100 m*

Illumination

Light intensity can be raised to increase the distance at which a sign is legible. Signs should give light for the normal human eye to see them at the required distance. If they are too bright however they may become illegible by 'blurring' and 'spreading'. The halation of visible tubing signs can be minimised by reducing current or by housing the letters in open trough sections to confine the spread of light.

Background

Background colour and intensity is particularly important for internally illuminated signs. Dark letters silhouetted against a bright background are especially difficult to read.

6.5 REGULATIONS AND BY-LAWS

Installation

All electrical wiring should be carried out in accordance with the Institute of Electrical Engineers (IEE) regulations so as to comply with the requirements of Local Electricity Boards. Cold cathode signs with high voltage installations require fire-switches conspicuously mounted and easily accessible and near the sign whether it is internal or external. Large buildings may be required by by-laws to provide fire escape signs on emergency doors leading to

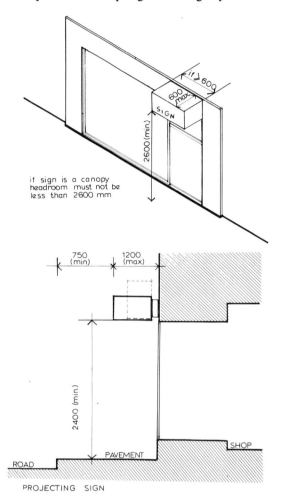

6.13 *Prescribed dimensions for projecting signs in Greater London*

escape routes. In such situations the electricity supply should be independent from the main supply to the sales floor.

Consents

Virtually all external illuminated signs require specific consent which must be applied for independently from that required for building works. Signs inside the shop are generally exempt. Consents must be given both by the landlords and by the Local Authority (who are concerned mainly under The Town and Country Planning (Control of Advertisements) Regulations 1960). The most important factors affecting decisions are overall size, brightness level and potential distraction to traffic (eg from flashing or animated signs and signs on the same level as road signs or traffic lights.

Brightness

The overall brightness permitted by Local Authorities varies considerably from area to area. In order to try and rationalise the levels of brightness permitted in different locations the Electrical Sign Manufacturers' Association (ESMA) produced a recommended code in 1964. This has been accepted by some Local Authorities but not by others. Its recommendations, converted into metric units, are as follows:

Table IV Recommended maximum level of brightness for new signs

Illuminated area	Location			
	Zone 1: recognised display centres	Zone 2: major shopping centres	Zone 3: secondary shopping centres	Zone 4: residential areas
(m²)	(lux)*	(lux)	(lux)	(lux)
0·5	no limit	95	45	30
0·5-2·0	no limit	70	35	25
2·0-10·0	no limit	45	30	20
over 10·0	no limit	30	20	10

*The lux is the unit for 'luminance'; it is used to measure the amount of light per m² which a sign emits on a surface one metre distant from it. It should be noted with internally illuminated signs that the luminance of the diffuser is the amount of light emitted and not the amount of light received.

Projection

It is necessary to make inquiries from the Local Authority concerning the restrictions which apply to signs projecting over public highways. Most Local Authorities have regulations similar to those made by the Greater London Council and illustrated in Fig **6.13**. Special consent is necessary if it is desired to exceed the dimensions prescribed.

7
SECURITY SYSTEMS

The degree of security to be provided in a shop will depend on the value of goods held in stock and on such considerations as the reductions which may be effected in insurance premiums if security precautions are increased. Thefts from shops are made by burglary or by shoplifting and different deterrent principles apply to each. Burglary prevention may be achieved through intruder detection methods using different kinds of alarm equipment or by using mechanical devices to form physical control barriers. Shoplifting can be prevented by using a wide range of surveillance and other equipment.

7.1 ALARM EQUIPMENT — INTRUDER DETECTORS

General principles
Some alarm equipment works on open circuits. Most quality alarms however use an electrical current flowing continuously within a closed electric circuit: if this system is inadvertently tampered with by an intruder the circuit is broken causing the alarm to go off. The way in which the alarm is actually triggered off is by means of a device known as the 'relay': electricity flows in a primary circuit passing through an electromagnet which keeps open a switch in the secondary circuit; breaking the primary circuit closes the relay contact thus making the secondary circuit 'live' and causing the bell to ring (Fig 7.1). To prevent intruders from discovering the position of detectors alarm systems may be 'tripped', meaning that they will only operate the bell at a pre-set time after detection. In addition circuits may be wired with double or triple poles to overcome attempts at looping the circuit. Here two or three sets of wires are kept together at all times in a single core cable. The problem of looping the appropriate pairs together to make the system inoperative is greatly increased because there is no way of knowing which wires pair off in the circuit.

Protective switches
Protective switches are used for the detection of unlawful opening of doors and windows. There are two types of switches: mechanical and magnetic. Mechanical switches rely on physical force to operate the mechanism. In its simplest form this system is seen in shops where the movement of the door knocks a metal rocker so that it completes a circuit and rings a bell to warn the shopkeeper of a customer's entrance. Mechanical switches contain plungers which operate micro-switches to complete the circuit when the door is locked. Opening the door breaks the circuit, and sets off the alarm. Normally the plunger mechanism is fixed to the door and the micro-switch is set into the door transom or the floor. Magnetic switches contain contacts which are held in a closed position by the permanent magnet (Fig 7.2). Opening the door removes the magnetic field and the contact opens to create an alarm condition. As no frictional movements are required to operate them, magnetic switches are more reliable, smaller and easier to conceal and connect. To overcome possible tampering by means of hand-held magnets both plunger and switch have a number of magnets laid in a field of opposite polarities so that any external magnetic field will trip the alarm even when the door remains closed. Protective switches provide a cheap and effective means of detection but they only detect the opening of a door or window. High risk shops should be provided with additional devices to detect breakage through glass or any other material.

Wired panels

Continuous wiring
This system is effective for doors, walls, floors, ceilings and cupboards. Continuous wiring consists of a blockboard panel on which are stapled fine wires carrying an electrical current (Fig 7.3). To reach his goal the intruder has to go through the wire barrier but when the wire is broken an alarm condition is created. The internal surface of the panel is usually covered with hardboard which protects the delicate strands of wire. The final decorative finish is

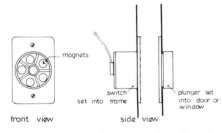

7.2 *Magnetic protective switch: the switch is fixed into the door or window frame and the plunger magnet in the jamb. Unlawful removal of the plunger causes the switch to activate the alarm*

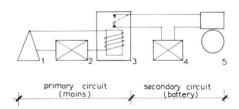

7.1 *Closed circuit diagram: breaking the primary circuit causes the secondary circuit (and hence the warning device) to operate* **1** *intruder detector* **2** *mains power* **3** *relay* **4** *rechargeable battery* **5** *bell or other audio device*

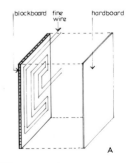

7.3 *Continuous wiring: a fine wire is stapled on blockboard forming a closed circuit. To go through the barrier the intruder has to break through the wiring, thus causing the alarm. The hardboard gives a protective covering against accidental damage*

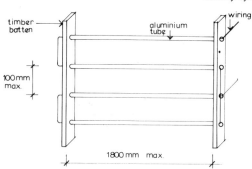

7.6 *Continuous wiring in hollow aluminium tubes: the fine wires are threaded in a haphazard pattern to overcome any attempts at looping. The tubes are used only to protect the wires and do not physically deter entry*

The tubes are not intended to act as a physical barrier but only to protect the wiring from accidental damage. They are fixed at distances of not more than 100 mm centres with wooden battens at either end. The wires can be threaded through in a haphazard pattern of polarity to avoid looping and are stapled to the battens. Each tube must not exceed 1 m in length. The main disadvantage of this system is that the bar-like tubes induce a caged atmosphere and must therefore be confined to rear areas not visible to customers. One variation of the system consists in having the tubes fixed to a removable frame which can be taken away from the window in the day and installed nightly by connecting it to detachable plugs. Another variation is the use of knock-out bars which can be removed when the alarm is not set. When fixed in position each bar is in contact with a micro-switch to form a closed circuit. Displacement of the bars creates an alarm condition. The maximum practicable span for this system is 1·8 m. Longer spans require intermediate battens for support.

Foil strips
A foil strip can be used for detection of glass breakages. It acts as a conductor in a closed circuit and is designed to break and trigger the alarm when the glass is broken. To fix the foil an adhesive

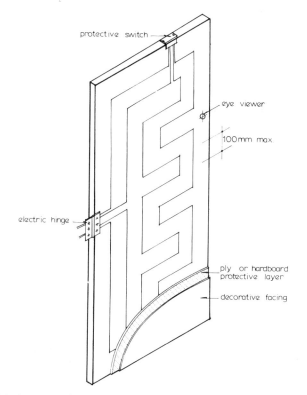

7.4 *A security door with continuous wiring*

applied over the hardboard. The effectiveness of this system depends entirely on the standard specified and the quality of workmanship of installation. BS 6746 gives recommendations for the specification of wiring and installations. Figure **7.4** shows a security door with continuous wiring.

Transverse wiring
If a standard higher than that provided by continuous wiring is required transverse wiring can be specified. Here the wiring is run both horizontally and vertically. When applied to doors the panel may be fixed as previously described but there is a flexible link between the door and frame. This link can be in the form of a flexible cable, a detachable plug connector or a special electrical hinge (Fig **7.5**). Continuous and transverse wirings are cheap and effective detectors but cannot be used near damp surfaces.

Hollow tubes
Continuous wiring can be used in hollow tubes for protection of windows and thin wall structures. It operates on the same principle as the above systems but instead of being sandwiched between boards the wires are laid inside light aluminium tubes (Fig **7.6**).

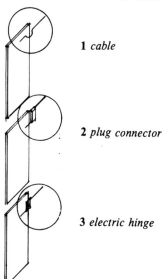

1 *cable*

2 *plug connector*

3 *electric hinge*

7.5 *Main types of flexible links between door and frame*

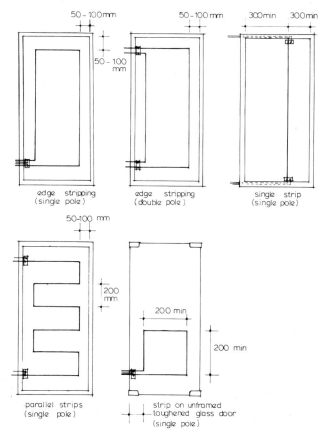

7.7 *Application of foil strips on glass doors*

(normally varnish) is applied along the window edge. The strip is then laid in position and covered over with another two coats of varnish. This system presumes that when the glass is broken the cracks will extend to the point where the foil is fixed. Foil strips are best used on plate glass. On ordinary glass they should be fitted over the entire surface at 200 mm centres because the professional thief can cut out the centre of the glass without cracking the edges (Figs 7.7 and 7.8). Foil strips are cheap and have a deterrent value but should not be relied on where there is a grave risk of burglary. They are prone to damage during window cleaning operations.

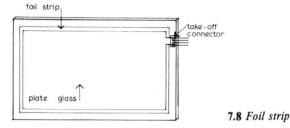

7.8 *Foil strip*

Vibration detectors

These may be used to detect breakages through windows, walls and ceilings. They consist of spring metal strips or inertia metal balls which complete a closed circuit; when vibrated these devices are displayed and set off the alarm. When specifying that this system is to be used architects should indicate the area and type of surface that is to be protected because a range of detectors is made to cover different surface areas and vibration transmission characteristics. Glass vibration detectors (also known as 'inertias') cover approximately 1·8 × 1·8 m of glass; they are not always reliable and need precise adjustment: if under too much tension they are prone to give false alarms and if under-tensioned they may fail to detect the breakage of glass. Vibration detectors are not recommended for use on shopfronts exposed to heavy vehicular traffic but they are very efficient at protecting internal walls, internal security doors and safes.

Ultrasonic sound detectors

There are two types of ultrasonic sound detectors: one for detecting the special ultrasonic wavelength that breaking glass creates and the other for monitoring sounds made by intruders inside the protected area. The system for detecting glass breakage consists basically of a microphone and amplifier with electronic filters to cut out ambient noise. Its advantages are that it leaves the protected glass totally unobstructed, that a single unit will cover any number of panes of glass within the protected area and that it can be used for any type of glass. The unit is usually housed within a range of 4 m from the protected glass; care must be taken that it does not point to telephones, vent grilles or external doors. The use of ultrasonic detectors for monitoring sounds made by intruders is discussed under the heading 'Space detectors' below.

Pressure mats

Pressure mats are used for internal detection. Each mat is about 4 mm thick and 600 mm square and is made from rubber or plastic containing two sets of metal strips kept apart by a layer of foam: the weight of an intruder stepping on the mat sets off the alarm by pressing the strips down and so bringing them into contact with each other. The system usually operates on the open circuit principle but it may also be connected to closed circuit alarms (Fig 7.9). The mats are best concealed under floor carpets placed where intruders are likely to tread. Ideal positions are across doorways, on stairs, under window sills and adjacent to security areas such as safes or showcases. Pressure mats should not be used under heavily worn materials, linoleum or damp or uneven floors.

Space detectors

Space detectors register the movement of intruders inside the shop.

There are three types: sound, micro-wave and infra-red. Sound detectors pick up all sounds in the protected area except ambient noises which are eliminated by audio filters. In order to minimise false alarms they may be fitted with a counting circuit. This records the pulses made by every new sound in the protected area until a capacitor is charged to the predetermined level which sets off the alarm; isolated noises which are not repeated within a set period are however eliminated through a decaying device so that only continuously recurring sounds are accumulated on the capacitor. Sound detectors suit quiet internal rooms but not noisy environments. Each unit covers approximately 60 m³. Micro-wave detectors use the 'Doppler effect' principle: a transmitter emits micro-waves of a fixed frequency over a defined area which are reflected back to a receiver; any moving object causes a variation in frequency which sets off the alarm (Fig 7.10). Infra-red detectors operate on the principle that current is generated by light falling on a photo-electric cell. If the light is interrupted the circuit breaks and activates the alarm. Only infra-red light is emitted and received by these devices because, unlike ordinary light, its frequency cannot be detected by the naked eye.

Choosing a suitable system

The following summary may be helpful in deciding which system is most suitable for deterring intruders in any particular set of circumstances:

Protected element	Detection principle	Hazard condition*	Detector device
Doors and windows	To detect unauthorised opening	Non-hazardous	Single pole magnetic switch or mechanical switch
		Hazardous	Double pole magnetic switch
		Extra-hazardous	Triple pole magnetic switch
Doors (solid portions)	To detect breaking through	Hazardous	Continuous wiring in tubes or continuous wiring covered with hardboard
		Extra-hazardous	Transverse wiring covered with hardboard
Doors (glazed portions)	To detect breaking through	Non-hazardous	Strip foil
		Hazardous	Knock-out bars contacted at one or both ends or continuous wiring in tubes with fixed or removable frames
Windows	To detect breaking through	Non-hazardous	Strip foil
		Hazardous	Vibration detector or ultra-sonic glass detector or continuous wiring in tubes with fixed or removable frames
		Extra-hazardous	Strip foil plus ultra-sonic glass detector
Walls, floors and ceilings	To detect breaking through	Hazardous	Continuous wiring covered with hardboard
		Extra-hazardous	Transverse wiring covered with hardboard or vibration detector or sound detector
Internal space	To detect intruder movement inside premises	Non-hazardous	Protective switches on internal doors or pressure mats, or infra-red detector
		Hazardous	Micro-wave detector or ultra-sonic detector

* This relates to the value of the merchandise eg non-hazardous: clothing, footwear toiletries; hazardous: leather goods, gifts, photographic goods; extra-hazardous: jewellery, objets d'art, furs, antiques.

7.2 CONTROL PANELS FOR ALARM EQUIPMENT

The control panel is the centre of any alarm system and should be carefully sited out of view, if necessary in a protected cupboard. It consists basically of a steel box housing the circuitry and an external display panel with the main on/off/test switch positions and a series of switches with light indicators for each independent circuit (Fig **7.10**). Items of special risk can be set on a 24 hour circuit and parts of the premises can be isolated or connected with the alarm as required. Power can be supplied to the control panel by batteries alone, by a mains transformer unit or by a combination of both. Battery-powered systems are the most economical to install but the batteries require continuous checking and are not always reliable. Mains transformer units (also known as 'power packs') reduce and stabilise the mains voltage to a level which suits the alarm system giving it a permanent supply of power so long as there is not a power cut. It is best however to combine the virtues of the first two systems and eliminate their vices by using a mains power pack as the normal source of supply and also having stand-by rechargeable batteries which take over when mains power fails. There are two basic ways of setting up the controls:

(a) The first of these is to fit an external shunt lock to the final exit door so that the actions of locking or unlocking this with a key from the outside set the control panel into the 'on' or 'off' position.
(b) The second way is to set the control panel so that the alarm will ring until the action of locking the final exit door closes the contact which stops it; a timer delay can be incorporated in this system which gives the shopkeeper a few minutes to lock up before the alarm can start to ring; on re-entry the bell will start ringing after the same period if the control panel is not switched off.

7.3 WARNING DEVICES FOR ALARM EQUIPMENT

Audible warning

A wide choice of warning devices is available. These may be classified according to the sounds they make as bells, sirens, bleepers, warblers, or whiners. Units are self-activating so that their internal batteries take over if they are cut off from the rest of the alarm system and are usually encased in strong steel casings

designed to delay any attempt to tamper with them. They should be mounted in positions over 3 m high on the outside of the structure so as to be a visible deterrent. They may be tripped to sound a few seconds after the alarm is broken and cut-out facilities may also be provided to limit the period for which the sound continues. It should be noted however that the general public tends to ignore alarm bells, perhaps because so often alarms are false ones. A bell howler alarm is shown in Fig **7.11**.

Telephone warning

This system may be used in addition to or instead of audible warning devices. In an alarm condition the control unit, which is

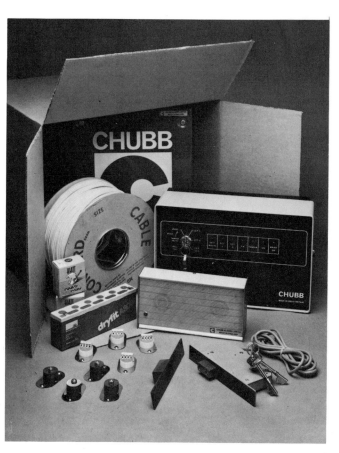

7.10 *A typical security kit for a small shop, consisting of protective switches, a lock for the front door, an ultrasonic movement detector, control panel, bell and accessories*

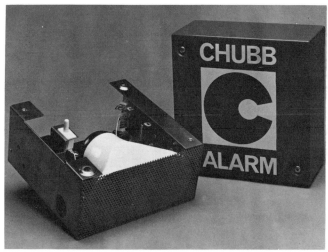

7.11 *Alarm howler with tamper-proof cover: more up to date version of the usual bell (Chubb Alarms Ltd)*

7.9 *Pressure mat: should be sited where intruders are most likely to tread on it eg in a doorway, on stairs or adjacent to the safe or to a counter holding goods of high value (Chubb Alarms Ltd)*

linked to a Post Office line, dials 999 and passes a spoken message (pre-recorded on disc or casette) to the police indicating an alarm condition and the location of the premises. If a dialling tone is unobtainable because the lines have been cut audible warning devices are activated. Alternatively, instead of dialling the police, the control unit may be programmed to dial any other number, usually a security firm's central station. Under this system a coded electronic digital message is passed within a much shorter time. The message is recorded at the other end on a print-out for reference and so that the appropriate action may be taken, eg if the message signifies that an intruder is on the premises the security firm must call both the police and the shop manager, if it signifies that there has been a personal attack they must call the police, and if it signifies that there is a fire they must call both the Fire Brigade and the shop manager. For higher security the transmitter in the control unit should be connected to an ex-directory, outgoing-only call line. This eliminates the risk of intruders phoning in and engaging the line.

Direct line

For maximum security, high risk shops may be connected to the police or the security firm's central station on an individual private Post Office line. In such situations a continuous signal is sent along the line and if this fails for any reason the alarm begins to sound. This system gives immediate warning and cannot be tampered with but is obviously very costly. To reduce line charges the private line may be connected only as far as the nearest telephone exchange from which it is then passed on over a shared line to the police or the security firm.

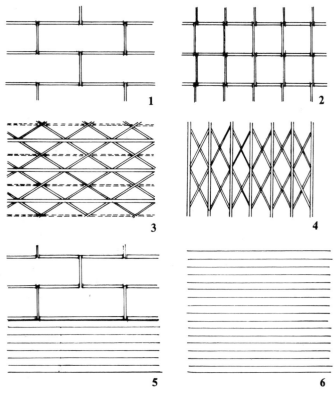

7.4 MECHANICAL SECURITY DEVICES

Whereas alarm equipment is intended to deter intruders by giving warning if intruders break in to shop premises, mechanical devices are designed to give physical protection to the goods on those premises which are most likely to be stolen.

Roller grilles

Roller grilles are commonly used in shops as a deterrent against burglary or vandalism. Different types are shown in Fig **7.12**. Rectilinear mesh, brick bond and square mesh grilles are constructed of vertical lines supported on horizontal rods encased in spacing tubes and assembled to form a mesh barrier of varying densities. Diamond mesh grilles are constructed from rolled or extruded flat sections jointed in the form of a lattice to horizontal channel bars. Where necessary, intermediary bars can be specified to reduce aperture sizes (see **3** in Fig **7.12**). Combined grille/shutters give additional protection against vandalism. The shutters are provided by fitting solid interlocking lath sections to the base of the grilles. This type of barrier also forms a trap against litter and vermin.

Table I Specifications and uses of roller grilles

Grille type	Typical aperture size (mm)	Applications
Brick bond	230 × 50	Doorways, windows protecting medium sized objects eg television sets, stereos, electrical goods
Square mesh	65 × 65	Windows displaying small objects eg cameras, handguns
Diamond mesh	125 × 50 125 × 25 (with intermediate bars)	Windows displaying small objects eg watches, jewellery, stamps
Combined grille/shutter	Grille apertures as above	Windows in areas of high vandalism
Solid shutter	No opening	Windows in areas of high vandalism where there are recurrent window breakages

Grilles are constructed of steel or aluminium. The finish of steel grilles may be sheradised, cadmium plated or coated with epoxy resin plastic in a wide range of colours. The finishes of aluminium grilles may be natural mill, anodised satin silver or anodised in a particular colour. Either kind may be operated by a hand chain, a cranked handle, an electric motor or a push-up self-coiling device

7.12 *Types of grille mesh*
1 *brick bond pattern (suitable for large objects such as items of furniture or television sets)* **2** *square mesh (for medium sized objects such as cameras or electrical goods)* **3** *diamond mesh (for small objects such as watches or jewellery: extra bars (dotted on diagram) can be introduced for higher security)* **4** *folding gate (for external use: where the gate stops lower than head height spearhead gates are normally used)* **5** *combined grille/shutter (lower shutter section protects lobby against litter and vermin)* **6** *shutter (interlocking lath sections give protection against vandalism)*

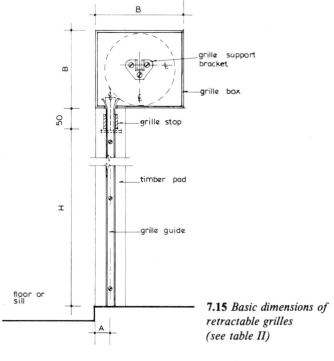

7.15 *Basic dimensions of retractable grilles (see table II)*

7.13 *Removable grille panel: fixing is by interlocking drop in hooks finally secured by padlocks (Baron Security Group)*

7.14 *Retractable roller grille: used externally in this case, locked by padlocks to side channels (Baron Security Group)*

(the last of these is suitable for small openings up to 8 m²; where the openings are larger they must be subdivided into smaller sections and run on removable extruded central mullions). During business hours the grilles are raised so as to leave unobstructed openings. The roller can be positioned internally, externally or under the lintel of the opening. Sizes for roller boxes may depend on the length of drop and manufacturers should be consulted to determine the appropriate ratio. The following table, which should be read in conjunction with Fig **7.15**, gives a guide to the dimensions of rectangular grilles.

Table II Dimensions for rectangular grilles

H (grille drop) (mm)	A (grille offset) (mm)	B (box dimension) (mm)
up to 950	40	225
915 to 1220	40	280
1220 to 1525	50	305
1525 to 2135	50	330
2135 to 3035	65	355
3035 to 3960	65	380

Collapsible gates

Collapsible gates, which may bunch separately or as a pair, are an alternative to roller grilles for protecting whole shopfronts, entrance doorways or arcades. They are constructed from heavy gauge steel pickets connected by steel diagonal lattice bars. The pickets are normally set at 150 mm centres but can be set at any other specified centres as required. Spearhead gates have pointed pickets projecting above the top track. Folding tracks may be used for small gates or permanently fixed ones for large gates. Extra large gates may be electrically operated. Figure **7.16** shows common ways in which gates may bunch and be recessed into pilasters. Collapsible gates are normally purpose-made to required dimensions. The normal minimum width is 0·9 m and the maximum dimensions are 7·0 × 7·0 m.

Burglar bars

Whereas grilles are temporary fixtures applied to the shopfront burglar bars are permanent and only to be used on rear openings. Bars should not be less than 12 mm in diameter and spaced not more than 100 mm apart. They may span up to 1000 mm in height after which tie bars must be deployed. Burglar bars are commonly supplied with welded square metal frames which allow for speedier site erection: after fixing the bolt head should be filed off.

Ironmongery

Locks and bolts are the major items of ironmongery that affect the

security of shops. The locks most commonly used are morticed deadlocks. These vary from 50 mm to 100 mm in size and may have two to seven levers. The security they provide is proportional to the number of levers and a four-lever deadlock gives fair security for a modest cost. An important point to remember is that the striking plate is as important as the lock: sometimes the plate may be ripped off the frame while the lock remains in perfect order.

Glazing

Types of glazing have been discussed in detail in section 5.5 above. Anit-bandit glass is commonly used in high risk windows displaying valuable goods such as jewellery or furs or in areas where vandalism is likely. This glass is a laminated type consisting of two or three layers of glass with polyvinyl butryal (PVB) interlayers and it normally withstands attacks from heavy implements such as crowbars and pickaxes. Although the glass will crack and craze when attacked with these implements the resilience of the PVB interlayers absorbs the energy of the blows, holds the glass in position and resists penetration. Substances for anti-bandit glass vary from 7·5 to 11·5 mm thickness and are covered in BS 5544. Bullet-resistant glass is constructed in the same way but is made in thicker substances which vary from 25 to 64 mm. BS 5051 sets various sets of standards which should be achieved against various types of firearms. The thickness and compounding weight of this type of glass sets limits to the sizes which can be manufactured and imposes restrictions on handling and fixing. Special framework and glazing techniques are required. As an alternative to laminated bullet-resistant glass, a composite panel, commercially known as Bristol Transparent Armour (BTA) may be used. This is as clear as

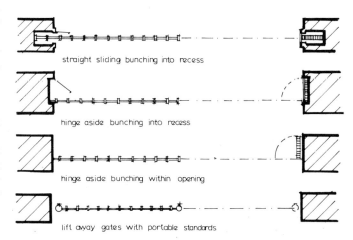

7.16 *Types of bunching for collapsible gates*

Comparison

The following is a summary of the information given on mechanical protective devices in this section:

Security method	Application	Comments	Advantages	Disadvantages
Roller grille	Used to protect doorways, entrances, windows and display cases; may be applied externally or internally	Size of mesh is determined by the size of merchandise it is meant to protect	Can be easily concealed when not in use; many bonding patterns and finishes available; can be motorised and connected to alarm system	
Collapsible gate	Used externally to protect arcades, doorways, and windows; can only be used externally	This is beoming unpopular and is being replaced by roller grilles	Quick to install; very strong	Unsightly; difficult to conceal when not in use; collects dust between lattice work and is difficult to clean
Burglar bars	For rear windows to toilets, stores or rooflights	Permanent and may be used where looks are unimportant	Quick to install; cheap	Unsightly; gives a prison appearance
Security glazing	For windows, screens, display cases	Available in various thicknesses depending on degree of security required	Neatest appearance; totally unobstructed	Costly; limited sizes of manufacture

glass and is manufactured from a composite of laminated glass and sheet polycarbonate located on the protected side of the panel. BTA is approximately one-third lighter and half as thick as laminated glass of similar qualities.

Table III Security glazing

Type	Nominal thickness (mm)	BS 5051 category	Normal maximum manufactured size	Approximate weight (kg/m²)
Anti-bandit	7·5		2600 × 1600 mm	15·8
	9·5		2140 × 1320 mm	21·6
	11·5		3210 × 2000 mm	26·6
Bullet-resistant laminated	25	G 0	3·5 m²	61
	25	G 1	3·5 m²	61
	42	G 2	2·0 m²	102
	64	G 3	1·25 m²	154
	43	S	2·0 m²	118
Bullet-resistant composite panels	13	G 0		21
	21	G 1		29
	28	G 2	2000 × 1200 mm	43
	51	G 3		80
	28	S		43

7.5 SHOPLIFTING CONTROL

Shoplifting, or 'shrinkage' as it is known in the store business, has reached such a high level that special desciplines and equipment have been evolved to fight it. Architects should take action on some of the points mentioned below and shopkeepers on others.

7.17 Anti-shoplifting notices have a deterrent value

Management policy

The most effective means of deterring theft is the action of alert and responsible staff. Large security firms provide courses and film programmes which give instruction to managers and staff on how to spot potential shoplifters and on the correct action to take when this type of theft is suspected or discovered. These also cover the legal aspects of shoplifting eg the requirement that shoplifters cannot be stopped and questioned or charged until they have left the premises.

Internal planning

Architects may contribute towards the success of security of a shop by careful planning. The main principles to be adopted are:

1 All entrances and exits should be well controlled.

2 Internal layouts should be planned with the minimum number of blind spots; fixtures in the middle of the sales floor should not exceed 1450 mm in height.

3 Unavoidable blind spots should be covered by surveillance devices.

4 The cash register, which must of course always be manned, should look inwards and be placed so as to have a commanding view of the shop floor.

5 Anti-shoplifting notices have some deterrent value and may be useful in self service shops; typical notices read 'Shoplifting is an offence — we *always* prosecute' or 'Shoplifting is a crime' (see Fig **7.17**).

6 Self service shops should be provided with shopping baskets or trolleys.

7 Signed price tags may be used so as to make it possible to identify the goods from the shop.

8 Turnstile units may be installed in supermarket entrances to control direction of customer exit.

9 Small luxury items should be housed behind security glass cabinets.

Electronic tag security

This method of surveillance only monitors the exits. Staff do not have to be on the constant lookout for potential shoplifters and blind spots no longer pose the traditional problems. All articles, or selected articles of high value, are individually tagged with proprietory tags that have been marked electronically; these are made from plastic or rubber and cannot be removed except by tag removal machines positioned at cash counters. Any unauthorised removal of articles through one of the exits activates detector units with audio or visual alarms. Tags removed at cash counters can be re-used and provide a useful double check on sales records.

An electronic tag security system is illustrated schematically in Fig **7.22**. The constituent elements of such a system are illustrated in Figs **7.19-7.22**.

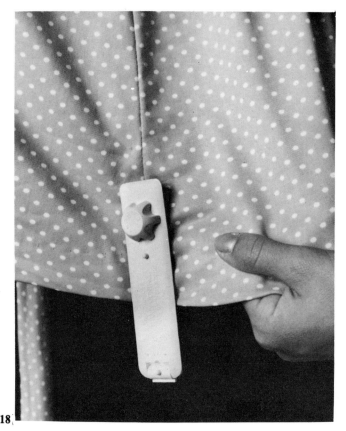

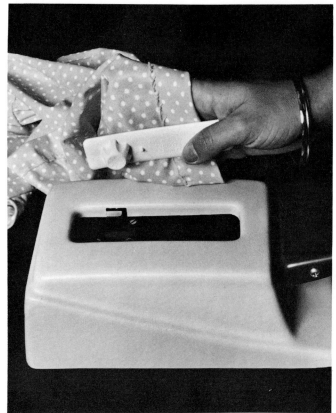

7.19

7.18 *Electronic tag security: articles are tagged*

7.19 *Tags are removed at cash desks by special machines. Tags are re-usable*

7.20 *Detector units detect articles which have not had their tags removed at the cash desk*

7.21 *Detector units give audible and visual alarm signals. With a system such as this one, the detectors do not have to be enclosed in free standing boxes as shown here: they may be incorporated into the planned design of the shop. (Photographs courtesy of Senelco Ltd, Slough)*

7.22 *Electronic tag security system: schematic diagram*

7.20

7.21

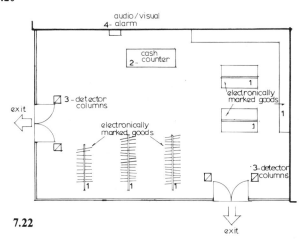

7.22

Mirrors

Ordinary one way mirrors, two-way mirrors or anti-theft mirrors may be used for surveillance. There are two basic types of two-way mirrors (see Fig **7.23**). One of these has a reflective surface indistinguishable from an ordinary mirror on one side and a clear observation surface on the other. The second type has silver stripes on the outer surface and is also clear on the inner side: this 'stripview' mirror is designed to be recognised as an observation mirror and that is what gives it its deterrent effect. One disadvantage of two-way mirrors is that they require observation rooms. Where it is not desired to have special rooms for this purpose observation posts can be provided in rooms designed for other uses, for example in the manager's office. Anti-theft mirrors may be convex, partly spherical or spherical in form. To produce a greater deterrent effect, they can be fitted with bright trims round their perimeter. Spherical or partly spherical mirrors are usually hung from the ceiling. Convex mirrors can be fixed to stationary points on walls or ceilings or alternatively to scanning units which automatically swivel the mirror through an arc of about 120° every 20 seconds or so. This scanning movement is intended more to make the mirror obviously visible to customers than to give staff better viewing angles. A swivelling anti-theft mirror is shown in Fig **7.24**.

Closed circuit television

Closed circuit television equipment is of the following kinds:
1 Fixed camera: this monitors exits, high value stocks, restricted access areas, etc; multi-directional types have a number of lenses in a stationary head to cover areas through 360°; selection of lens may be automatic or hand controlled.
2 Automatic panning camera: this swivels through a predetermined angle to permit inspection of wide areas.
3 Remote control camera: this makes it possible to have precise inspection of large areas; it can be fitted with zoom lenses for close-up surveillance.
4 Low light level camera: this is used for surveillance in near-darkness; the system can be fixed to the main intruder alarm.
Because it is so expensive to install and operate closed circuit television can only be accommodated in high risk shops or large retail units. Swivelling dummy television cameras have been used quite successfully in small shops. These can be fitted with scanners and blinking operating lights so as to be indistinguishible from 'live' closed circuit cameras. Closed circuit television requires constant monitoring and is only as effective as the operator behind the console panel. A camera is shown in Fig **7.25** and monitors in Fig **7.26**. Photographic surveillance can be installed as a more economical alternative. In this system the camera must be activated by an operator. It will then take an individual picture or a series of pictures at a rate of two per second for a five minute period. This system is mainly used where violent crime is expected.

Security chains

Merchandise on open display can be protected by securing it with a flexible chain or with nylon-coated steel wire. The chain threads through a number of goods making the removal of any item impossible. To enable staff to release individual items without disturbing the lot chains can be fitted with a series of opening links at intervals of 750 to 900 mm. Another type of chain is available for attaching to moulded plastic coat hangers and is used for the protection of expensive garments and furs.

Electric loops

Electric loops operate on the same principle as chains but are connected to an electrical circuit: if an intruder breaks the loop he causes the alarm monitoring box to sound the alarm. They usually operate from batteries although mains types are available. The circuitry is designed to run on a minimal electrical consumption. Only when the loop is broken and the alarm activated does the battery appreciatively run down; the alarm may be re-set by turning the control key. Where goods do not have handles or openings through which the loop can be threaded adhesive discs or pads may be used: these have to be fastened to each article which it is desired to protect. An electric loop and a security chain are illustrated in Figs **7.27** and **7.28**.

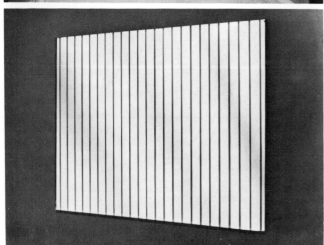

7.23 *Two-way mirrors allow monitoring from one side*
1 *Clearview: the customer is observed surreptitiously*
2 *Stripview: the customer is made aware that he is under surveillance (Volumatic Ltd)*

7.24 *Convex anti-theft mirror with swivel arm: if the mirror is mounted on a rotating arm its movement gives it a higher deterrent value (Volumatic Ltd)*

7.25 *Closed circuit television camera (Volumatic Ltd)*

7.26 *Closed circuit television central monitors (Pye Business Communications Ltd)*

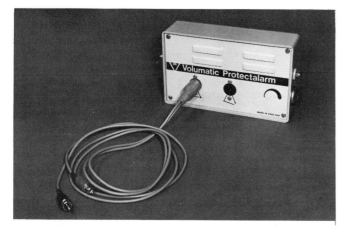

7.27 *Electric loop: this is linked to an electric alarm*

7.28 *Security chain: this gives physical protection only*

8
ENVIRONMENTAL SERVICES

8.1 LIGHTING

Aims

The correct use of lighting in shops can have an important influence on sales. Artificial lighting must not be regarded solely as an alternative to daylight but as one of the essential features of good interior design. The main purposes which interior lighting has to fulfil in shops are:

1 To show the goods on display as clearly and attractively as possible in a way that attracts customers' attention.

2 To employ colour in a manner that suits and complements the display.

3 To be flexible enough to accommodate changes in display or layout.

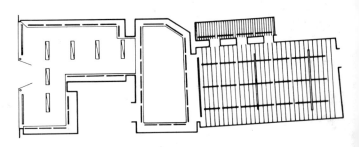

8.2 Lighting plan for a stationery shop. Branch of Ryman Lamport Gilbert in Reading designed by Robin Gilbert of the Ryman-Conran Design Group. The areas of continuous suspended lighting in the front and middle section of the shop have perimeter lighting using batten fittings behind vertical baffles; shallow surface-mounted fittings create a built-in impression. The rear area of the existing premises had an exposed pitched roof structure, and the lines of tubes here are effectively screened by a series of lateral white-painted baffles in 230 × 25mm boarding at 380mm centres. Initially the three 5m runs of electrified track in this area have been fitted with high-intensity spotlights for 100W crown-silvered lamps, while the 2·4m length in each window has adjustable holders for 150W blown-bulb reflector lamps; the arrangement can of course be readily changed if it is thought desirable

⊢———⊣	fluorescent tubes supported by spring clips (remote control gear)
⊢═══⊣	batten fittings for one 65W tube mounted in recess in ceiling
o	recessed downlight
•	special surface-mounted cylinder with 50W 12V lamp
◉	adjustable spotlight for 50W 12V crown-silvered lamp
✗	special surface-mounted cylinder with 150W reflector lamp
O	special surface-mounted cylinder with 125W mercury reflector lamp
⊕	low-brightness recessed fitting for 150W PAR 38 lamp
⊕	semi-recessed fitting for 100W pearl lamp
⊘	decorative aluminium penant for 100W pearl lamp
⊓⊓⊓	wall fitting (5 × 40W clear tubular lamps)

8.1 Lighting plan for a shoe shop. Branch of Dolcis Ltd, Brompton Road, London SW3 designed by Ellis E. Somake, Chief Architect, British Shoe Corporation. The drawings give simplified layouts of the lighting equipment in the areas shown, namely A hosiery section and staircase just inside the main entrance B display windows and C handbag counter and display in a corner of the ladies' main salon on the first floor

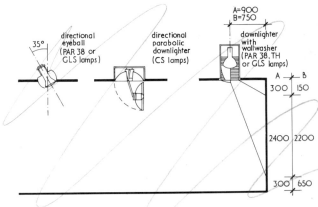

8.3 Types of directional downlighters

4 To use the correct illumination level for each task and avoid the uneconomical use of electricity.

5 To avoid glare.

Typical lighting plans for two types of shop are shown in Figs **8.1** and **8.2**. Downlighters (Figs **8.3** and **8.4**), spotlights (Fig **8.5**) and reflectors (Fig **8.5** to **8.13**) are devices which may assist in producing satisfactory results.

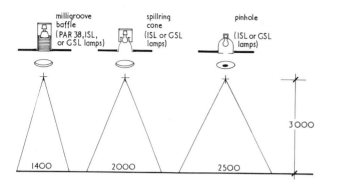

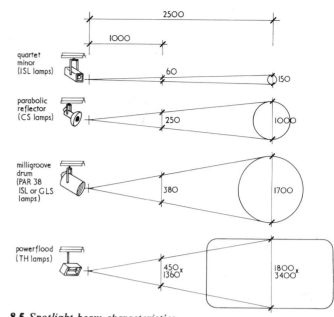

8.4 *Beam characteristics of downlighters*

8.5 *Spotlight beam characteristics*

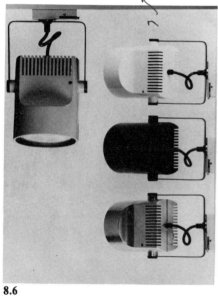

8.6

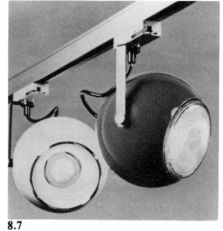

8.7

8.8

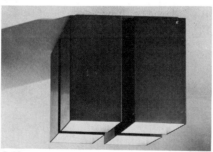

8.10

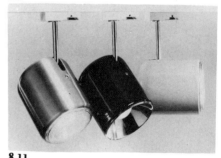

8.11

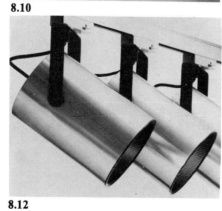

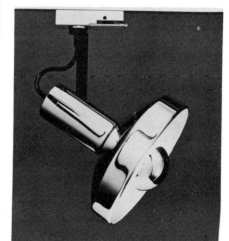

8.9

8.12

8.6 *Proprietary types of reflector. Mainline spots* **8.7** *Globe spots* **8.8** *CS spot* **8.9** *TH Unifloods* **8.10** *Square downlighters* **8.11** *Acorn spots (Merchant Adventurers Ltd)* **8.12** *Milligrove drums* **8.13** *Standard CS spot*

8.13

The shop window

The degree to which shop windows should be illuminated depends on whether the general lighting level of the neighbourhood in which they are situated is high, medium or low. As a general guide 600 to 900 watts per metre window run is suitable for a district of high lighting level (eg the central shopping centre of a large town), 300 to 600 for one of medium level (eg the main street of a large town) and 150 to 300 for one of low level (eg the main street of a small town). The apparent brightness of windows is affected by the reflectance factors of the materials displayed in them: these vary according to texture and hue (for example black velvet has a reflectance factor of 0·5 per cent, polished silver of 86 per cent). The following table gives guidance on how reflectors could be spaced, according to district brightness and window size.

Table I Guide for spacing reflectors in shop windows

Window size Height (m)	Depth (m)	District brightness level	Spacing of reflectors (mm) 60W	75W	100W	150W	200W
2·0	1·0	L	525	-	-	-	-
		M	250	350	500	-	-
		H	-	-	325	500	-
2·0	1·5	L	450	600	-	-	-
		M	-	300	425	-	-
		H	-	-	300	450	-
2·5	1·2	L	400	500	-	-	-
		M	-	250	375	575	-
		H	-	-	250	375	550
2·5	1·8	L	350	450	-	-	-
		M	-	-	350	500	-
		H	-	-	450×2	350	475
3·0	1·5	L	325	425	600	-	-
		M	-	-	300	450	-
		H	-	-	400×2	325	450
3·0	2·5	L	275	350	500	-	-
		M	-	-	250	400	575
		H	-	-	350×2	275	375
3·5	1·8	L	250	300	475	-	-
		M	-	-	250	375	550
		H	-	-	350×2	275	375
3·5	2·5	L	250	350	475	-	-
		M	-	-	450×2	350	475
		H	-	-	325×2	250	350
3·5	3·5	L	-	275	400	600	-
		M	-	-	375×2	300	425
		H	-	-	250×2	400×2	575×2

Notes on abbreviations in the above table:
L = Low brightness (main street of small town)
M = Medium brightness (main street of large town)
H = High brightness (central shopping area of large town)
×2 after figure denotes two rows

The usual method of lighting shop windows is to place the lamps on the upper part of the window so as to distribute light evenly on the window bed where the merchandise is displayed. People do not normally look up at an angle of more than 45°; nevertheless if the lights in a window are powerful they should be screened by baffles, louvres, pelmets, or reflectors. Other positions for window lighting are on the window bed and vertically behind the window frame. These positions may only be used where windows have a closed back: otherwise they produce excessive glare inside the shop. Where window displays play an important part in sales policy the lighting must be flexible enough to permit layouts to be rearranged and fittings changed to suit display requirements. Lack of flexibility is a serious drawback and the effect of a rigid pattern may be to draw the eye away from the merchandise. It is normal for window lighting to be controlled by a timer switch to suit the requirements of members of the public who wish to go window shopping after closing hours. Lighting for an enclosed and for an open display window is shown in Fig **8.14**.

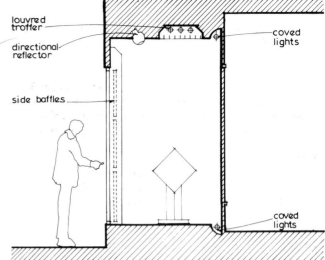

Enclosed display window

Closed display window

8.14 *Lighting for an enclosed and for an open display window*

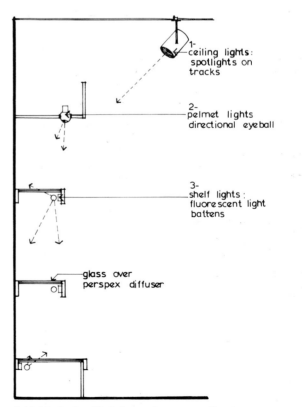

8.15 *Methods of lighting a showcase wall unit*

The interior

The requirements for interior lighting will vary according to the size, shape, type and character of shop.

Ceiling

Light fittings may be integrated or independently suspended from the ceiling; a dark background visually lowers the ceiling whereas a bright background increases its apparent heights; ceilings should not be too brightly lit or they will become too dominating.

Walls

Indirect lighting on walls produces a hazy quality that is sometimes desirable; wall light fittings are not always suitable if they compete for space with storage or display fixtures.

Displays

Directional reflectors can be used to make displays stand out from backgrounds.

Showcases

These can be internally lit with concealed fittings and kept alight after closing time by using a time control; the use of trailing flexes should be minimised. Three ways of lighting a showcase wall unit are shown in Fig **8.15**.

Counters

Lights can be suspended from the ceiling or from an overhanging canopy; care should be taken to avoid reflections on glass tops; freestanding fixtures require built-in sockets to avoid trailing flexes.

8.16 *Proprietary decorative interior lighting (Yubido Ltd)*

Fitting rooms

Lighting should be placed so as to illuminate the customer, not the mirror; soft diffuse lighting is usually preferable to harsh lighting; quality shops may have lamps of several colours so as to allow customers to view clothing under different lighting conditions; an illuminated 'Engaged' sign can be installed outside the cubicle.

Standard lighting levels

Table II taken from the IES (Illuminating Engineering Society) Code 1973 equates standard illuminance values (measured in lux) with the IES Limiting Glare Index (a scale calculated according to a method adopted by the IES which enables the degree of discomfort caused by glare from a lighting installation to be classified in order of severity and permissible limits to be prescribed):

Attractions within a uniform background

In plain very symmetrical lighting layouts the customers' attention is not drawn to any particular point of the store and this results in a tendency for them to remain congregated near entrances. A receding line of lights may be planned in such circumstances to attract the eye towards the rear of the store. When this is done there should be a culmination in a brightly lit display at the end. Where the background lighting is mainly uneventful, decorative lighting (which usually gives little light) may be employed to draw attention and give sparkle. Typical examples of such a technique are the use made of chandeliers in luxury shops or of art-deco lamps in boutiques or antique shops. A cubic chandelier is shown in Fig **8.16**.

External lighting

In most shops, external lighting (floodlighting) of the shopfront tends to distract attention from the windows without producing any conspicuous advantage. To be effective floodlighting has to be done on a generous scale (which may not be acceptable to local authorities). Adequate external lighting may be provided by illuminated signs (see section 6.3 above).

Emergency lighting

Two categories of emergency lighting may be considered desirable: escape lighting and stand-by lighting.

Escape lighting

Escape lighting is needed to enable the building to be evacuated quickly and safely. It must come into operation immediately the normal lighting system fails. In some areas it may be permanently switched on. Escape lighting must be fed from power sources independent of the main lighting system. The following factors

Table II Standard service values of illumination and limiting values of glare index

Sectional area	Standard service illuminance (lux)	Position of measurement	Limiting glare index
A Sales floor			
1 Conventional with counters	500	Counters (horizontal)	19
2 Conventional with wall display	500	Display (vertical)	19
3 Self service	500	Vertical on displayed goods	19
4 Supermarket	500	Vertical as above	22
5 Hypermarket	500	Vertical as above	22
	1000	Horizontal on working plane	22
6 Showroom			
— car	500	Vertical on cars	19
— general	500	Merchandise	19
B Offices			
1 General office with mainly clerical staff doing occasional typing	500	Desk	19
2 Executive office	500	Desk	19
3 Business machine and typing office	750	Desk	19
4 Filing room	300	Filing	19
5 Conference room	750	Table	16
C Ancillary rooms			
1 Stockrooms, packing and dispatch	300	Vertical on displayed goods or worktop	22
2 Cloakroom, toilets	150	Basin	22
3 Workrooms			
— general	500	Workbench	22
— drawing board	750	Board	16

should be taken into consideration when planning escape lighting:

1 All escape routes and exit doors should be clearly visible.

2 All changes in level, ramps and stairs should be specially illuminated.

3 There must be no interference with ventilation and sprinkler systems.

4 Incandescent lamps (which can operate on either alternating or direct current) are the simplest type to use (fluorescent lamps give higher illumination and last longer but require higher voltages).

Stand-by lighting

Stand-by lighting is needed to allow activities to continue during a power failure and is usually suitable only for the larger department stores.

Light fittings

Light fittings may be broadly divided into three categories:

1 Decorative fittings: intended to attract the eye rather than to give optimum lighting distribution and performance.

2 General utility fittings: intended to be economical and efficient at producing adequate background illumination; the main types and the directions in which they cast light are the direct (downwards), the semi-direct (mainly downwards, sometimes upwards), the semi-indirect (mainly upwards or sideways, but sometimes downwards) and the indirect (upwards or sideways).

3 Special fittings: these have designed optical arrangements such as reflectors, baffles or filters to suit particular conditions (some reflectors may also be classified as decorative fittings).

Light fittings should be strong enough to withstand handling, erection and cleaning operations. Ideally they should obscure the lamp from direct view so as to reduce glare. If they do not do so the lamp should present a large surface area of low brightness. With fluorescent fittings the function of reducing glare is performed by diffuser panels which may be any of the following types:

(a) Opal: a simple acrylic panel for use where glare ratings are not important.

(b) Prismatic: available in a range of patterns to give varying degrees of light control.

(c) Polarised: a sheet panel used where strict control of glare is desirable.

(d) Louvred: available in plastic, anodised aluminium, or stove-enamelled aluminium and suitable for producing a surface area of low brightness.

Types of lamp

Lamps are usually incandescent or fluorescent. Incandescent lamps are small and very bright and produce a bright, sparkling quality of light with sharp shadows. Fluorescent lamps give about three times more light than incandescent lamps for a given electrical consumption. They are much cheaper to run and give out less heat into the building. In order to employ both types of lamps to their best advantage fluorescent lamps should be used to give general background illumination and incandescent lamps used discriminatingly to give sparkle to merchandise. High pressure discharge lamps are sometimes used to illuminate large space users such as supermarkets, hypermarkets and shopping precincts.

Incandescent lamps

The main types of incandescent or filament lamps are:

GLS (General lighting service): 15 to 200 watts; average life 1000 hours; low cost general purpose lamps. The envelope may be clear, pearl, silica coated or coloured. The light output is approximately uniform in all directions. Clear lamps give a sparkling effect, pearl or silica coated lamps give a diffuse effect. The main colours in which lamps are made are amber, green, pink, yellow, and red.

ISL (Internally silvered reflector lamp): 25 to 150 watts; average life 800 hours. Lamps have a built-in reflector producing accurately controlled beams. They are used for spotlighting.

PAR (Parabolic aluminised reflector lamp): 100 to 300 watts; average life 2000 hours. These are made from heat resistant glass with built-in reflector and lens front designed with either spot or flood distribution. A coolbeam variant produces light with reduced heat component in the beam. Lamps are clear or coloured.

CSL (Crown silver lamp): 100 watts; average life 1000 hours. These are designed for use with parabolic reflectors to provide beam with little spill or filament glare.

TH (Tungsten halogen lamp): 300 to 500 watts; average life 2000 hours. These have a high light output and long life with virtually 100 per cent light output maintained throughout their lifespan. The lamp envelope is more robust than others because of use of quartz material.

Fluorescent lamps

Fluorescent lamps are normally from 10 to 125 watts and their average life is 7500 hours. A range of both 'warm' and 'cold' colours is available. The light produced is diffuse in quality reducing form and shadow. Lamps require special start control gear. S/S (switchstart) fluorescents flicker when switched on. Q/S (quickstart) light immediately but are more expensive. Lamps are available in straight lengths 150 to 2400 mm, in circular tubes 200 to 400 mm diameter, and in U-shaped tubes. It is recommended that fluorescent lamps should be used for shop lighting as follows:

Tube colour	Colour rendering quality	Colour appearance	Applications
White	Fair	Intermediate	General display lighting requiring maximum light output but without the need of good colour quality: office, stockrooms
Plus white	Good	Intermediate	General lighting where reasonably good colour rendering is required covering the complete visible spectrum
De-luxe warm white	Good	Warm	Gives filament lamp effect: furniture shops, restaurants, reception
Natural	Good	Intermediate	Jewellery, glassware, china, hardware, tailors (main shop area), clothing and footwear
De-luxe natural	Very good	Intermediate	Florists, fishmongers, butchers, grocers, supermarkets and brightly coloured merchandise
Kolor-rite	Good	Intermediate	Where true reproduction of colour is required (gives the effect of a sunny day): showrooms
Home-lite	Good	Warm	For interiors requiring a warmer appearance than provided by filament lamps
Northlight	Good	Cool	Produces a cool effect: furriers and tailors (colour matching areas)
Gro-lux	-	-	For plant growth purposes and aquarium lighting where it stimulates aquatic plant growth: plants and fish look more vivid
Coloured	-	-	Green, gold, red and blue: for special decorative effects; pink produces a very warm effect

Discharge lamps

Discharge lamps may be high pressure or low pressure types. Low pressure types emit a distinct yellow light so that all colours except yellow appear brown or black. Light colours appear grey. This poor colour rendering makes them unacceptable in commercial use and consequently they are only used on roadways and industrial areas. High pressure discharge lamps however have reasonable colour rendering. Added to their other qualities of high light efficacy and long life, they become attractive for retail use. Mostly they are used in situations where the interior space has high bays or where lamp maintenance is difficult or costly.

High pressure discharge lamp characteristics are as follows:

Lamp type	Colour rendering	Operational characteristics
Mercury Halide (MBI)	Equal emphasis to greens and blues, mostly yellow. Red rendering variable according to manufacturer.	Run-up period to full light output about 5 minutes less if special circuits used. Clear outer bulb.
Mercury Fluorescent (MBF)	Emphasises yellows and blues which shift towards violet. Subdues reds.	Run-up and ignition times as for MBI. Outer bulb with fluorescent coating.
...ure ...ON)	Emphasises yellow strongly, reds to lesser extent. Greens acceptable. Blues which shift towards violet strongly subdued.	Run-up period to full light output about 2 minutes. Diffuse outer bulb.

Maintenance

Light fittings require comprehensive maintenance. Their efficiency is affected by the accumulation of dust on lamps, reflectors and diffusing panels. To prevent serious loss seasonal cleaning is necessary, if not by the staff, then by a maintenance contractor. Incandescent lamps with an average life of between 1000 and 2000 hours require replacing at about six-monthly intervals. Fluorescent lamps with longer life last up to 7500 hours but with higher daily use may require replacing every two years. A maintenance contract can be provided on this basis, to arrive at a compromise between constant cleaning or constant replacement. This is invariably on the basis that all incandescent lamps should be replaced and all fluorescent lamps and all fittings cleaned every six months, and that all incandescent and fluorescent lamps should be replaced and all fittings cleaned every two years. To avoid excessive wastage lamps which are scheduled for replacement but found to be still in working order can be continued in use but confined to a specially designated area where it can then be known that every lamp has an uncertain length of life. By this means lamps on the sales floor can be guaranteed a trouble-free period of life while those in the designated area can be replaced as necessary. This arrangement overcomes the disruption caused on the sales floor whenever a lamp fails.

8.2 HEATING

General considerations

When planning for heating services, as well as for ventilation or air conditioning services, the following considerations should be taken into account:

Locality: how the shop is orientated bearing in mind the effects which may be expected from the weather in a particular place.

Site: a densely built area such as a town centre provides more shelter than a suburban or resort site which may be severely exposed.

Insulation: the efficiency of the insulation and the total area of glazing in the building as a whole.

Internal gains: the amount of heats and humidity expected to be generated by occupants, lighting and machinery.

Comfort: the standard of comfort which it is desired to provide for customers and how this is to be achieved on the budget available. In Great Britain statutory regulations made under the Offices Shops and Railway Premises Act 1963 require that the internal temperature in shops shall not fall below 16°C but this is a minimum figure and the temperatures which should be recommended are 18°C for the sales floor, 20°C for general offices, staff rooms and canteen and 16°C for the working area in stores, and for cloakrooms, lobbies and general circulation.

Types of system

The heating systems suitable for use in shops fall into the following categories:

Electric unit heaters: pre-packaged units with wire coil-heating elements, electric fans and adjustable louvres to direct heated air. Ducted warm air: heated by electricity or other fuels in a central plant and distributed in overhead ducts.

Low pressure hot water: service pipes take hot water to outlets fitted with fan convectors for more efficient distribution.

In considering the type of installation suitable for a particular situation, the following points will affect the final choice:

1 The system should be cheap to install and economical to run.
2 The sales floor should be kept as free from heating equipment as possible.
3 The equipment should have a rapid response capability to external temperature changes.
4 The equipment should require the minimum attention and be thermostatically controlled.

Electric unit heaters

This is the most popular system for heating small shops. The heaters are independent units and can therefore be distributed as required. This gives great flexibility because it is possible to use only those units which are required at any particular time. The main advantages of this system are:

1 Quick and low installation costs.
2 Adjustability for position or direction.
3 Immediate response capability.
4 The assurance that the whole heating system cannot break down at the same time.
5 Absence of fumes or products of combustion.
6 Easy removability when layouts have to be changed or a department is closed.

There are three basic types of electric unit heaters:

(a) Fan heaters: most models have variable control up to their maximum of 3 to 15 kW heat output. In summer units may be set to operate so as to give air movement but no heat. Models may be either portable to plug into socket outlets or permanently fixed to walls or ceiling. One special type fits above the entrance door to combat the effect of draughts by blowing a downwards current of hot air. These light slimline units may be used singly for single door-width openings or in series for multiple banks of doors. They are commonly referred to as 'air-curtains' or 'thermo-screens'.

(b) Night storage radiators: these operate on off-peak tariffs and are therefore more economical to run. But they are heavy and bulky: they cannot therefore be wall- or ceiling-mounted and they compete for floor space with display units and restrict the planning of layouts. The most acceptable positions are at the end of gondolas or storage racks. It should be made clear that storage radiators rated at 3 KW do not produce 3 kW of heat in the same way as ordinary electic heaters: the figure refers to their charging rate. Thus during an average off-peak charging period from 11 pm to 7 am such a heater will store 3 kW an hour for 8 hours (24 kW hours of heat). This is released over the next 16 hours to give an average output of 1·5 kW per hour. The sluggish response of storage heaters to heat demand makes them an unpopular choice.

(c) Radiant heaters: these consist of a single sheathed element in a compact reflector which produces infra-red radiation. Ratings range from 0·75 to 1·5 kW. The units are usually wall-mounted in a high position and operated by a pull cord. They are suitable for use in toilets, store rooms and food shops (such as delicatessens) where warm air would damage the food.

Ducted warm air

Ducted air systems involve relatively high installation costs which make them unsuitable for small shops. Large retail units prefer this system because it can be combined with ventilation or air-conditioning systems. It makes the best possible use of space because the ducting can be concealed above the false ceiling to leave the sales floor totally clear. Its central heating plant may be supplied by electricity, gas, oil, or solid fuels. Electric heaters may be on direct heating coils or on storage heaters which charge up overnight on off-peak tariffs. Other fuels require adequate provision for the discharge of exhaust gases and liquid fuels also require storage facilities which must comply with local regulations and by-laws.

Low pressure hot water

This system consists of conventional low pressure hot water service pipes serving radiators fitted with fan convectors. The radiator units may be fixed to walls or ceilings and may incorporate additional electric heating coils for immediate response. The system allows for air circulation in the summer without heating and provides for constant hot water facilities. If required it is possible to circulate cool water or refrigerants through the pipes so as to produce a cooling effect but the refrigeration plant is of course very expensive to fit. Like that used for warm air systems the central plant may be served by electricity, gas, oil or solid fuels.

8.3 VENTILATION

Aims

Proper ventilation is an important requirement in achieving the following aims:
1 Control of temperature and humidity
2 Adequate supply of oxygen
3 Efficient extraction of smells and smoke
4 Preventing the deterioration of merchandise.
The following general standards for ventilation have been laid down by the Institute of Heating and Ventilating Engineers (IHVE) (the precise number of air changes which is desirable must also depend on the number of persons expected to occupy each particular area of the shop):

Table III Recommended ventilation rate

Type of shop	Number of air changes per hour	Outdoor air supply per m² of floor area (litre/s)
General shops		
sales floor	8	3·0
offices and lavatories	6	1·3
stores, cloakrooms, lobbies and circulation	2 to 3	1·0
Special shops		
hairdressers, laundries, fishmongers, shoe repairs, workshops	10 to 15	–

Ventilation systems

Ventilation may be natural or mechanical. Natural ventilation requires effective temperature differences or winds to induce air movement. With mechanical ventilation air movement is induced by power driven fans. These can be either of axial or centrifugal type and may be mounted on walls, glazing (including the shopfront), or roofs (if site conditions permit). Most models run at pre-set speeds (typically, low, normal and boost). Variable speed controls can be achieved quite easily with the incorporation of auto-transformers. Other additional fittings are air and grease filters, flexible ducting and terminal grilles for connection to false ceilings (which permit ventilation of shops where the interior is subdivided by internal partitioning). The methods which can be used for ventilation can be classified as follows:

1 Natural inlet and extract: this applies to small shops where occupancy is low. Adequate ventilation is achieved by the natural cross flow of air between the front entrance doors and openings at the rear (openable windows or controllable shutters).

2 Natural inlet and mechanical extract: with this method a negative pressure is set up inside the shop causing air to leak inwards rather than outwards. The system is suitable for supplying fresh air but not for extracting smoke unless the supply of air is adequate to balance the volume which has to be extracted.

3 Mechanical inlet and natural extract: this method delivers air to the interior through ducted systems, allowing extracted air to pass out through door openings. Facilities for filtering and heating air are usually incorporated.

4 Mechanical inlet and extract: this method is capable of the widest application because distribution, pressure and temperature can all be controlled.

Where exhausting is through walls ventilator fans should be protected by baffles or made to discharge in a vertical direction upwards or downwards: this avoids the considerable noise and the reduction in volume of air exhausted which is caused if a current of air is allowed to blow in the opposite direction to the fan discharge.

8.18 *Small ventilator units: this one is suitable for fixing through glass*

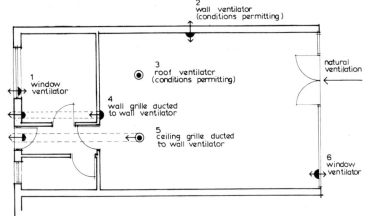

8.17 *Siting of ventilator units in a small shop. For general extract the units should be sited as high as possible, particularly over sources of steam or smell. To give the best results they should be well distributed and allow for cross ventilation*

8.19 *Same. This model is suitable for wall or false ceiling mounting*

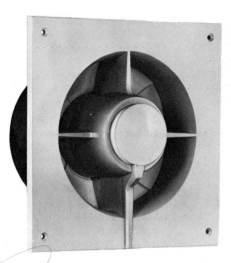

8.20 *Same. A panel-mounted model*

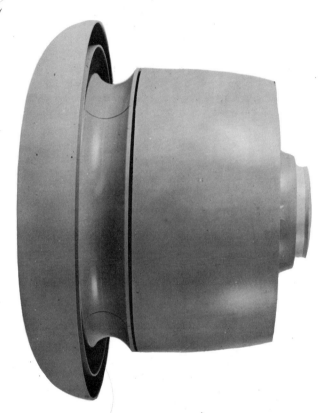

8.21 *Same. One of the models available for roof fixing*

8.22 *Same. Darkroom model (Vent-Axia Ltd)*

Where exhausting is through windows glazing sizes and glass substances should take into consideration vibration stresses from the exhaust fans: the following table gives a guide to the sizes which it is not desirable to exceed:

Table IV Recommended maximum sizes of glazing and glass substances to accommodate window fan ventilators

Glass substance (mm)		Maximum glazing sizes (m²)
Normal conditions	Exposed conditions	
4	5	1·0
5	6	1·5
6	10	2·0

Internal wall or ceiling 'punkah' type of fans should not be considered as providing ventilation. They merely stir air round the interior and in so doing provide a mild cooling effect. A selection of small ventilator units is shown in Figs **8.17** to **8.21** and Fig **8.22** illustrates a scheme for siting ventilators in a small shop.

8.4 AIR CONDITIONING

Aims

Whereas ventilation systems involve the delivery of air which may or may not have been warmed, air-conditioning systems involve the delivery of air which has been warmed or cooled and has had its humidity raised or lowered. In summer the requirement is a supply of fresh air which has been cleaned and cooled: as the cooling process increases the relative humidity of the air a dehumidifying process is necessary; this may be accomplished by exposing the air to cold surfaces or cold spray whereby the excess moisture is condensed. In winter the requirement is a supply of fresh air which has been cleaned and warmed: the warming process lowers the relative humidity and some form of humidifying plant such as a spray washer is therefore necessary. Air conditioning may be suitable for use in any of the following types of building:
1 Stores where large crowds of people congregate at any one time.
2 Stores where natural ventilation is inadequate due to the depth of the core behind window areas.
3 Stores which experience considerable heat gains from solar exposure or incidental sources such as lighting, occupants and any heat-producing equipment.
4 Exclusive stores where the comfort of customers is a major priority.

Heat gains

Solar heat gain
Solar heat gains can be considerable and may make up a significant part of the total heat gains. Values are dependent on geographical location, site orientation, extent of vertical or horizontal plane occupied, month of the year and time of day. (Calculations for such heat gains are complex and beyond the scope of this section.)

Heat from occupants
Heat is emitted from the human body at approximately the following rates:

Table V Heat from occupants at 20°C and 60% relative humidity

Activity	Heat emission per occupant (Watts)		
	Total	Latent	Sensible
Light desk work (offices)	140	40	100
Walking (customers)	160	50	110
Light manual work (sales staff)	235	105	130
Heavy work (goods handling)	440	250	190

The heat emitted from the human body is partly sensible heat and partly latent heat from perspiration and vapour in the breath. Sensible heat alone affects the internal temperature of a room. The number of customers at peak periods may be taken as one person per 2·32 m² of the sales floor ares.

Heat from lighting

Heat produced by lighting can be easily calculated by adding up the wattage ratings of all lamps without involving any conversions.

Heat from machines

Machines, in particular refrigerated cabinets, can produce considerable heat gains. Where the wattage consumption is known, the formula to estimate heat output (Q) is:

$$Q = W (1-E) \text{ watts}$$

where E is the efficiency ratio (usually between 0·75 and 0·92). Where the wattage is not known, but the motor rating is given in horse power the formula to estimate the heat output is:

$$Q = 746 \times \text{h.p.} \left(\frac{1}{E}-1\right) \text{ watts.}$$

Types of system

Various air conditioning systems are available to suit various types of buildings. These most commonly employ central plant, zoning or self-contained units. Heat pumps are a recent development which is finding favour with some high street multiple shop operators.

Central plant

This system is suitable for supermarkets and hypermarkets where there is one large space to be air conditioned (ie only one set of conditions has to be provided for). The elements of the system (fans, filters, refrigeration plant, heating coils, humidification plant and control system) are all housed in the central plant.

Zoned system

This is a system suitable for department stores and large variety stores where there are a number of rooms or floors to be served. The building is divided into zones with as similar conditions as possible. Units receive an air supply conditioned to an average temperature and humidity from a central plant. Each zone is supplied with its own local recirculating fan and booster cooler and heater. In such a system each floor may form an independent zone but under certain conditions it may be desirable to have separate zones within floors (if, for example, one elevation of the building faces north and the other south).

Self-contained units

These are suitable for small shops and premises where duct systems are not possible. The units are 'packages' complete in themselves. They are mass produced to make them as cheap as possible and are not therefore tailored to suit specific requirements. They are designed either solely for the purpose of recirculating internal air or for drawing in fresh air through an intake. Small units are suitable for single rooms and generally have an air cooled condenser. Much larger sizes are available and in these the condenser may be water cooled. Otherwise the only services needed are an electrical supply and a connection to drain away any condensed moisture. 'Split' systems have the relatively small distribution and central unit housed separately from the bulkier compressor unit: this allows the former to be fitted indoors in the area which is to be air conditioned leaving the latter to be placed outdoors or on any other suitable indoor site.

Heat pump

A heat pump has the facility of providing either heating or cooling. In some circumstances 'heating only' may be specified but in general the capital costs can only support the dual role.

The heat pump borrows the principle of the refrigerator. The refrigerator extracts heat from a confined space near the evaporator and gives it off in the condenser. In the refrigerator this heat is lost in the air, but it could be used as a source for heating air or water. When the condenser is used for heating purposes, it is called a heat pump. If the system is used in a building, the evaporator can be used for cooling in summer and the condenser for heating in winter. The external coil which is located outdoors extracts heat from any available source such as air, water (river, pond, lake) and the ground.

Present apathy towards heat pumps is mainly because of higher plant costs compared with traditional systems and of low outdoor air temperature in winter months. With increasing fuel costs however, heat pumps are becoming competitive. To supplement the heat output from the condenser coil during very cold spells a boost heater may be incorporated in the unit which is automatically switched on once the outside air temperature falls below a preset level.

9
ENGINEERING SERVICES

9.1 ELECTRICAL SUPPLY

IEE regulations
Electrical installations are subject to codes and regulations produced by the Institute of Electrical Engineers (IEE). These stipulate standards of quality, performance and protection in the interests of safety to occupants. Briefly their aim is to avoid leakage of current and outbreak of fire and to ensure proper earthing so as to avoid users getting electric shocks.

Site supply
The electrical service cable normally terminates inside a building in a mains cut-off which is situated as near as possible to the service cable entry. Everything up to and including this cut-off, including the meter, is the responsibility of the Electricity Board. The electricity supply in Great Britain is normally single phase, 240 volts, at 60 Hz. If three-phase supply is required it can be obtained by lodging an application with the local electricity board. The four core cable used for this form of supply (colour coded red, yellow or white and blue for phases and black for neutral) will run via an isolating switch or circuit breaker to the mains distribution board. This may operate at 415 volts between any two phase conductors or 240 volts between any phase conductor and neutral.

Fuses and circuit breakers
Protection must be provided in a circuit to safeguard the wiring, appliances and equipment connected to it against the flow of larger currents than the circuit has been designed to carry. The protective device used should be capable of detecting an overloading so as to isolate the faulty circuit before damage can occur.

Re-wireable fuses
These are used extensively on low voltage systems with ratings up to 200 amps and 250 volts, but there are some disadvantages:
1 The high temperature at which the fuse operates causes it to oxidise and contract.
2 The amount of excess current needed to operate the fuse cannot easily be forecast.
3 It may take several seconds for the fuse to break if a fault occurs.
4 The fuse takes a long time to replace.

Cartridge fuses
These are more efficient and more easily replaced than re-wireable fuses. The fuse wire is held together between two metal caps in a glass tube filled with insulating material.

Circuit breakers
These are mechanical devices for making and breaking the circuit and may be operated by hand as well as automatically. It is usual for them to be provided with a delay so that they are not affected by moderate short term overloading and break instantaneously under heavy load or short circuit conditions. Although more expensive to install than alternative systems circuit breakers offer a number of advantages because they can be easily re-set after an electrical fault has been repaired thus causing little loss of time and disturbance to customers. When circuit breakers are used in three-phase systems all three phases are opened simultaneously when failure occurs on one of them.

Electricity cupboards
Electrical control gear must be protected from damp, heat and hazard. This calls for the housing of the equipment in an electricity cupboard measuring approximately 750 mm wide × 450 mm deep × 1500 mm high. The control equipment which this has to house consists of the service cable, a single or triple pole supply head, one electricity meter (or three if the supply is three-phase), a mains switch, a fuse box or set of circuit breakers, time clocks and a bank of master switches. Other equipment requiring the same storage conditions can be housed with the electrical control gear (eg Post Office power and relay units and fire and security control units) and in this case the cupboard should measure 750 mm wide × 450 mm deep × 2500 mm high. A minimum clear space of 750 mm must be allowed in front of the cupboard for access.

Distribution systems
Trunking
Where a large number of cables has to be run along the same route it is more economical to enclose them in trunking than to install a number of separate conduits. Trunking is manufactured from sheet metal or plastic and the most common sizes are 50 × 50 mm, 75 × 75 mm, 100 × 50 mm, 100 × 100 mm and 150 × 150 mm. Metal trunking is bolted together but to ensure satisfactory earthing copper earthing straps should be fitted over each joint. Trunking can be obtained with subdivisions so that various cables for other services may also be included in the same enclosure. Trunking systems should include outlet boxes at frequent intervals to give maximum flexibility of use.

Conduit
In this system plastic or rubber insulated cables are run in metal tubes. They are completely protected and can be replaced wherever necessary. Two types of conduit system are available, the continuity or grip joint conduit and the heavy gauge screwed conduit, seamless or with welded joints.

Plastic sheath
This system uses plastic insulated cables contained in a plastic sheath. If these are used on the surface the sheath must be carefully protected from mechanical damage. If they are buried in plaster they are usually additionally protected by short lengths of conduit.

Mineral insulated metal sheath
This is known as the Pyro system. It uses expensive and very high

quality fire resistant cable. The sheathing is copper and the insulation a special heat resistant mineral. Sometimes the outer copper sheath is covered with PVC. The copper sheath acts as a conductor and can contain one, two or three other conductors inside. The Pyro system is usually installed without additional protection. Landlords or Local Authorities may stipulate that it must be used if the shop is part of a building subject to stringent fire regulations.

Socket outlets

Socket outlets may be single or multiple, switched or unswitched, surface of flush mounted and with or without indicator lights. The normal recommended height is a minimum of 150 mm above the floor or 1200 mm if over a worktop. Usually double sockets are preferred to two single sockets because they are considerably cheaper and discourage the use of adaptors. Socket outlets should normally be placed
(a) on perimeter walls or in floor boxes or ceiling outlets;
(b) so as to be readily accessible using only the shortest lengths of flex;
(c) so as to be away from exposed or frequently used areas;
(d) so as not to be obscured by any likely rearrangement of furniture or fittings;
(e) as built-in fixtures so as to avoid trailing lengths of flex.

Demand loads

In order to decide what the total current carrying capacity of an electricity system is going to be, the ratings of the conductors which should be used in it, and whether it should operate on single phase or three-phase supply it is necessary to make separate calculations for the respective demand loads which will be placed on it by lighting and by electrical equipment.

Lighting load

This can be calculated from the specifications for all the lighting equipment to be used or it can be estimated on the basis of the average loads to be expected in different parts of the shop. Estimates of this kind may be made on the following basis:

Table I General lighting load

Area	Average load (watts/m²)
Sales area	30 to 65
Staff, office areas	55
Stockroom, toilets	25
Electrical appliances shop	50 to 120

Electrical equipment loads

The loading produced by electrical equipment can be established by making an overall assessment from the manufacturers' specifications for all the equipment which is to be used including heating, air conditioning equipment and specialised items like refrigerated cabinets. As a general guide the values to be taken are:
Heating: allow 35 to 50 watts per m³ of the space to be heated

Water heating:
$$\text{No. of watts} = \frac{\text{No. of litres} \times \text{Temperature rise in } °\text{C}}{\text{Time in minutes} \times 2}$$

Motors: allow 1000 watts per unit horsepower
The estimated demand load must include capacity for future expansion. An allowance of 20 to 30 per cent over the maximum load is adequate.

Planning

Early consultation between the architect, electrical contractor and the Electricity Board is essential to determine the satisfactory installation of the electrical supply. The following points should be determined at the planning stage:
1 The estimated load (whether the existing supply is adequate).
2 The point of entry of service cables (for any new supply).
3 The type of installation (whether there is need for a three-phase supply).
4 The need for protection of switch gear (electricity cupboard).
5 Where additional gear (Post Office units, security alarms, fire alarms) is to be housed.
6 Distribution (routing of vertical and horizontal cable runs).

Emergency power

Stand-by generators may be required in some premises to provide power for emergency lighting and essential services such as fire fighting pumps or refrigerated cabinets in case of mains power failure. Most generators are diesel operated and are automatically brought into action on power failure. They should be installed in non-combustible enclosures with adequate air supply for the prime mover. Exhaust gases must be safely dispersed and any noise reduced as much as possible. Storage facilities for liquid fuels must comply with the relevant by-laws and regulations. Where lighting is the only service which has to be provided for in an emergency power can be supplied for it from local individual batteries attached to the light fittings. Alternatively this power supply can be centralised in a battery room. Most installations use lead/acid batteries, or nickel/alkali batteries. Batteries are housed on racks and the battery room must be provided with acid-resistant walls and floors. Ventilation must be adequate to dissipate the gases produced during the charging-up operation. Planning and siting of battery rooms should take into account the needs for delivery and storage of carboys of acid and distilled water.

9.2 WATER SUPPLY

Cold water

A supply of water is required for the purposes of drinking, cleaning, washing, heating, and possibly fire fighting.

Use	Requirement
Drinking	Piped water direct from mains; otherwise a supply of pure water must be kept in containers and be renewed daily; drinking vessels if not disposable must be rinsed in clear water
Personal washing	Running hot and cold water or at least clean warm water drawn from a storage tank
Cleaning	General water from storage tank
Water closets and urinal cisterns	General water from storage tank
Boilers, heating plant etc	Stored and circulated independently
Fire fighting: sprinklers	Water mains or pressurised storage tanks
hoses	Water mains or break tanks

Sufficient water (equal to at least 100 per cent of the daily requirement) should be stored to ensure continuity of supply and a suitable constant pressure. An allowance of 37 litres per member of staff is adequate to cover a 24 hour period.

Hot water

Hot water may be supplied either from a central or from a local system.

Central

Water is heated in the boiler room by a cheap fuel which is also used for space heating and distributed to taps throughout the building. This method is only suitable where there is a large continuous hot water demand close to the central plant.

Local

Water is heated by gas or electricity adjacent to the appliances from which it is to be drawn. This method is suitable for most shops or large premises where use is intermittent or drawn-off points are scattered. There are two kinds of heater: the instantaneous type and the thermal storage type. Instantaneous heaters provide a continuous flow of hot water; those operated by electricity range from about 3 kw to 12 kw and deliver a flow of about 2 to 5 litres per minute; those operated by gas deliver a greater flow (between 10 and 20 litres per minute) but require gas exhaust outlets. Thermal storage heaters work on a different principle. Within each unit there is a thermostatically controlled immersion heater which warms and stores water. When the tap is turned on cold water enters the lower part displacing the heated water above. Once the capacity (5 to 25 litres) runs out time must be allowed for the new supply to be heated up.

9.3 REFUSE DISPOSAL

Disposal methods

Provisions must be made for collection, storage and disposal of waste. The nature and quantity of waste will dictate its storage and disposal conditions:

Type of waste	Method of disposal
Clean waste paper, cardboard and wrappings	1 Taken to baler or compactor and collected by waste paper merchant, or 2 Collected by Local Authority
Dirty waste paper, floor and non-returnable sackings	1 Collected by Local Authority, or 2 Collected by private contractors
Organic matter: meat trimmings, fruit and vegetable waste	Kept in air-tight containers to await collection by: 1 Local Authorities 2 Specialist firms
Canteen and restaurant waste	1 Ground up by sink waste disposal unit and removed through drains, or 2 Collected by specialist firm, or 3 Collected by Local Authority
Returnable materials or those for re-cycling	Stored in a clean dry place for collection by firm's or manufacturer's agents

Refuse containers

The most popular forms of refuse containers are:
1 Paladins: cylindrical containers on wheels; they measure 1220 mm in diameter × 1830 mm high; their approximate weight when full is 70 to 90 kg.
2 Box containers: rectangular containers measuring about 1·0 × 0·5 × 3·0 m high; their approximate full weight is 70 to 90 kg.
3 Dustbins: the general household type measures approximately 460 mm in diameter × 610 mm high; its approximate full weight is 15 to 20 kg.
4 Disposable sacks: these are wet strength paper or plastic bags fixed to a metal ring with a hinged cover; they may be freestanding or bolted to the wall; they are cheap, hygienic and easily disposable; they measure about 400 mm in diameter × 750 mm high; their approximate capacity is 0·10 m³.

Refuse yards

A minimum capacity of 2·3 m³ should be allocated for each refuse store. The frequency with which collection is made by Local Authorities or specialist firms should be determined so that enough bins can be provided. It is always cheaper to provide for additional bins than to pay for more frequent collection. Refuse yards should be situated near loading docks and should comply with the requirements of Local Authorities. These are usually as follows:
1 The floor of the yard should be of smooth and impervious material such as concrete or asphalt laid to falls to allow for adequate drainage.
2 The floor should be able to withstand impact on loading without damage.
3 Yards should be provided with hoses and water supply for washing down.
4 Yards should be securely enclosed to protect them from unauthorised entry and scavenging animals.

5 Tall refuse containers such as paladins should be placed alongside a concrete platform over 300 mm high to allow for easy tipping-out.

9.4 LIFTS AND ESCALATORS

Passenger lifts

Positioning
Lifts should not be positioned adjacent to entrances because this may restrict circulation or make waiting unpleasant because of the movement of people passing through. A lift lobby of adequate size should be provided in a position unaffected by other circulation but if possible visible from the entrance.
If planned in groups lifts require lobbies at least twice as deep as the lift car; if planned in straight banks they require lobbies at least one and a half times as deep as the car. Figure **9.1** illustrates typical arrangements. It is always desirable to group lifts together to satisfy the following objectives:
1 To make maximum use of lift wells and machine room.
2 To simplify structural design and maintenance.
3 To use floor areas more effectively.
4 To reduce waiting time.
Machine rooms for electrically operated lifts should be placed immediately above the lift well. This position reduces the loading on the structures, allows the use of a smaller lift well and reduces installation and maintenance costs. Machine rooms for hydraulic lifts may be positioned adjacent to the lift shaft, or elsewhere so long as the position is convenient. In this type of system the left car is pushed up the shaft by a hydraulic ram. Speed is generally lower than that of electric lifts but the loading capacity is greater. The motor room must therefore be located at the bottom level and a roof-level motor room is not required.

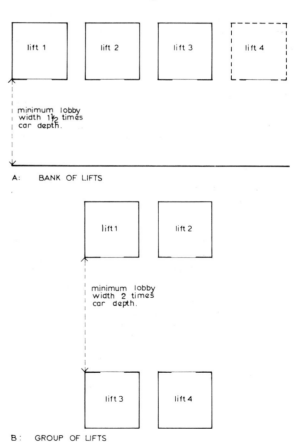

9.1 *Passenger lift arrangements*
A *a fourth car in the same line is not normally recommended because it increases the distances passengers have to walk, decreases visibility and impairs efficiency* **B** *the width of the lobby will determine the size of the motor room located above it*

Table II Standard dimensions for typical service lifts

Aspect measured	Car capacity				
	5 kg	12 kg	20 kg	50 kg	100 kg
A Width of tower	350	710	815	890	1170
B Depth of tower	230	335	355	685	925
C Height of hatch opening	405	610	760	760	865
D Width of hatch opening	235	485	560	635	915
E Sill height	1065	1065	915	915	840
F Aperture through floor	350 × 450	455 × 810	475 × 915	815 × 990	1040 × 1270
G Car inside width	235	485	560	635	915
H Car inside depth	195	255	280	610	840
J Car inside height	405	545	710	735	840

Control

Lifts may be controlled in the following modes:

1 Operator: suitable for prestige department stores; operation can be set for automatic or collective control when operators are not on duty.

2 Automatic: this system is not suitable for use in shops; on setting the lift in operation no further calls are accepted until the lift is again at rest.

3 Collective: the lift car stops at all landings where calls are waiting or where passengers wish to stop on either the upward or downward journey.

4 Group collective: up to four lifts may be grouped together so that only the closest lift moving in the desired direction will respond to a call.

5 Programmed operation: collective and group collective systems may be programmed to suit particular patterns of lift operations; this system (also known as 'lift logic') involves programming lifts to home to the ground floor during opening hours and to wait higher up the building closer to possible calls during closing hours; when lifts are full they may ignore calls until the load has been reduced thereby saving time when no more passengers can be taken.

Calculating the requirements

Calculations should be based on the total estimated number of passengers, the desired waiting interval, the number of floors to be served and on whether any special service may be needed.

$$\text{Number of lifts required} = \frac{\text{Total number of people to be served}}{\text{Number of people discharged by one lift}}$$

$$\text{Number of people discharged by one lift} = \frac{\text{Lift capacity} \times 30 \text{ minutes}}{\text{Time for round trip}}$$

The following data may be used for calculations:

1 Number of persons to be served:
It is normal to expect that 65 per cent of the population on the second floor and above will be served by lifts for a period of 30 minutes. To calculate the number of persons per floor allow the following figures:
Sales floor: one person per 2·32 m² of floor area for peak load
Offices: one person per 5·57 m² of floor area
Note that figures for offices should not normally be included in the calculation if staff use the lifts at different times from customers.

2 Time for round trip:
The time interval between round trips may be taken as an average of 30 seconds. Alternatively timing may be calculated from the manufacturers' data on lift performance and probable number of stops. If the latter method is entertained the following figures may be used:
Normal lift speed in shop use = 1·50 to 3·50 m/s
Allowance per person entering lift = 2 seconds
Allowance for waiting time at each landing = 8 seconds
Allowance for waiting time on ground floor = 20 seconds.
Suitable dimensions for lifts carrying intensive passenger traffic are shown in Fig **9.2**.

Goods lifts

General duty

The type and size of goods lift required is generally determined by the kind, type and size of the goods which need to be transported. Goods lifts are usually located near the loading dock so that goods brought in may be taken directly from the unloading vehicle to the stockroom. Lobby dimensions should measure at least one and a half times the depth of the lift car to allow trolleys or carts to be manoeuvred without damage to walls. To suit planning requirements, lifts can be accommodated with one front door only, with front and rear doors, with front and side doors, or front, rear and side doors (see Fig **9.3**). the collapsible steel gates commonly used are noisy and provide no barrier to smoke. Shutter gates with vision panels which open with a concertina effect are preferable and can be made to conform to a minimum period of two hours fire resistance. The loading capacities of goods lifts range from 500 to 2000 kg. The speed with which they travel (normally 0·2 to 0·45

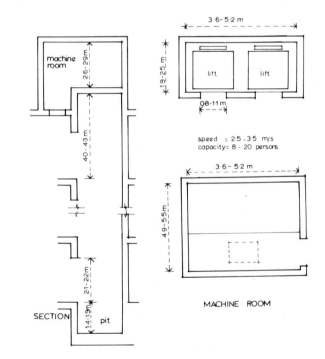

9.2 *Dimensions for lifts suitable for carrying intensive passenger traffic*

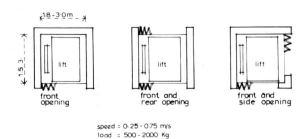

9.3 *General duty goods lift*

m/s) is not important because the time taken up by movement is less that that needed for loading and unloading.

Service lifts

Small service lifts such as 'documents lifts' or 'dumb waiters' are ideal for the vertical movement of small goods linking areas such as sales floor and stockroom, sales floor and workshop or canteen and kitchen. Service lifts are commonly used in shoe shops, electrical goods shops and bakeries where stockrooms or workrooms have to be on different levels because of restricted space on the sales floor. The motor and control gear can usually be accommodated in the same plan area as the well size, and within the headroom given, provided access can be made for servicing. This eliminates need for the traditional lift pit and ancillary motor room. Landing doors may be vertical sliding or bi-parting vertical sliding (known as 'rise and fall shutters'). They may be finished to manufacturers' specifications or clad to suit internal decor. Standard finishes include wood veneers, plastic laminates, PVC-coated steel and stainless steel. Service lifts are mostly self supported on prefabricated steel members and do not require brick or blockwork shafts. If the fire regulations stipulate that the enclosure shall be lined with a fire insulating material this is commonly fixed between the steel structure and the external cladding. Signalling may be by indicator lights, adjustable volume buzzer, or both. Typical loading capacities range from 5 to 100 kg; car sizes are from 200 × 250 × 400 mm high to 850 × 950 × 850 mm high; and car speeds range from 0·2 to 0·5 m/s. Sill height should vary from 1050 mm for a 10 kg car down to 850 mm for a 100 kg car. The following table of dimensions should be read in conjunction with Fig **9.4**.

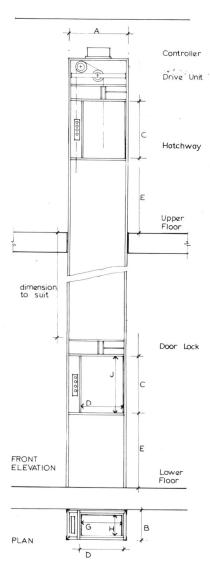

9.4 *Dimensions for typical service lift (see table II)*

Basement hoists

Basement hoists are more commonly found in older properties. They consist of a platform running between two steel guides and they are normally operated by a lifting chain which is attached to the top of one guide, passes under the platform, runs up the other guide and then down to a winding drum. Typically their loading capacity is 1000 kg, platform size 1100 × 1300 mm and speed 0·1 m/s. The machine enclosure measures approximately 2400 × 1500 mm. Some hoists may be hand-powered and take loads up to 100 kg but these are not recommended for frequent use.

Escalators

Planning

It is better to use escalators in large stores because they move larger numbers of people, require no waiting time, and occupy less floor space than the equivalent number of lifts. New escalators are usually made in a complete factory-tested unit. This minimises the amount of work needed to erect them on site and thus saves time and expense. Site preparations should be completed in advance and provision should be made for access into the building. Installation is normally carried out at night so as to reduce any disruption caused. Escalators can be planned to serve several floors and typical arrangements (illustrated in Fig **9.5**) are as follows:

1 Continuous: a continuous line of escalators only allowing travel in one direction (the space below can be filled with showcases or counters).

2 Superimposed: giving interrupted travel in one direction only.

3 Single crossover (also known as corkscrew or scissors arrangement): giving continuous travel in one direction.

4 Double crossover (also known as double corkscrew or double scissors arrangement): giving continuous travel in both directions.

Table III Discharge capacity of escalators

Nominal width (mm)	Clear width of step (mm)	Overall width (mm)	Usable space	Capacity (persons/hour)
920	600	1230	One adult only	5000
1230	910	1540	One adult and one child per step	7000
1330	1010	1640	Permits passing on outer lane	8000

Escalators may have an angle of incline of either 30° or 35°, but the 35° type is unsuitable for a rise of over 6·10 m. Allowing 2·5 m at each end for circulation purposes their length in plan in either case should be approximately 1·7 times their rise (floor to floor height) plus 9·0 m. Their typical speed is between 0·45 and 0·50 m/s and their direction can be reversed for 'tidal flow' situations. Typical dimensions are shown in Fig **9.6**.

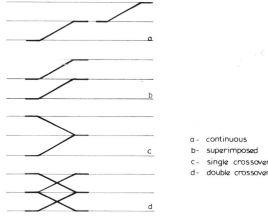

a - continuous
b - superimposed
c - single crossover
d - double crossover

9.5 *Types of layout for escalators*

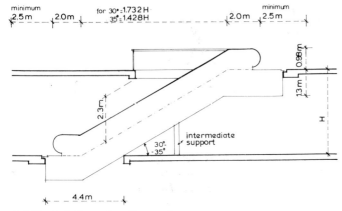

9.6 *Typical dimensions for escalators*

Fire protection

Where fire regulations limit the cubic capacity of any section or sections of the building (Part E of the Building Regulations 1976 requires division into compartments not exceeding 2000 m² or 7000 m³) escalators must be enclosed within fire proof construction and their openings protected by automatic fire doors and sprinklers.

9.5 FIRE FIGHTING APPLIANCES

The degree of fire protection to be taken in a shop will depend on the requirements of local fire authorities, the conditions stipulated in the leases to the properties, and the reductions in premium given by the insurance companies. Large stores and shops on the lower floors of large buildings may require elaborate fire alarms and fire fighting appliances but for most shops ordinary hand-held extinguishers are adequate.

Portable extinguishers

Portable extinguishers provide a fairly adequate form of protection and are very cheap. The types of extinguishers suitable for dealing with the various types of fire are as follows:

Fire classification	Cause of fire	Suitable type of extinguisher
Class A	Carbonaceous material (paper, cloth, rubber, wool, wood, plastic, etc)	1 Water 2 Dry powder
Class B	Flammable liquid (petrol, grease, oil, paint, etc)	1 Dry powder or foam 2 CO₂ or BCF
Class C	Gas (butane, propane) or electricity (wiring or other combustible equipment)	1 CO₂ or BCF 2 Dry powder

Each type of extinguisher has its characteristic method of extinguishing fire:

Water: this type puts out the fire by cooling it down and prevents rekindling by soaking the material; it must not be used on Class B or C fires.

Dry powder or foam: these types extinguish the fire by permitting the existing supply of oxygen to be consumed at its source and preventing any new supply from reaching it.

CO_2 (Carbon dioxide) or BCF (BromoChlorodiFluoromethane): these types extinguish by displacing the existing oxygen and excluding any new supply; because both are gaseous elements they cause no material damage and are useful in dealing with electrical fires.

Portable extinguishers must be positioned in readily visible and accessible places and some must be provided near fire exits to allow fire combatants a route of retreat in case the fire gets out of control.

Sprinklers

Sprinklers extinguish fire by soaking the burning material and charging the atmosphere with excessive water vapour so that it will not support combustion. Sprinkler systems may be supplied by water mains or, if this will not do, by pressurised storage cylinders of 22·5 to 50 m³ capacity usually housed in the basement or on the landlord's part of the premises.

Sprinkler head pipes to take up to 18 heads measure 25 to 50 mm in diameter. 150 mm diameter pipes are required if more than 150 heads are used. The heads are made of glass and designed to break at a predetermined temperature ranging from 68 to 180° C. Such breakage releases a high pressure jet of water which strikes a serrated metal plate and spreads over an area of about 10 m² in a fine spray. Sprinkler heads are normally planned on a 3 m square grid. It should be noted that sprinkler heads may be required both above and below the false ceiling if the ceiling voids between structure and false ceiling exceed 750 mm. Sprinkler systems have the disadvantage that as much damage is generally caused by the water they spray as by the fire it extinguishes. Sprinkler stop valves must therefore be located as near as possible to the final exit to allow the system bo be turned off as soon as possible.

Fire hoses

Unlike sprinklers (which are indiscriminate) fire hoses are directional and controllable. They may be connected to the mains so long as the mains pressure is adequate. Otherwise break tanks are required. These are usually of 1150 litres capacity and may feed the hoses by gravity or by mechanical pumping. The hydraulic requirement is that hoses should be able to deliver 22 litres of water per minute at a distance of 6 metres from the nozzle and that three nozzles may be in operation at any one time. Hoses are made of rubber, usually 18 mm or 25 mm in diameter, and are in standard lengths of 20, 25 and 30 m. Hose-reel drums should ideally be recessed into walls and hinged so as to swivel outwards in the desired direction. A sufficient number of hoses should be provided of adequate length to enter every room and reach within 6 m of

Table IV General characteristics of the different types of portable fire extinguisher

Type of extinguisher	Canister colour	Capacity (litres)	(kg)	Weight (kg)	Discharge range (m)	Discharge time (seconds)	Canister height (mm)	Canister base (mm)	Recharging procedure
Water	Red	5		10·8	9 to 13	50	500	150	Refill with water and replace CO₂ cartridge
		9		15·4	9 to 13	80	450	175	
Dry powder	Blue		5	9	4 to 6	11	480	150	Empty remaining powder from container, hose and syphon tube; refill with powder mixture and replace CO₂ cartridge
			6·5	13	4 to 6	13	650	150	
			10	19	4 to 6	24	750	175	
Foam	Cream	9		16	6 to 10	42	620	175	Refill foam compound and water; replace CO₂ cartridge
Carbon dioxide	Black		1·2	4	3 to 4·5	8	420	100	Return to supplier
			3·2	8·8	3 to 4·5	15	500	150	
			4·5	11	3 to 4·5	20	620	150	
BCF	Green		0·7	1·5	2 to 2·5	12	250	125	Return to supplier
			1·5	3	2 to 2·5	16	300	150	

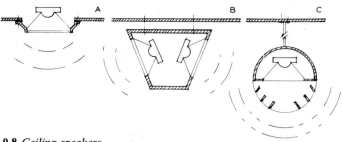

9.8 *Ceiling speakers*
A *panel unit: ideal for use with suspended ceiling systems*
B *bi-directional unit: suitable for large covered areas* **C** *pendant globe type: suitable for high ceiling areas*

every part of the floor. Hose points should be readily accessible and sited near means of escape so that fire combatants may guide themselves back to safety if the floor is filled with smoke.

Fire alarms

Fire alarms may be automatically or manually operated. Automatic types operate on the principles of heat sensing or smoke detection and are linked to the main alarm system and central indicator; if required they can also be arranged to call the fire station automatically. The detector units employed in such systems cover areas of between 20 and 100 m². The most common manual system is the 'break glass — push knob' alarm which gives warning of fire and its position. When this is used in shopping complexes individual shop units' alarms may be connected to the landlord's central indicator for immediate investigation and action. Manually operated systems have the advantage over automatic ones that they give rise to fewer false alarms.

9.6 AUDIO SYSTEMS

Uses

Audio systems provide facilities for the selection, amplification, and distribution of music from radio, records, tapes or cassettes. Where desirable microphone imput and alarm signalling may also be incorporated in the same system.

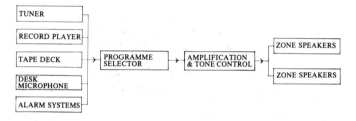

9.7 *Typical operations of audio system*

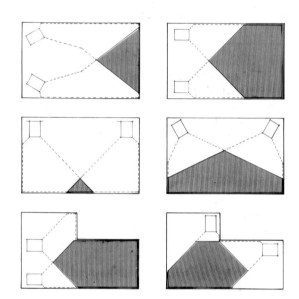

9.9 *Arrangement of column speakers: shaded areas show stereo receiving zones*

Figure **9.7** illustrates typical operations. Audio systems may be required to provide a musical background (a) in fashion businesses catering mainly for the young (eg boutiques or trendy shoe shops); (b) where music is the main concern (eg shops selling records or cassettes); or (c) where a soothing atmosphere is otherwise specially desirable (eg showrooms, fashion displays). They may also be used by large composite shops such as department stores to announce bargains, sales or other events taking place in any particular section of the premises.

Speakers

Speakers may be of the cabinet type either fixed to walls, freestanding or concealed above an open grid ceiling. Types of ceiling speakers are shown in Fig **9.8**. There are also proprietary models resembling spotlights which are mounted on tracks and may be moved at will. Other types are manufactured to fit on to most types of false ceiling panels. The best place to put them is still largely a matter of trial and error. Corner positions provide the maximum base but produce reflections which cause distortions in quality. Figure **9.9** shows typical positions for various types of floor plan. In open layouts it is generally desirable to have the speakers raised at least 200 mm from the floor and placed between 2200 and 3600 mm apart. Where the layout is obstructed by internal fittings the speakers may be mounted off the ceiling and hung at least 2100 mm above the floor.

Audio-booths

Record shops may require audio-booths for customers who wish to listen to records prior to buying. To avoid damage by scratching the record is usually played at a control desk by a qualified assistant. It is thence transmitted to any of a series of audio-booths at one end of the store. One record player or record deck is required per booth. Booths require to:

(a) have a minimum floor area of 1·0 m wide by 1·2 m deep;
(b) form an enclosed space with walls, floor and ceiling lined with sound-absorbing material;
(c) have a glass panel 750 to 1800 mm high fitted in the door (so that occupants can avoid claustrophobia by being able to see out, whether they are sitting or standing);
(d) be equipped with a speaker unit mounted on ceiling or wall plus audio-sockets or headphones; and
(e) be furnished at least with a chair, an ashtray or no-smoking sign and a coat hook.

9.7 COMMUNICATIONS SYSTEMS

Telephones

The telephone system to be adopted will depend on the type and size of business as well as the degree of intercommunication desired within the premises. The main systems provided by the Post Office include:

System	Feature
Single exchange line	Allows one person to make and receive calls on one exchange line; when fitted with extensions allows up to three people to make and receive calls as well as to communicated with each other
Double exchange line	Allows up to ten people to make and receive calls on up to two lines with consecutive numbers, as well as to communicate with each other

System	Feature
Private branch exchange (PBX)	Manual (PMBX) and automatic (PABX) systems are available taking up to ten lines and forty extensions per switchboard
Special line	Special lines may be negotiated for linking computer terminals and for security alarm calls

Telephone systems are usually installed in the later stages of shopfitting and too often, if adequate provisions are not made, the process of putting them in causes inconvenience and damage to finishes. The position and arrangement for the entry of the GPO cable should be discussed with the Post Office engineers at an early stage. The cable is invariably buried under the pavement, sleeved through a basement wall, and then carried up to the point where the distribution frame is to be placed. Telephones are operated on 50 volts by batteries which are automatically rechargeable by an autocharger connected to the main electricity supply. Service ducts should be provided whenever possible for the housing of cables. These protect and conceal the cables as well as providing accessibility for repairs and extension. Other services which may also be accommodated are fire and burglar alarms, radio and television aerials and audio, lighting and power systems. Proprietary skirting trunkings are widely available in metals or plastics with an average cross-sectional area of 2000 mm². Separation between the communications system and the lighting and power systems is essential and this is provided by internal compartmentalisation within the trunking. In large stores a switch room will be needed to accommodate the distribution frame and switchboard operator: good ventilation and dry conditions are essential here.

It is always desirable to make allowances for extra extensions and extra lines, because the substitution of a larger size switchboard causes considerable inconvenience and expense. The typical size of a switch room incorporating equipment cabinet, battery cell, mains unit and distribution frame is 2400 × 2700 mm. Figure **9.10** shows the layout and recommendations for a PABX switch room.

Telex

The telex system allows a recorded typewritten message to be transmitted with the same ease and speed as a conversation on the telephone. Telex is suitable where it is important to have a record or to be accurate, for example when orders or complicated messages are sent. The teleprinter and dialling unit can be fitted to a table space of about 1000 mm high × 710 mm wide. The total weight is 114 kg. Allowing adequate room for the operator's chair and for maintenance purposes, the installation requires a floor space of 1600 × 1250 mm. Figure **9.11** shows the dimensions.

Internal communication

Post Office telephones fitted with extensions can usually be used for internal communications. In circumstances where independent internal telephones only are required, these may be bought or hired. Hiring usually includes servicing. Small private extensions are usually limited to 6, 8, or 12 hand-sets. Larger installations may accommodate up to 50 instruments per board, enabling up to 5 persons on different hand-sets to speak at the same time. Frame boards measure about 0·9 × 0·45 × 1·8 m high. The space taken by the autocharger is quite small, about 0·6 × 0·3 × 0·3.

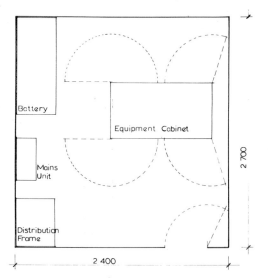

9.10 *Layout and dimensions recommended for a PABX switchroom. The accommodation should have adquate heating, lighting and ventilation and the minimum headroom should be 2300 mm*

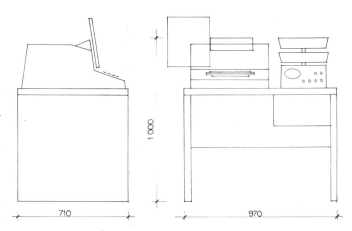

9.11 *Dimensions of telex with teleprinter*

Pneumatic conveyors

Pneumatic tube conveyors serve to dispatch documents, receipts, cash and small pieces of equipment between two or more points. Traditionally this system was used for such communication between the sales floor and the central cashier's office. Improved models now however allow for ring distribution with automatic selection of destinations. Both round and square tubes are commonly used. Round tubes vary in diameter from 50 to 150 mm and rectangular tubes measure up to 380 × 130 mm. Movement is possible in all directions including the vertical and there is no practical limitation on length of runs. The number of stations varies between 80 and 120 per ring main. Planning at an early stage with manufacturers is essential to establish the right positions for tubes, bends, stations, and plant room for the air exhauster unit.

Table V Typical switchboard sizes

Type of switchboard	Width (mm)	Depth (mm)	Height (mm)	Weight (kg)	Max. no. of lines	Max. no. extensions	Max. no. extensions (multiple switchboard)
Manual (single unit)	660	840	1420	135 to 180	10	40	200
Cordless manual (desk top)	500	380	220	11	5	20	

10
IMPLEMENTATION

10.1 BRIEFING CHECKLIST

A General data

1 Location

Evaluate:

(a) the quality of the neighbourhood (eg exclusive, popular or low grade area).

(b) the standard of finishes, the intensity of window lighting and illuminated signs of adjoining premises.

(c) local economic activity and data (eg direction of main pedestrian flow, position of local 'magnets' such as department stores, transport terminals, etc).

2 Site

Determine:

(a) the type of site the unit is situated in (eg off a straight or curved street, at a road junction or T-junction, on a sloping site or in a shopping centre).

(b) the critical dimensions: frontage, depth, heights, gross and nett areas, position and sizes of internal structural members.

3 Client

Determine what type of client is concerned with the proposed work (eg independent retailer, large retailing organisation, or developer). If the client is a large organisation determine which individuals will be directly involved in the project and what are their respective areas of interest. Usually types of interest may be broken down into planning and administration, stock and staff control, services and engineering department, and branch manager.

4 Stock

Establish:

(a) the type of goods to be sold and the methods of display.

(b) the respective quantities to be displayed and to be held in stock.

(c) which goods, if any, require special handling or storage.

(d) what methods of delivery are planned (eg random delivery by different types of vehicles or organised delivery by the client's own fleet of vehicles).

5 Staff

Determine the numbers of male and female staff in full time or part time employment and their job classifications (eg management, administration, buying, sales, maintenance or cleaning).

6 Customers

Determine what type of clientele the shop is supposed to serve and the degree of customer comfort to be provided (eg whether the intended unit is an exclusive shop providing personalised service or a popular shop providing assisted service or self service).

B The shopfront

1 Relationship with neighbouring shops

Investigate whether the shopfront may be treated independently or whether it should relate to neighbouring shops. Dimensions to look for in adjoining shops are fascia height and size, height of window soffit and bed, and stallboard height. Other factors which may influence design are construction details and materials, size, type and illumination level of signs, and areas of glazing.

2 Shopfront type

The type of shopfront which should be chosen is influenced primarily by length of frontage, type of merchandise to be displayed, relationship of area available for shopfront to sales floor, and relationship with neighbouring shops. The choice lies between the following types of shopfront (any of which may be single or multi-storey):

(a) Open: this gives maximum display of medium to large sized goods.

(b) Enclosed: this provides concentrated display of small luxury goods.

(c) Flat front: this is an economical means of achieving maximum display and use of internal areas.

(d) Arcaded with recessed lobby: this may be straight, curved, splayed or modelled, and may include island or wall showcases; it generally provides shelter for customers to inspect goods from the back and sides as well as the front.

3 Display windows

Determine required window dimensions by type of goods to be displayed. The controlling dimensions are depth, bed height and soffit height. Window backs may be open, glazed or enclosed with opaque partitioning but consideration should be given to providing access for heavy or bulky goods and to removal of goods from the window for direct sale. Establish whether the client prefers temporary or permanent lining finishes. Check whether any display fixtures are required in particular intermediate display levels. Examine neighbouring shops to determine the intensity of their window lighting. If the client is concerned about the amount of external reflection consider means of reducing it by tilting the glass, using curved glass sections or installing a blind or canopy.

4 Sunblinds

If the window is exposed to solar radiation it is advisable to fit a sunblind or a permanent canopy in order to reduce internal heat gain, protect displayed goods from fading and reduce reflection problems. Blinds may be positioned above or below the fascia and may be operated manually or electrically. The main modes of action are by telescopic or folding arms. Consider whether any sign is to be imprinted on the blind material.

5 Signs

Determine the position for the main shop sign. This may be external (on the fascia, pilaster, stallboard or entrance recess) or internal (hung from the window soffit, on the soffit bulkhead, signwritten on the glass or on the window bed). Check whether the client has an established logo or letterstyle which is to be adopted and whether it is proposed to reproduce this on articles used inside the shop such as labels or carrier bags.

6 Entrance

Where there is any choice about where to put the main entrance the following factors should be taken into consideration: relationship with other shops, pedestrian circulation, traffic flow, and proximity to car parking and bus stations. Check the number of doors required by the client, the size of opening needed, and the mode of action desired (ie pivoted, hinged, sliding, folding, revolving, or automatic). Establish the degree of security required in terms of locks and contact alarms. Entrance doors can be decorated or inscribed by various techniques including signwriting, screenprinting, film application, acid etching, sand blasting, and gilding. Consider what types of handles and letter plates are needed.

7 Other shopfront elements

Establish the client's requirements, preferences or responsibilities concerning materials, finishes, dimensions and maintenance of all other outstanding shopfront elements:

Fascia and shopfront paving: these may have to be related to adjoining premises.

Pilasters: the client may be responsible for their whole width or for only half of it.

Stallboard: this may or may not be required.

Mat and mat well: fittings may be permanent or removable and may have open or closed mesh.

C The sales floor

1 Selling method

Find out whether the selling method is to be self service, assisted service or counter service.

2 Goods

Establish the types and quantities of goods to be on display and the methods of display and storage. Divide up the commodities into categories and subcategories and determine the amount of space to be allocated for each and the position to be allotted on the sales floor.

3 Design

Establish client's preferences concerning design (eg masculine or feminine, straightforward or sophisticated, period or modern). After the design has been fully established determine the colour scheme which is preferred.

4 Fixtures and fittings

Determine which types of fixtures and fittings are to be standard and which are to be specially made. The main items to be considered include:

Wall units: these may be with or without canopies or concealed lighting; the respective heights and numbers of shelves required must also be determined.

Counters: these may be solid or glazed and their number and respective heights, positions and functions require to be decided.

Cash desks: these may be localised or dispersed and the number of cash register machines or till drawers has to be decided as well as the question of whether a cash office is required.

Gondolas: the respective heights and numbers of shelves needed have to be established.

Furniture: a schedule should be prepared showing all the items required and their respective positions (eg chairs, tables, stands, etc).

Special items: the need for specialised items should be determined (eg storage or display equipment such as refrigerated cabinets, display turntables, fashion display models, etc).

5 Finishes

Establish the client's preferences concerning materials, finishes and maintenance (eg whether these are to be dark or light, textured or glossy, permanent or temporary). Determine requirements for the following:

Ceiling: this may either be painted or covered with a false ceiling; in the latter case open crate false ceilings may make it necessary to disguise the true ceiling and the service pipes and ducts with an inconspicuous coating of paint. Suspended ceilings are either of the strip type or the frame and panel type with the frame exposed or concealed. The need to integrate the lighting and services with the type of ceiling chosen must be considered.

Walls: wherever these are exposed they can either be painted or covered with a wall covering material or cladding. Consider whether application should be straight or in panels.

Floors: the choice of flooring material is highly influenced by the type of goods for sale and is generally between impervious materials (where a high standard of hygiene is required) and soft materials (where customer comfort is the main consideration).

6 Lighting

Consider the types of lighting required for ceiling, walls, displays, showcases, counters and fitting rooms. Also decide whether background lighting, decorative lighting and emergency lighting are needed. Determine the types of fittings to be used and how to achieve greatest flexibility for alterations and additions.

D Non-retail areas

1 Staff entry

Establish client's requirements for staff car parking. If a separate entrance is required for staff determine how their entry and exit are to be controlled. Investigate needs for clocking-in machines, staff storage racks, notice boards and accommodation for doormen.

2 Staff lavatories and cloakrooms

Statutory requirements determine the minimum lavatory accommodation which must be provided for each sex. Establish if separate accommodation is required for senior and general staff and whether customers are to have access to staff lavatories. If a cloakroom is to be provided find out what facilities are needed (ie type, size and number of lockers).

3 Staff restroom

Determine the kind and extent of accommodation needed and what provisions are required for making refreshments. Prepare a schedule of furniture. Establish whether the restroom is to be used after closing hours and if so whether it will then require to be supervised.

4 Offices

Establish the precise requirements for administrative offices (their functions are generally broken down into management, accounts, administration, personnel, security, and sales). Establish needs for conference rooms, customer interview rooms, cash offices and any other requirements.

5 Cafeteria

Determine the location of any accommodation required in relation to kitchen and vertical transportation. Determine the seating density and the number of seats to be provided.

6 Workshops

There are two types of workshop: one is concerned with servicing and maintenance of the store and the other with the repair or alteration of goods sold in the store. Determine which type is required and exact requirements in terms of space, planning and equipment.

7 Delivery and dispatch

Ascertain how goods are to be delivered (eg unloading off the front pavement and bringing goods through the sales floor; unloading off the front pavement and delivering through side, rear, or basement entrances; unloading in a protected area at the side or rear; or unloading in a sheltered loading dock). Also find out whether goods are to be dispatched according to an organised system or at random and the types of vehicles which will be used.

8 Handling equipment

Investigate the methods which will be used for handling goods (eg horizontal movement: carts, trolleys, and conveyor belts; inclined movement: rollers, belts, and chutes; vertical movement: lifts and hoists).

9 Stockrooms

Establish the percentage of total space to be allocated for the storage of stock. Investigate if any goods need special storage conditions (eg refrigerated stores).

E Environmental and engineering services

1 Lighting

Establish requirements for background lighting, decorative lighting and emergency lighting. Determine what types of fittings are required and methods of achieving greatest flexibility.

2 Heating

Establish degree of customer comfort to be provided and the budget allocation for this. The main types of heating systems are electric unit heaters, ducted warm air and low pressure hot water.

3 Ventilation

Investigate if natural ventilation is adequate or if mechanical ventilation is required. Ducted systems may be incorporated with heating and air conditioning systems.

4 Air conditioning

Establish if air conditioning is required. The circumstances where it may be desirable are:
(a) where large numbers of customers are expected.
(b) where natural ventilation is inadequate.
(c) where heat gains are excessive.
(d) where customer comfort is a major priority.
Air conditioning may be provided by a central plant, by means of zoned systems or by self contained units.

5 Security

Establish the extent to which the intended security system has to provide protection against burglary, shoplifting or fire. Determine the hazard condition (see section 7.1 above) which is related to the methods used for displaying goods and to their value. The main detector devices for protection against burglary include:
Contact switches: for doors and windows.
Wired panels: for doors, walls and ceilings.
Wired tubings: for windows and thin wall structures.
Foil strips: for windows and doors.
Vibration detectors: for windows, walls and ceiling.
Sound detectors: for internal detection.
Pressure mats: for internal detection.
Space detectors: for internal detection.
Although most alarm systems are installed after completion of shopfitting works, precise requirements must be established at the outset so that concealed cables can be accommodated with minimum disturbance and cost. Discuss with the client his preferences for anti-pilfering methods which include security conscious planning, anti-shoplifting notices, closed circuit television, normal or anti-shoplifting mirrors, lockable chains, electronic loops and electronic tags.

6 Fire fighting equipment

Establish requirements for fire fighting equipment from the client, local authorities, the landlord and the client's insurance company. Find out whether portable extinguishers will be adequate or whether sprinklers or hoses are required.

7 Audio systems

Check whether audio systems are required and if so what facilities are to be incorporated in them (eg radio, records, tapes, cassettes, microphone input and alarm signalling).

8 Communications

Determine requirements for external and internal telephones, telex, computer terminals and direct alarm lines to police or security firm's office. Ascertain whether systems are to be installed to convey documents or cash.

9 Refuse disposal

Establish with the client the nature and quantity of waste expected. The main types of waste to be expected usually fall into the broad categories: clean paper and wrappings, dirty waste, organic matter and returnable materials. Check if the client wishes to enter into an agreement with a specialist firm for the disposal of organic waste.

10 Lifts and escalators

Establish if lifts or escalators are required and if so the extent to which they will be used (a) for carrying passengers and (b) for transporting goods.

10.2 BUILDING WORKS

Operation methods and procedures for shop building works are largely dependent on the size of the project, the intended time scale and prevailing site conditions.

1 Large building works

The complexity of building and structural work may require the employment of specialist consultants. These may include a quantity surveyor, a structural engineer, and mechanical and electrical engineers dealing respectively with heating, ventilation and air conditioning, lighting, acoustics, refrigeration and communications. A clerk of works may be employed for site supervision and quality control. The contract is usually placed with a building contractor of adequate size to handle the job and he may subcontract such specialist work as shopfront or fixtures and fittings to a shopfitting firm.

2 Standard 'unit' works

This type of work covers most individual shops and may involve erecting new premises or remodelling existing ones. The work is normally carried out by the architect on his own with the help of any consultants he may require. Architects' drawings usually carry more information than they would for other types of work because shopfitters prefer to have as much detail on them as possible so that they do not need to refer to the specification. Work is normally placed with shopfitting firms on competitive or negotiated tender. Some large firms provide a comprehensive service from design to completion and enter into a direct contract with the client right from the outset.

3 Remodelling works

Remodelling works fall into two categories: reconstruction on change of user, or reconstruction for alterations. In both cases the time element is important, but more so in the latter because the client may wish to continue trading during shopfitting. Preplanning stages require careful attention to minimise the actual building period. It is normal practice for shopfitters to prefabricate as much as possible, which requires accurate setting-out and detailing. To avoid on-site problems architects should check all the contractor's full size setting-out drawings, commonly known as 'rods'. The building operation is usually carried out in stages to permit trading during shopfitting. Shopfronts and major internal works are carried out over weekends, if possible over bank holiday weekends.

10.3 PLAN OF WORK

The following plan of work follows the work stages recommended by the Royal Institute of British Architects:

A Inception
1 Preliminary discussion between architect and client to define responsibilities, terms of engagement, fees, contracts, client organisation, etc.
2 Advise the client on consultants and their direct employment.
3 Examine the feasibility of the project in terms of time scale, financial limits, etc. Determine date of possession of property, desired completion date, and client's budget.
4 Develop all preliminary information for the project. Determine if the client is negotiating the lease, is in possession of the lease, or is already trading on the premises and in the latter case whether he will continue trading during shopfitting.

B Feasibility
1 Prepare the brief. Determine what further information is needed to develop the final brief: see Briefing Checklist (section 10.1 above).
2 Determine if plans are available or if a survey is required. Drawings should include plans, sections, elevations, existing shopfront details (if applicable), existing fixtures and fittings (if to be retained). A written report should indicate whether existing services and building structure are in sound condition or whether upgrading or complete renewal is required. Services investigation should include soil and surface water drainage, water mains, local electricity board cables, GPO cables, gas mains and any other services. Investigation of building structure should include dry rot, woodworm, damp patches, settlement cracks, walls bulging out of plumb, ceilings, beams or lintels sagging or cracking and any other defects.
3 Determine what consents are required from authorities, organisations, or persons having jurisdiction over the project. Confirm the number and type of drawings required and obtain the relevant forms. The main actions needed are:
(a) Legal: obtain from client's solicitor all relevant leases, covenants etc and determine what consents are required. Normally this concerns the landlord and adjoining owners.
(b) Planning: planning consents are required for new shopfronts and external signs which should be submitted independently. Check if the site is in a conservation area and if so what restrictions may be imposed on design and choice of materials.
(c) Local authority: determine what consents are necessary for the erection of temporary structures, street lighting requirements, special access for heavy or large loads. Check building lines and improvement lines.
(d) Building regulations: check which authorities have responsibility for building regulations, means of escape and under the Offices Shops and Railway Premises Act.
(e) Services: check which departments have jurisdiction over the supply of essential services. Determine the dates by which applications for supplies have to be made in order to fit into the building programme.
Water supply: determine location of water mains, metering requirements, position of intake and stopcocks etc.
Gas supply: determine location of gas mains, position of intake and stopcocks etc. Check if permanent or temporary supply is required.

Electricity supply: estimate load if possible to determine whether single or three-phase supply is required. Determine position of intake duct and metering requirements.
GPO: establish location and clearance for underground cables and the position of intake ducts.
4 Report to client. Consultants' reports can be incorporated into the architects report or be appended as separate documents. The report should summarise the contents of the brief, mentioning design constraints which might affect proposals, state the situation regarding consents and their effect on the schedule and include an assessment of the cost for the total project (any such assessment should include separate breakdowns of figures for contract items (building works), for direct contract items (furniture and fittings etc) and for professional fees for architects and consultants).

C Outline proposals
1 Investigate all alternative design solutions and prepare outline scheme. Prepare outline plan with quantity surveyor.
2 Present report and outline scheme to client for discussions. Make recommendations and check that client is in agreement with finalised design proposals.

D Scheme design
1 Prepare full scheme. Check design and outline specification against design criteria. Issue drawings to consultants. Review and discuss proposals. Finalise scheme design, outline specification and cost plan.
2 Report to client and advise that there should be no changes in requirements after this stage.

E Detail design
1 Carry out detail design. Review details, standards of finishes and equipment. Review service installations and cost plan.
2 Check that all consents are obtained as far as possible. Advise client of any outstanding consents which may cause delay.

F Production information
1 Prepare groundwork for tendering procedure. Compile list of possible contractors, take up references, discuss list with quantity surveyor and client. Issue invitation to contractors.
2 Prepare list of subcontractors and suppliers. Consider which elements are to be the subject of separate quotations. Issue documents for invitation to tender. If drawings are required from subcontractors or suppliers in order to complete production information consider the issue of a letter of intent. Consider the issue of advance orders to comply with long term delivery dates.

G Bill of quantities
1 The client should advise on any detail decisions still outstanding and should agree on the tender list.
2 The architect and consultants should hand over to the quantity surveyor all drawings and documents to enable him to prepare the Bill of Quantities. Where no Bill of Quantities is required the drawings and specification should be finalised and put out to tender.

H Action on tenders
1 Issue tender documents. On receipt of tenders prepare to report to client with recommendations. Obtain client's formal acceptance of tender.
2 Check that there are no restrictions on the project (eg outstanding consents, ownership, statutory conditions etc). Advise client on risks he runs where consents are outstanding.

J Project planning
1 The architect should prepare contract documentation and arrange for copies to be signed by the client and contractor.
2 Sets of production information should be issued to the

contractor. The contractor should be instructed to accept nominated subcontractors' and suppliers' quotations. The contractor's programme should be drawn up and reviewed by the architect. Critical dates are contract start and finish dates, subcontractors' and suppliers' dates and sectional completion (phasing) dates, if applicable.

3 The contractor should send a setting-out team to the site to take accurate measurements for the manufacture of the shopfront and built-in or prefabricated equipment.

4 Hold preliminary site meeting for introductions, discussion of site management, future site meetings, architect's instructions, communications, quality control, programme, finance and consultant matters.

K Operations on site

1 Check all contractors' setting-out drawings, known as 'rods'. Maintain general supervision of the project. Hold regular site meetings. Issue instructions, drawings, certificates. Authorise dayworks as necessary.

2 Initiate action for commissioning and testing of mechanical and electrical installations. Arrange for client's representative to attend operations so as to be instructed on operating all systems.

3 Keep client informed of progress and financial position.

L Completion

1 Inform client of handover date. Advise him of his need to insure the building and contents prior to handover.

2 Inspect building, list all outstanding works and instruct contractor to make good. Check that all works are done to required standard and issue certificate of practical completion.

3 Arrange for final inspection. Prepare schedule of defects and ask the contractor to prepare a programme of works for all outstanding items. When all defects have been made good issue certificate of making good defects, certificate of payment of retention money, and final certificate of payment.

10.4 MAINTENANCE

Planned maintenance

Maintenance in shops may be carried out as an organised and planned procedure or as an emergency operation if an urgent situation arises. Small shops, including most of the independents, tend to rely on emergency maintenance whereas the large, exclusive or multiples may have some forms of planned maintenance. The advantages of planned maintenance are that emergency situations are less likely to arise; when they do so the maintenance contractor with a full case history will provide a better and speedier service than a strange contractor. Also standards are likely to remain high, administration procedures are easier and there is less of a problem in terms of security.

Types of maintenance

Maintenance comes broadly under one of the following types:

Preventive

This is a form of planned maintenance. Details of what may be needed are usually provided by equipment manufacturers' instructions. General plant equipment may be on a maintenance contract with service contractors. Specialist equipment will be on a contract with the manufacturers' service department.

Corrective

A form of planned maintenance. This is dependent on the management policies, budgets and set standards. Maintenance contracts

may be placed with the main contractor responsible for the initial shopfitting or with a specialist contractor.

Emergency

This is unplanned and results from plant or equipment breakdown.

Life cycles

Lighting equipment requires the most comprehensive maintenance because accumulation of dust in fittings reduces light output and lamps suffer from a short life cycle. Incandescent lamps have an average life of 1000 to 2000 hours and require replacing at every six months. Fluorescent lamps with a longer life of 7500 hours require replacing every two years. Maintenance contracts placed with electrical contractors invariably take the following form:

At every 6 months: replace all filament lamps, clean all fluorescent lamps and clean all lamp holders and diffusers.

At every 2 years: replace all filament and fluorescent lamps. Clean all lamp holders and diffusers.

Life cycles and the consequential replacement of plant, fixtures and decorations due to wear and tear are difficult to establish precisely. They depend on the initial quality of the item in question and on the extent to which it may be misused. Table I gives a guide to the life cycles which may be expected for various items. Many of these may last longer than the periods shown but it has to be assumed that they will require renewal by the time these elapse if good standards are to be maintained.

Table I Life cycles and replacement schedules for internal shop elements

Element	Period	Maintenance contractor
Lighting	6 months (filaments) 2 years (fluorescents)	Electrical or General
Decor, furnishing fabrics	2 to 4 years	General
Carpets	4 to 6 years	Carpeting
Fixtures and fittings	4 to 8 years	General
Electrical, communication control, accounting and security equipment	5 to 8 years	Specialist or Manufacturer
Engineering plant	10 to 15 years	Specialist or Manufacturer

Factors for consideration

Replacement of materials and renovation work is affected by the following factors:

1 Changes in market conditions: whether the standards set require to be upgraded or whether they can be retained; whether there must be any changes in the use of the amount of floor space available.

2 Flexibility of existing design and construction: whether these can accommodate changes of layout or other interruptions.

3 Permanence of materials and equipment.

4 Capital costs, disturbance and loss of revenue.

Major works should be planned to be carried out in low seasons so that disturbances to customers and losses in revenue may be kept as low as possible. Their main effects are:

1 Loss of revenue due to closure of the shop or parts of it for works.

2 Loss of customer goodwill because of disturbance and interruptions.

3 Safety and security risks and possible infringement of legal and insurance requirements.

The maintenance of external areas at sites such as shopping centres is generally undertaken by agencies employed by the landlord under the terms of the lease.

Appendix 1
PROPERTIES AND SUITABILITY
OF MATERIALS

A Cladding and paving materials — stone

Material	Thickness (mm)	Size (mm)	Colour	Texture	Properties	Application	Wearing qualities	Cost
Granite	10 to 32 for plain surfaces 22 to 52 for textured surfaces	Up to 1830 × 910	Grey, Red, Pink, Blue, Black	Polished, matt and a variety of tooled textures eg hammered, grooved, riven, random sawn, tooled hammered and relief textured	Virtually indestructible, impervious to water, resistant to staining and requires minimal maintenance	Exterior and interior work of all types; letters can be engraved in 'V' incisions or flat profiles; suitable for heavy duty use	Excellent	High
Quartzite	10 to 20	152 × 152 up to 229 × 229	Grey, Green, Buff, Yellow	Riven, split-face	Virtually indestructible, resistant to staining and abrasion	As for granite	Excellent	High
Marble	As for granite	Up to 1500 × 910	Green, Blue, Purple, Black, Grey, Buff (sealing intensifies the colour)	From sanded to very fine polish, filled or unfilled, can be tooled as for granite	Very hard but slightly porous and if not sealed stains easily	As for granite; also suitable for stairways, counter tops and fixtures	Good	High
Natural stones	15 to 40 and 50	600 × 600 and 1500 × 910	Grey, Buff, White	From sawn to high polish	Soft or porous varieties should be avoided	Wall claddings and floor paviours	Good	High
Slates	19 to 25 and 32 to 40	381 × 381 and 1500 × 910	Green, Blue, Purple, Black, Grey (sealing intensifies the colour)	Riven, sawn, sanded, rubbed, polished	Very good resistance to abrasion; slippery if polished and stains if not sealed	Wall cladding, steps and floors	Good	High

B Cladding and paving materials — tiles

Material	Thickness (mm)	Size (mm)	Colour	Texture	Properties	Application	Wearing quality	Cost
Brick	65	102 × 215	Wide range of natural clay colours	Usually plain, laid in various patterns	Various qualities; engineering bricks have excellent resistance to impact, corrosion and wear	Walls and floors, internally or externally	Good	Low
Quarry tiles	19 to 38	102 × 102 up to 305 × 305 also hexagonal and other geometric forms	Red, Buff, Brown, Blue, Black	Plain, ribbed, studded or granulated	Similar to equivalent bricks; moderately non-slippery	Internal and external floors, cladding to walls columns and pilasters	Good	Low
Ceramic tiles	8·5 to 22·2	76 × 76 up to 254 × 254 also hexagonal and other geometric forms	Black and White plus a wide range of monochromes and mingled colours	Matt, semi-gloss, gloss and some non-slip surfaces	Accurate size and shape; good resistance to staining and water penetration; easy to maintain	Internally or externally where impervious surfaces are required; can be laid inconspicuously or in patterns	Good	Medium to low
Mosaic	4 to 10	13 × 13 to 25 × 25 usually supplied bonded to sheets up to 800 × 800	As for ceramic tiles; also available in glass and marble	Glazed, matt, rice-grain and some non-slip survaces	Similar to ceramic tiles of equivalent thickness	Glass mosaics are not suitable for floors; other materials suitable for floors and walls: many design potentials	Good to medium	Medium

B Cladding and paving materials — tiles (continued)

Material	Thickness (mm)	Size (mm)	Colour	Texture	Properties	Application	Wearing quality	Cost
Terrazzo (pre-cast tile units)	19 to 38	200 × 200 up to 500 × 500	Wide range	Plain or polished	Accurate size and shape; resistant to staining and water penetration; cold, hard, noisy and slippery when wet	External and internal floors where impervious surfaces are required	Good	Medium
Concrete (pre-cast tile units)	16 to 25	151 × 151 up to 305 × 305 also hexagonal and other geometric forms	Natural Grey, White or coloured by pigment or aggregates	Plain or ribbed	Properties vary widely (as for in-situ concrete) but with benefit of factory manufacture; stains easily	External and internal floors	Good	Low

C Hard flooring materials

Material	Thickness (mm)	Size (mm)	Colour	Texture	Properties	Application	Wearing qualities	Cost
Linoleum	2 to 6·7	229 × 229 or 305 × 305 also sheet rolls	Wide range of colours and patterns including marble, granite, jasper and geometrical	Semi-matt	Wear is proportional to thickness; hardened grades have good resistance to impact and abrasion; quiet and warm; easily cleaned	Internal floors	Medium	Low
Flexible vinyl	1·1 to 3·2	Up to 305 × 305 also sheet rolls	Wide range of colours and patterns including marble, travertine, mosaic, mosaic, timber, bricks etc	Semi-matt plain or embossed	Very quiet with resilient backing; embossed types are non-slippery	Internal floors	Good	Low to medium
Thermoplastic 'asphalt tiles'	3·5 to 4·5	229 × 229	Limited range of dark colours	Semi-matt	Noisy and hard; prone to cracking if unevenly bedded; slippery if highly polished	Internal floors	Medium	Low
Rubber	3·8 to 13	Up to 1829 × 910 also sheet rolls	Black and white plus a wide range of colours	Various textures including studded grooved and panelled	Wear and resilience are proportional to thickness; plain surfaces are slippery when wet; damaged by ultra-violet radiation	Internal floors	Good	Low to medium
Cork	3 to 25	Up to 305 × 305 also sheet rolls	Honey to dark brown plus dyed colours	Matt to gloss plus deep relief natural textures	Damaged by dirt and water if not sealed; warm and non-slippery	Internal floors and walls	Good	Low to medium

D Soft flooring materials

Material	Appearance	Properties	Application
Wool	Dyed many colours and woven to any design	Warm, soft, resilient and fire resisting	Woven carpets; usually mixed with 20% nylon
Jute	Coarse texture	Brown fibre from plant stem	Predominantly used as backing to main carpet
Sisal	Natural colours, coarsely woven	Light brown fibre from plant stem; either used pure or blended with other fibres	Coarse carpet tiles or fine cord carpeting
Coir	Rich gold orange colour	Dirties easily; difficult to clean; harsh coarse texture	Coir matting
Animal hairs	Many dyed colours	Hard wearing; does not collect dust; fire-resisting	Cord carpeting and carpet tiles
Acrylic	Many colours: nearest of the man made materials to wool	Warm, resilient, wears well	Woven or tufted carpets
Nylon	Many colours and patterns	Very tough and durable; attracts dirt and prone to static electricity	Woven or tufted carpets; either used 100% pure or blended with wool or viscose rayon

D Soft flooring materials (continued)

Material	Appearance	Properties	Application
Viscose rayon	Many colours and patterns	Not hardwearing or dirt resistant, but inexpensive	Mostly blended with other fibres
Polyester	Many colours and patterns	Soft and easy to clean; hardwearing	Often blended with nylon

E Wallcovering materials

Material	Appearance	Properties	Application
Lining paper	Smooth light coloured paper	Available in various weights; one type is pitch coated for use on damp walls	Applied under main wallpaper to give smooth surface
Ceiling paper	Plain or embossed textures	Heavier and thicker than lining pepers	Covers ceiling cracks in preparation for paint
Flock	Many colours and patterns; velvet texture	Made from wool, silk or nylon fibres	Decorative finish
Vinyl	Many colours and printed patterns; plain or embossed surfaces	Tough, waterproof and easily cleaned	Decorative finish
Anaglypta	Embossed designs in high relief	Made from cotton fibres; strong and resilient	Decorative finish used to cover irregular wall or ceiling surfaces
Hessian	Many colours; slight texture of fine or coarse weave	Tough material, some backed on foam, paper or latex; can be flame resistant	Can be painted on
Textiles	Natural colours of dye colours; close, medium or open weave	Can be backed as for hessian	Decorative finish; unbacked materials are suitable as stretched panelling on light frames
Felt	Many colours	Tends to collect dust but can be vacuum cleaned; soft finish	Suitable for jewellery display
Silk	Very fine texture; cheap vinyl 'silk' imitations have similar appearance	Usually glued on a backing paper; damages easily	Decorative finish
Grass cloth	Natural colours with rough texture	Grasses, honeysuckle and bamboos are held together by thread and mounted on backing paper	Decorative finish
Rollywood	Natural colours	Thin wood slats, square or circular, are woven together with thread and backing	Decorative finish
Cork	Natural and dyed colours; various textures from fine to rough natural bark	Available as compressed tiles or backed on coloured foil paper	Decorative finish; if applied on fixtures it should be sealed with clear polyurethane
Foil	Metallic silver or gold foil plain or with printed patterns	Tough, waterproof and easily cleaned	Decorative finish
Leather	Light or dark tan; simulated 'leather' in PVC looks inferior	Tough, wears well; simulated leathers are backed by foam material	Mounted to blockboard and cladded on walls or fixtures
Suede	Natural or dyed colours; many simulated 'suedes' available	Easily stained; requires great care	Mainly used in fixtures

F Timber

Material	Appearance	Properties	Application
Pine	Varying from pale to reddish gold; curvy grain and knotty; suitable for painting, staining or clear sealing	Various types of pine are available among which are: Douglas Fir, Parana, Red Baltic, Norway Spruce, Cedar and Yew; inexpensive	Suitable for all uses from carcassing to decorative application such as tongued and grooved panelling
Teak	Long even grain; middle brown colour	Hard, resistant to rot and decay; moderately water resistant cheaper woods which resemble Teak are Afromosia and Iroko	Joinery, furniture and flooring; also used as veneer
Beech	Straight grain; pale light colour	Very strong wood which can be machined to a high quality of finish; polishes up well	Internal fixtures, shopfront framing, and fascia, decorative panelling, veneers
Mahogany	Even grain; pale to deep rich red	Easily worked on; similar varieties are Gaboon, Sapele and Utile	Veneers
Rosewood	Dark brown or purple with irregular dark strips	Hardwearing	Veneers
Walnut	Dark brown with curly black veins	Can be machined to a high quality of finish	Veneers
Oak	Light coloured but darkens with age and polish	Hardwearing and expensive; can be used externally	Veneers

G Metal

Material	Appearance	Properties	Application
Steel	A wide range of colours are available, depending on the type of treatment; finishes can be gloss semi-gloss or matt	General treatments for steel are primed under-coated and painted, stove enamelled, vitrious enamelled, or plastic coated; enamelled and plastic coated finishes are permanent and require no maintenance due to the durable finish	Small fixtures, claddings, and anywhere where strength and durability is required; steel chequered plates are available plain, studded or ribbed
Chromed steel	Highly polished silver surface	Chromed steel quality depends on the quality of the steel base as well as on that of the plating; hard, durable, very easy to maintain	Decorative internal fixtures
Stainless steel	Satin or polished	Quality depends on the thickness of the anodic film; generally hardwearing, non-corrosive and heat resistant	Internal and external use; where used externally in urban or urban-marine locations loss of appearance through tarnishing and pitting sometimes occurs
Aluminium	Plain or anodised; satin, silver, bronze, gold and black; can be painted on or PVC coated; surfaces finished matt, polished or brushed	Extruded or in sheet form; strong, light and non-corrosive	Exterior and interior work of all types including glass framing, strip ceilings, decorative wall coverings and fascia claddings
Bronze	Bright finished or toned naturally or chemically	Bright finishes are subject to atmospheric tarnishing and require frequent burnishing; chemically induced toning is initially soft, but given time it will mellow and harden	Signs, cast letters and small fixtures; because of high costs, it is mostly replaced by bronze anodised aluminium
Brass	Bright finished	Natural finishes require constant burnishing to prevent tarnishing; may be protected with clear lacquer	Decorative items and small sign plates

H Thin surface finishes

Material	Appearance	Properties	Application
Oil paint	Very wide range of colours; surface finishes include gloss, semi-gloss, eggshell and matt	Protects wood and metal; prevents moisture penetration into plaster; washable and durable, especially when made with synthetic resins; its disadvantage is that it shows surface irregularities, takes a long time to dry and needs good ventilation	Internal and external finishes
Emulsion paint	Range of colours as wide as for oil paints; surface finishes include silk, satin and matt	Should not be used directly on wood or metal; easy to use, quick to dry and produces little smell	Internal finishes
Special property paints	Generally in a very limited range of colours	Paints are available with different properties eg water and chemical resistant, heat resistant, fire retarding, fungus resistant and luminous	As required
Wood stains	Various colours and wood tones	Modify the colour of the wood without obscuring the grain; preservatives and water repellants can be incorporated	Internal or external finishes
Varnish	Clear varnish does not affect the appearance of wood; surface finishes include high gloss, semi-gloss and matt	The hard surface of the varnish protects the wood; other treatments producing similar clear finishes include wax polishing, french polishing, lacquering and oil sealing	

Appendix 2
LEGISLATION

The following Acts of Parliament and statutory regulations are particularly relevant to the planning of shop buildings in Great Britain:

Fire Precautions Act 1972
Food and Drugs Act 1955
Health and Safety at Work Act 1974
Highways Act 1974
Licensing Act 1964
London Building Acts 1930 to 1939
Offices Shops and Railway Premises Act 1963
Town and Country Planning Acts 1972 and 1976
Town and Country Planning (Control of Advertisements) Act 1969
Weights and Measures Act 1963
The Building Regulations 1976
The Building Standards (Scotland) Regulations 1971 and 1975
The Food Hygiene (General) Regulations 1970

The more important provisions of three of these, the Offices Shops and Railway Premises Act 1963, the Building Regulations 1976 (Part E) and the Food Hygiene (General) Regulations 1970, are summarised below.

OFFICES, SHOPS AND RAILWAY PREMISES ACT 1963

Objectives
The objectives of the act are to safeguard the health, safety, and welfare of the employees in premises not covered by the provisions of the Factories Acts.

Definition
The Act defines 'shop premises' as:
(a) a shop;
(b) a building or part of a building, being a building or part which is not a shop but of which the sole or principal use is the carrying on there of retail trade or business;
(c) a building occupied by a wholesale dealer or merchant where goods are kept for sale wholesale or part of a building so occupied where goods are so kept but not including a warehouse belonging to the owners, trustees or conservators of a dock, wharf, or quay;
(d) a building to which members of the public are invited to resort for the purpose of delivering there goods for repair or other treatment or of themselves there carrying out repairs to, or other treatments of, goods, or part of a building to which members of the public are invited to resort for that purpose.
(e) any premises (in this Act referred to as 'fuel storage premises') occupied for the purposes of trade or business which consists of, or includes, the sale of solid fuel, being premises used for the storage of such fuel intended to be sold in the course of that trade or business, but not including dock storage premises or colliery storage premises.

Minimum working space
Working space for people habitually employed to work in a room is to be calculated at a minimum of $3.7\,m^2$ or $11.3\,m^3$ per person excluding furniture. (This figure is always exceeded on the sales floor but applies for ancillary workrooms and offices.)

Temperature
Provision must be made to ensure reasonable temperature, and a temperature of not less than $16°C$ should be aimed for. (This is not necessary on sales floors or where its maintenance would cause deterioration of goods: in such cases employees must have access to warming themselves.) A thermometer must be provided on each floor and employees must be permitted to use the thermometer to check the temperature of the room in which they work.

Lavatories
Lavatories and washing facilities are required in conveniently accessible places for the use of employees. The Act lays down required numbers (see section 3.3 above, tables V and VI).

Drinking water
The provision and maintenance of an adequate supply of wholesome drinking water is required for employees, but this does not have to be a piped supply.

Clothes storage
Arrangements must be made for clothing not worn during working hours, and for the drying of clothing if reasonably practicable. (Coat hooks in a normally warmed and ventilated space should be adequate, though larger shops will require the provision of coat rooms with lockers.)

Eating facilities
Where employees eat meals on the premises, suitable and sufficient facilities should be provided for them to do so.

Fire precautions
Wherever the number of employees exceeds twenty, or where more than ten people work on floors other than ground floors, the employer must obtain a Fire Certificate (which details the actual means of escape). Once this certificate is issued, no material structural alterations should be made without first informing the

Occupant capacity of room or storey	Number of exits required
1-60	1
61-600	2
601-1000	3
1001-1400	4
1401-1700	5
1701-2000	6
2001-2250	7
2251-2500	8
2501-2700	9
Over 2700	9 plus one additional exit for every 300 persons in excess of 2700

Fire Authority that issued the certificate.

The number of exits required from any room or storey is as above.

THE BUILDING REGULATIONS 1976

These regulations apply to all types of buildings except those exempted under Regulation A4. The section most significant to shop design is likely to be Part E which is now structured in two sections:

Section I: Structural Fire Precautions

Section II: Means of Escape (originally introduced as Part EE when the Building Regulations 1972 were first amended).

Structural fire precautions

General principles of Section I

The main danger of fire is its spread either within a building or from one building to another. Spread of fire is dependent on four factors:

1 Use to which the building is put (purpose group).

2 Resistance of the structural elements to fire and of the finishes to spread of flame.

3 Size of the building.

4 Degree of isolation between buildings or parts of buildings.

Purpose groups

Shops are classified under Group V, which is defined in the regulations as:

'Shop, or shop premises, meaning thereby premises not being a shop but used for the carrying on there of retail trade or business (including the sale to members of the public of food or drink for immediate consumption, retail sales by auction, the business of lending books or periodicals for the purpose of gain, and the business of a barber or hairdresser, and premises to which members of the public are invited to resort for the purpose of delivering there goods for repair or other treatment or of themselves carrying out repairs to, or other treatment of, goods'.

Compartmentation

The principal concept adopted in the regulations for provisions for resistance to the spread of fire is that of compartmentation. This does not apply to shops which do not exceed 2000 m² in area or 7000 m³ in volume. Shops which do exceed these dimensions must be subdivided into compartments bounded by compartment floors and compartment walls, which are defined in Regulation E 1. (This principle of compartmentation is likely to affect department stores, variety stores, hypermarkets, and any other shop likely to be large enough in plan area or volume.)

Table I Periods of fire resistance for shops of more than one storey

Maximum dimensions			Minimum period of fire resistance	
Height (m)	Floor area (m²)	Cubic capacity (m³)	Elements part of ground or upper storey (hours)	Elements part of basement storey (hours)
7·5	150	No limit	0	1* †
7·5	500	No limit	½	1
15	No limit	3500	1‡	1
28	1000	7000	1	2
No limit	2000	7000	2	4

* No fire resistance is required if the elements form part of a basement storey which has an area not exceeding 50 m².

† Applies only to building, not compartments.

‡ This period is reduced to ½ hour for a floor which is not a compartment floor, except as to beams which support the floor or any part of the floor which contributes to the structural support of the building as a whole.

Periods of fire resistance

Every element of structure of a building must have a minimum fire resistance. An 'element of structure' is defined as:

(a) any member forming part of the structural frame of a building or any other beam or column (other that those forming part of the roof structure only)

(b) a floor, including a compartment floor, other than the lowest floor of a building

(c) an external wall

(d) a separating wall, defined as a wall or part of a wall which is common to two adjoining buildings

(e) a compartment wall

(f) any structure enclosing a protective shaft

(g) a loadbearing wall or loadbearing part of a wall

(h) a gallery

Table II Periods of fire resistance for single storey buildings

Maximum floor area (m²)	Minimum period of fire resistance (hours)
2000	½
3000	1
No limit	2

Restriction of surface spread of flame

The provisions are designed to control the use of materials which permit the spread of flame across the surface. They classify materials as follows:

Class 0 non combustible material, or very thin material backing on a non combustible background

Class 1 a surface of very low flame spread

Class 2 a surface of low flame spread

Class 3 a surface of medium flame spread

Class 4 a surface of rapid flame spread

This classification applies to walls, ceilings and soffits, but not to floors. Class 3 materials should be used for small rooms not exceeding 30 m², Class 1 materials for other rooms and Class 0 materials for circulation areas and protected shafts.

Means of escape in case of fire

Application of Section II

This new section applies to all shops larger than 280 m² per floor. It requires provisions for means of escape to comply with the recommendations set out in CP3: Chapter IV: part 2: 1968 (Shops and Department Stores).

Objectives

The objectives of the code of rules laid down in Section II are:

1 To safeguard the lives of employees and customers in shops of any floor area and height in the event of fire.

2 To facilitate fire fighting in buildings with upper floors beyond the reach of mobile fire appliances operated outside the building.

Stage I: Horizontal route to staircase enclosure

The following rules should be observed:

1 Obstructions:

The route should be clear of any obstructions at all times and clearly indicated throughout its length.

2 Number of staircases:

If any point on a sales floor is more than 12·2 m from the nearest staircase or exit, a second one should be built in such a position that the angle subtended by a line joining the two and any point within the sales floor is not less than 45°. The angle subtended by the lines joining any two adjacent staircases or exits to any point on the sales floor should not be less than 45°.

3 Travel distance:

This should be not more than 12·2 m when escape is only possible in one direction and not more than 30·5 m when escape is possible in alternative directions to different exits. Travel distance should not be obstructed by any obstacle exceeding 9·1 m in length.

4 Width of exit:

This should be not less than 1070 mm for the first 200 people plus 152 mm for each additional thirty people. Where two exits are required each should be wide enough for the total number of occupants of the building (employees and customers). Where more than two exits are required the aggregate width of all exit openings less one (it is assumed that one exit will be unusable because of fire) should be adequate for the full number of occupants. Except where the number of customers is known the number must be estimated by calculating the gross area of total sales floor space and dividing this by the anticipated density expressed as the number of square metres per person. For shops trading in common consumer goods such as food, hardware, clothes, cosmetics, fabrics etc the density for this purpose can be estimated as 1·9 m^2 per person. For specialist shops selling such goods as bespoke tailoring, furs, furniture, jewellery, carpets etc the density can be estimated as 7·0 m^2 per person.

Stage 2: Vertical route — staircases

Recommended rules for planning staircases are as follows:

1 Minimum number of staircases:

Two or more staircases should always be provided for escape purposes (other than accommodation stairs and escalators which are not included in means of escape measurement) and should be enclosed throughout their height.

2 Entry to staircase:

There should be entrances to staircase enclosures at each floor level:

(a) where it is not more than one floor above ground floor the entrance should be through a single fire check self closing door;

(b) in shops with more than one storey above ground entrances should be through a lobby between fire check doors from the sales floor and the doors into the staircase; in some cases the lobby may need to be ventilated;

(c) in all shops with any floor more than 18·30 m above ground floor level certain staircase entrances should be through a ventilated lobby with openable windows of not less than 1·4 m^2 and with a permanent free opening of 0·046 m^2; the lobby should have a minimum area of 5·57 m^2 and should be arranged to allow easy use of a fire hose;

(d) no store, cleaners' cupboard or other fire risk should open directly into a staircase enclosure or lobby;

(e) it is preferable for all escape stairs to the basement to be entered only from the open air at ground floor level, and for them to be placed so that smoke from any basement fire will not obstruct any exit serving the ground and upper floors;

(f) in shops with more than one stair available for escape from upper floors one of the staircases may be taken down to the basement provided that the stairs are fully enclosed and protected by fire check lobbies at ground floor and basement levels and that the lobby at ground floor level is ventilated;

(g) because of the difficulty of fighting fires in basements, alternative access should be provided to every storey below ground level which exceeds 230 m^2.

3 Calculation of width of staircases:

(a) assume that one stair is unusable.

(b) a 353 mm unit of width allows the passage of 100 people in 2½ minutes. A width of 1070 mm should however be considered as the minimum for a staircase; each additional 152 mm of stair width allows for the passage of 30 people;

(c) staircases should have a minimum width of 1070 mm measured between walls or 990 mm between a wall and the inside of a balustrade and having a continuous handrail on one side; the stair should be not less than 255 mm and the riser not more than 190 mm with not less than three or more than sixteen in a flight; staircases

over 2130 mm wide should have a central handrail in addition;

(d) to calculate the aggregate staircase width, first determine the area at risk which may be one floor if totally separated, or any number of floors if they are interconnected; the total area of all interconnected floors divided by the recommended density factor will give the total aggregate width of staircase necessary to evacuate the area in 2½ minutes.

4 Ventilation of staircases:

It is generally preferable for all staircases to be ventilated but staircases not exceeding three storeys may be unventilated providing the lobby at first and second floor is adequately ventilated; fire fighting staircases must always be ventilated together with the lobby at each floor level.

5 Lighting:

All exit routes should be provided with artificial lighting and with a secondary system independent of the main supply.

Stage 3: From base of stair to exit

The following rules should be observed:

1 The route from the stairs should be directly to the open air through exit doors or through an entrance hall window display lobby directly to the open air.

2 Accommodation staircases (similar conditions apply to escalators) need not be enclosed provided they do not serve more than two storeys and that neither storey is connected by an open staircase to a third storey, and that the staircase does not pass through a compartment division. The foot of the staircase should not be more than 15 m from an exit door into an enclosed staircase or the open air.

Marking escape routes

Exits should be indicated by signs at the head of stairs and over doorways and if necessary by arrows indicating the direction of exits. It should be possible to see any one of these signs from any part of the shop used by the public. Emergency exits not normally used should be marked 'Fire Exit'. Doors which could be mistaken for an exit should be marked 'No Exit'.

THE FOOD HYGIENE (GENERAL) REGULATIONS 1970

The above regulations apply to 'food businesses': a definition which covers all retail food shops and premises where food is prepared or packaged.

Objectives

The regulations are concerned with the behaviour of people handling food as well as with the premises where they do so. The stress is on maintaining high standards of hygiene and avoiding contamination.

Design

Architects may contribute towards high standards of cleanliness by detailing premises with hygiene as a major factor. Unnecessary crevices or ledges should be avoided and materials should be selected for their hardwearing qualities so that they do not roughen in use and can be easily cleaned.

Other requirements

Other requirements in the regulations are generally in line with the Offices Shops and Railway Premises Act 1963. They include provision of WCs and basins, water supply, and space for storing clothes and first aid materials. Lavatories must be situated where odours cannot penetrate from them into a room where food is being handled. Clothing must not be stored in rooms where food is being handled and it must be housed in cupboards or solid lockers. No room in which open food is handled may communicate directly with sleeping places. The regulations further demand that sufficient and suitable lighting and ventilation shall be provided in food rooms.

Bibliography

Books and articles

Alison Adburgham: *Shops and shopping 1800-1914*, Allen and Unwin, London, 1964

G. Barker and E. Funare: *Shopping centers, design and operation*, Reinhold Publishing Corporation, New York, 1951

A. Bartram: *Fascia lettering in the British Isles*, Lund Humphries, London, 1978

Wilfred Burns: *British shopping centres*, L. Hill, London, 1959

N. Chapman: *Heating*, Macdonald, London, 1971

F. Chatterton: *Shop fronts*, G. W. Keuhny, Cleveland, 1927

S. O. Curtis: *Shopfitting and setting out*, Pitman, London, 1939

Clive Darlow (ed): *Enclosed shopping centres*, Architectural Press, London, 1972

J. Debaigts: *Shopfronts*, Architectural Book Publishing Co, New York, 1974

Dodge: 'Design for modern merchandising: stores, shopping centres, showrooms', *Architectural Record*, 1954

A. T. Edwards: *Architecture of shops*, Chapman and Hall, London, 1933

O. Faber and J. R. Kell: *Heating and air-conditioning of buildings*, Architectural Press, London, 1936, 6th edition 1979

J. A. Fernandez: *The speciality shop (a guide)*, Architectural Publishing Book Co, New York, 1950

David Gosling and Barry Maitland: *Design and planning of retail systems*, Architectural Press, London, 1976

W. Grub: *Boutiquen, shops und schicke haden*, Verlag Georg, 1974

Victor Gruen and Larry Smith: *Shopping towns USA*, Reinhold Publishing Corporation, London 1960

A. P. Hartnell: *Shop planning and design*, Bloomsbury, London, 1943

G. Hasler: *Integrated alarm systems*, 1960

J. S. Hornbeck (ed): *Stores and shopping-centres*, McGraw Hill Book Company, New York, 1962

K. Kaspar: *International shop design*, Thames and Hudson and Andre Deutsch, London, 1967

M. Ketchum: *Shops and stores*, Reinhold Publishing Corporation, New York, 1954

George E. Kline: 'Modern supermarkets and superettes', *Modern Grocer*,

London shop survey 1978, Newman Books, London, 1978

Claude R. Lyon: *Self selection*, Camford Press, London, 1958

E. D. Mills and N. Beddington (ed): *Planning, buildings for habitation, commerce and industry*, Newnes Butterworths, London 1976

G. M. Pain: *Planning and the shopkeeper*, Barrie and Rockliff, London, 1967

L. Parnes: *Planning stores that pay*, Dodge (Arch Rec), Yale, N.Y., 1948

Trevor Perry: *Modern shopfront construction*, Technical Press, London, 1933

Retail Directory 1978, Knight, Frank and Rutley, London, 1978

L. J. Ridley: *Shopfitting construction*, Pitman, London, 1939

R. Scrubbe: *Small commercial buildings*, Reinhold Publishing Corporation, New York,

Ellis E. Somake and Rolf Hellberg: *Shops and stores to-day*, Batsford, London 1956

M. L. Turner and D. Vaisey: *Oxford shops and shopfitting*, Oxford Illustrated Press, Oxford, 1972

B. and N. Westwood: *The modern shop*, Architectural Press, London, 1952, revised edition 1955

Pamphlets and other sources

Architects' Journal Information Sheets: *Shop building design guide*, Architectural Press, London, January-June 1966 and 31 July 1968 (metric summary)

Board of Trade: *Report on the census of distribution and other services*, HMSO, London, 1971

British Lighting Council: *Shop design*

British Lighting Council: *Shop lighting*

British Plastics Federation Ltd: *Corrugated plastic sheeting*

Civic Trust: *Shopfront design*

Co-operative Union: *Supermarkets*, 1964

Department of Employment and Productivity: *Fire fighting equipment*, HMSO, London,

Distributive Trades Economic Development Council: *The future pattern of shopping*, HMSO, London, 1971

Electrical Sign Manufacturers Association: *A journey into light*, 1954

Electric Lighting Manufacturers Information Bureau: *Shop lighting*, 1955

Electricity Council: 'The interior retail environment', Conference paper, 1974

Flat Glass Association: *Glazing manual*

Gas Council: *Gas in shops*

Illuminating Engineering Society: *Code of recommendations for good interior lighting*, 1968

Institute of Heating and Ventilation Engineers: *IHVE guide 1970*

Institute of Heating and Ventilation Engineers: *Energy notes for shops*

Lighting Industry Federation Ltd, Electricity Council and Electrical Contractors Association: *Lighting for shops, stores and showrooms*, 1969

Milton Keynes Development Corporation: *Central Keynes central area — a handbook for tenants*

Patent Glazing Conference: *Patent glazing plans: a pedestrian shopping centre*

Royal Institution of Chartered Surveyors: *Shopping and retailing — the future*, conference report

Stainless Steel Development Corporation: *Building with stainless steel No 7*

Index